QUANTUM HURTING

Where Autoimmune Diseases and Other Spiritual Illnesses Lie in Wait

JJ JONES

QUANTUM HURTING

AUTHOR'S NOTE/DISCLAIMER:

I am not a doctor, licensed therapist, or counselor, so the information presented in this book is not meant to diagnose or determine a course of treatment for any individual. It is a presentation of a collection of research data and findings, as well as 30 years of my firsthand experience and the results of my research based on that experience.

DEDICATION:

To my father, who unexpectedly left us much too soon...
You helped to give me a great life, coached many of the teams I played on,
especially softball. I truly believe you are up there guiding. I feel you were
the driving force behind why my youngest son got unnecessarily kicked
out of his father's house and moved back in with me to go to summer school
in college where I stumbled across the online Criminology book from
his class and the contents that opened my eyes and led me to these major
realizations. My father was retired law enforcement...

THANK YOU'S AND ACKNOWLEDMENTS:

There are so many people I would like to thank for helping me along the way during this grueling journey—friends and family members who provided fantastic support and positive reinforcement. I will be forever thankful!

I'd like to begin by thanking the Salcido (Salsweeto) family—like every single one of them—who are amazing people! My cousin Pam inspired me to go to real estate school and imparted her wisdom when necessary. Elaine, thank you for recruiting me for my current position, which I love. I never realized there was such a thing as a "GREEK FIRECRACKER" until I met her!

I'd especially like to thank my mom. She was pretty helpful during this process. She provided me with ongoing encouragement and support, as well as all of the sky/storm photos you see in this book. The beautiful images were taken from her backyard. She was also instrumental in helping me with editing. Although not a professional editor, she is a retired high school English Teacher. Without her, I think this book may have ended up as one big long run-on sentence, a literary nightmare, full of way too many commas, (I like commas) quotes, and dangling participles. It may not be perfect, but it's better than it was!

I must also thank my children for providing me with unwavering support and encouragement. They, along with my granddaughter, are *my reasons. My whys.* The reasons why I scratched and clawed my way back to life. To health. The reasons why I fought my way back into society. These are the reasons why I fought my way back into a heavy career after being sick and away for almost 25 years—the reasons why I went on this truth-finding journey. Finally, I want to share this information so they can be a part of breaking the generational curses that bind so many families, as well as sharing this legacy of human healing.

Lastly, I want to thank #source. That invisible fabric of higher intelligence that connects us all and allows us to be our highest and best selves when we actually give it a chance and learn how to tap into it. GOD/the quantum field/the place where placebo effects come from, etc. That's the #source I'm talking about. I have learned from profound first-hand experiences (not all discussed in this book) that #source is always around us, waiting to be accessed and integrated, regardless of what we call it.

"STEAL MY SHOW..."
~TobyMac

Cover design: JJ Jones
Storm photos: Bobbie Jones

"Sorrow prepares you for joy. It violently sweeps everything
out of your house, so that new joy can find space to enter. It shakes
the yellow leaves from the bough of your heart, so that fresh, green
leaves can grow in their place. It pulls up the rotten roots, so that new
roots hidden beneath have room to grow. Whatever sorrow shakes
from your heart, far better things will take their place."

~RUMI

TABLE OF CONTENTS

Part 5

INTRODUCTION

*"THE DEVIL USED TO WHISPER IN MY EAR, "YOU'RE NOT STRONG ENOUGH TO HANDLE MY STORM".......
TODAY, I TOLD THE DEVIL, "I AM THE STORM…AND I'M COMING FOR YOU AND YOUR KIND…"*

(Written in 2018)

My name is JJ, and I created the website IAMTHESTORMWARRIOR.COM (Currently also known as QUANTUMHURTING.COM in 2024) to educate, raise awareness, advocate, and heal. I experienced some profound life-altering events, which I almost did not survive. You see, I was married to a man for nearly 30 years who turned out to be a legitimate " Narcissistic Psychopath"; I just didn't realize it! I knew he was "something"; I just didn't know "what" exactly. A few short years after my marriage began and after some "bombs" had been dropped on me, compliments of my husband's severe personality disorder and the corresponding rising tension, volatility, and chaos, I started getting sick. I mean really sick, like serious autoimmune disease sick. First, I developed fibromyalgia, then shortly after, Systemic Lupus Erythematosus (SLE~the kind that completely turns your life upside down leaves you jobless, incredibly weak, exhausted, and in bed with massive amounts of pain and inflammation.) One that leaves you with absolutely ZERO quality of life, and my doctors and I couldn't figure out why. Fast forward nearly 30 years later and shortly after my divorce, I noticed I mysteriously started healing, so I investigated, and along with some golden hindsight and a crazy coincidence (or a little divine intervention???), I was finally able to identify so many of his abusive behaviors. I came to understand that I had been enduring some pervasive domestic abuse...mostly the "invisible" kind, which just so happens to be the most damaging, especially over time. It was this realization that led me to the fact that it was this abuse that had caused my illnesses!!! MASSIVE EPIPHANIES AND REALIZATIONS FOLLOWED!!! This compelled me to go on an educational, truth and fact-finding journey, which has allowed me to come full circle with my traumatic experiences and with the ability to understand and the vocabulary to describe in detail my experiences, personal insights, and the subject matter relating to these main areas of; (1) Abusers (namely narcissists, sociopaths, and psychopaths, all aka. antisocial personality disorder), (2) Domestic and child abuse/violence and intimate partner violence, and the newer research coming out of the areas of (3) neuroscience, developmental psychopathology, and interpersonal neurobiology and epigenetics. This research information, much of which hasn't even reached doctors yet, much less the general public, has shown us that, surprisingly, it is the "invisible" verbal, emotional, and psychological abuses that are the MOST insidious and damaging to the psyche and to our physiology. These include excessive yelling, neglect, abandonment, and rejection. In fact, this science and research show us exactly how verbal, emotional, psychological abuse, neglect, oppression, trauma (from war, natural disasters, etc.), adversity, and the corresponding strong tormenting emotions and opposing internal impulses are CAUSING THE VAST AMOUNT, IF NOT THE MAJORITY OF, AUTOIMMUNE DISEASES AND "PRE- AUTOIMMUNE DISEASE" ILLNESSES, SUCH AS, CHRONIC FATIGUE SYNDROME, FIBROMYALGIA, IBS, PTSD, ASTHMA, THYROID DISORDERS AND MORE. This new information explains this process from beginning to end, something science has not been able to do with most other known causes of autoimmune diseases.

After two failed attempts at filing police complaints against my ex and learning about the systemic failures of law enforcement and the laws designed to protect the abusers, I also want to put a warning sign around the "collective neck" of these abusers because the law failed me at this… TWICE. This is ***unacceptable***!

After weathering some pretty wicked storms and realizing that I had apparently been "sitting" on some very valuable experiences and information, I made the decision to share it with the public, not just as a therapeutic and constructive way for me to heal but because I see all the confusion out there regarding these "difficult to talk about" subjects, especially with autoimmune diseases. These writings contain my own private blood, sweat, and tears and encompasses all that I've experienced, learned, and gained wisdom from up to this point in my life. I bravely and proudly present this to you as a place to educate, heal, and connect with others who have suffered from similar experiences.

~~~~~~~
~~~~~~~

THE MOST IMPORTANT GAME…

When my teammates and I were playing in the National Championship game of Division I Softball in 1991 against the much feared and defending champion *Juggernaut* that was the UCLA softball team, I thought for sure they would be the "toughest" adversaries I would ever have to face (especially for this small town girl), but boy, was I wrong! Adulthood and life had a few juggernauts of its own that it was waiting to hurl at me. **Some things** and **someone** much more powerful, insidious, and destructive than anything I had ever experienced. Things for which I had neither practiced nor prepared for. I had never felt these feelings before, and I had no *strategies* or a *game plan* for what I was about to face. I also didn't understand the gravity of what any of them would eventually mean. The UCLA softball team, on that day, was not the toughest I'd ever have to battle, but it sure was great practice!

Fast forward about 34 years, and "POOF" here I am…barely! Hold on a second while I finish picking myself up off the ground, dusting myself off, and re-attaching my spine, backbone, and self-esteem… OK… I've made it to the other side, and I may have come crawling out looking like I just met the wrong end of a Spanish bullfight, but dammit, I'm still standing!!!

Now, I'm writing about my experiences because they are unique in several ways, which makes them a valuable tool for helping and inspiring others. The writing part (purging the toxicity within me) is extremely healing for me! So have you ever heard of that book, "The Sociopath Next Door"??? Well, I lived a real-life version of that, except the sociopath wasn't next door; he was sleeping with me in my bed, and he wasn't a sociopath. He was a ***narcissistic psychopath*** *(and there is a difference).* He was my husband, and I was with him for almost 30 years…It's just too bad I didn't know it or even realize it until it was much too late.…

But first, I want to bring you back to the present day, 2024, by beginning with my Quantum Hurting section. I feel this is the most critical and current information, so it gets the first spot!

~~~~~~~
~~~~~~~

PART 1

(QUANTUM HURTING 2024- ENTRY)

What started as an attempt at self-therapy by writing down my thoughts has now, several years later, turned into something that, well, I don't even know what to call it. It is massive. It *feels* massive, like a monster (a good one, though), anxiously waiting to be unleashed into the world at its proper time. That's what it has come to feel like to me. It's been an undoubtedly *guided journey*. Unnervingly *guided* at times. Merging several different topics that are very relevant and vital in their own right but now all interrelated in a way that creates even more new issues to be discovered and explored. I think the timing is divine. I don't believe the general public would have been ready to receive this piece of work in 2018 as it will now be able to in 2024.

Back in 2018, the vast majority of people had no clue that abuse/ trauma/adversity was causing inflammation or that inflammation was what was driving these diseases. I know this as a fact because I would conduct little "social experiments" to find out the average person's scope and depth of knowledge concerning autoimmune diseases. People not only were not aware that inflammation was the "secret sauce" to these specific diseases but would argue with me that it wasn't and that these diseases had to be caused by a virus, bacteria, heavy metal, etc. (They could never produce any kind of valid study or any other type of literature or information backing their claims.) Fast forward to *NOW*, and we know that is not the case. I think I would have gotten absolute pushback and a bunch of blank stares if I dared even mention, well, anything in the Quantum Hurting section! Not that I had realized any of that myself in 2018, anyway. It was between then and now that I had even stumbled onto the quantum hurting aspect and realizations, so again, a perfect example of divine timing! We first, collectively, had to evolve in the last several years by gaining new knowledge and understanding regarding the true and accurate big picture of the world we live in, how it works, and who is really in control. We *had* to, in order to evolve to a place where we would be able to receive this type of information in a way that makes sense to us and doesn't totally freak us all the fuck out!

~~~~~~~
~~~~~~~

<u>QUANTUM HURTING INTRO</u>
"The truth shall set us free…"

Here it is, October 18, 2023, and now I understand why "something" was blocking me from returning to my book writing, which I left off in 2019. I remember wanting to get back to it, but every time I looked over at my desk, it was like there was a big brick wall blocking my access to it. I could see it in my head, a big gray wall…of the cinder block variety, to be exact.

That didn't really make much sense to me at the time. All I knew was that "a significant force" was preventing me from simply physically walking over to my designated little writing nook, where my desk was located, sitting down, and resuming. Weird! It was a cool antique desk, too, parked right in front of a big old school bay window with expansive views as far as the eye can see of the gorgeous high desert and mountains. I live here in beautiful Southern Arizona, and the views are magnificent. It's not like it was a bad place to be! Well, never in my wildest could I have imagined what that "something" might be. It was actually a tremendous realization! Now I know the "WHY" and how that all ties into the big picture of what my book is about, the direction I want to take it, and the many messages it is trying to convey, as well as the newer sciences I am helping to introduce. Had I continued where I left off at the time (approx. five years ago), I would have missed what I believe to be the absolute real underpinning of the "root cause" of WHY people really develop autoimmune diseases. I am not just talking about identifying the root cause of these full-blown autoimmune diseases from the typical medical standpoint but going much deeper than that and identifying the "why" behind your body's reaction to trauma/adversity in the first place, especially when the offender is a parent, family member, loved one or trusted superior and the abuse/trauma is sustained over a prolonged period. Very much like a toddler just learning to talk and asking, "But why?" after one question was answered. I asked "why" until I found the end to that initial question I had in the beginning. *The very end.* After exhausting my research into the traditional supposed known causes of autoimmune diseases and not finding any answers, on a hunch, I looked to the quantum field. It was here that I found my answers. I was not finding them anywhere else. The quantum field, precisely the Quantum Hurting aspect (180* opposite of Quantum Healing), is where I believe autoimmune diseases lie in wait. It's the place where science, religion, and spirituality all intersect, and we are learning more about it every day.

I think that, at this point, most of us have learned in the last several years that autoimmune diseases are driven by inflammation. OK, great, that is progress, but what is "initiating and driving" such a massive amount of inflammation (and what's causing *that*, by the way...) that your body switches into "self-attack/self-betrayal" mode? It's not because you're eating too many fries, not exercising enough, "doom scrolling" excessively, or being too sedentary. Sure, those things can cause and exacerbate inflammation, but not the massive amount and type it takes to brew up these internal storms known as autoimmune diseases. So far, I have researched toxic materials and metals such as lead, mercury, cadmium, and uranium. None of those studies I looked at clearly show a cause-and-effect relationship between any of those toxic metals and the sustained illness of a full-blown autoimmune disease. Yes, these metals cause autoimmune "features" and disorders (similar to autoimmune symptoms, etc.), and there are correlations/associations shown between variables, but no distinct causation is listed in any of those studies. I'll go even a step further by adding that not only is there not a clear cause-and-effect relationship established, but I don't believe those older studies, at the least, properly controlled for trauma/abuse/adversity within their test subjects (which turns out to be the most significant cause of these illnesses after the fact). So doesn't that make those studies inherently flawed and therefore invalid anyway?!? Most of these studies also mentioned that there were few studies done in this area. I am wondering if it is because the previous studies were not promising enough in their findings to continue with an abundance of more studies. I saw a lot of "may trigger," "is associated with," and "has in common" type explanations. It is also essential to know and distinguish the difference between an immune reaction, dysfunction, disorder, and features vs a full-blown sustaining autoimmune disease.

(Note: to anyone who has seen a study that does definitively show any of the above or other metals or toxic materials as an actual cause, please send it my way. I would love to take a look at it.)

Since I couldn't write for the last few years due to a severe writer's block case, I kept myself very busy. I took a big chance and went to real estate school, and I am now selling new homes for a major builder in a new community here in Southern Arizona. I knew writing, publishing, and marketing a book would be costly, so I needed a way to fund my venture! I also ended up absolutely loving my new career and company, and in the meantime, I continued my truth-finding journey. What I ended up learning is astonishingly deep. Because of my personal first-hand experiences and previous research, I learned that when an individual develops an autoimmune illness from the abuse/trauma of a loved one, specifically their caretakers or significant other, their "spirit/soul" becomes damaged and eventually broken; as a result, the body begins developing/ manifesting the same overall set of symptoms, which ultimately end up as a full-blown autoimmune disease. A psychoanalyst researching abuse in children by the name of William Niederland developed the term "soul murder" because of the effect it had on its young victims. An effect that consisted of the "erasing of awareness and cultivating denial that is often seen as essential to survival, but the price is that you lose track of who you are, of what you are feeling, and of what and whom you can trust." That always stuck with me because that is precisely what the perpetrator/abuser is doing (on purpose), whether their victim is a child or adult. They are trying to badly injure and even kill your spirit, your very essence, and, therefore, your soul. Their abuse is designed to get you to try to doubt yourself and then hate yourself and make you believe you have all types of deficiencies and are, therefore, inadequate or faulty. They want to breed self-directed anger, dislike, and hatred within you. All the very low vibrational and frequency emotions (the ones evil prefers to wallow in.) *They want to dull your shine*. Now, being naturally a very spiritual person, I came to a massive realization that with the above in mind, does that not make autoimmune diseases *SPIRITUAL AILMENTS/ILLNESSES, FIRST*, before they even chemically then physically manifest?!? Hmmmm ...I think and *feel* so.

During this time, I also had to come to the harsh realization that there are an awful lot of evil and evil people in this world. No, I mean profound, dark evil that goes beyond anything we could have ever imagined. And it is real and it is powerful. Those who partake literally enjoy imparting harm and destruction on good, God-loving, and innocent people and watching, inhaling their pain, like the drug and fuel that it is to them, many times with a twinkle in their eye. Now, with that in mind, doesn't that sound an awful lot like attempts to purposefully annihilate someone's spirit and soul as well as inner happiness and shine? That is one of the overall goals of the big-picture dynamics of the Good vs evil war, isn't it?

Then I dove even deeper...I wanted to know about the worst of the worst, what the most depraved psychopaths are capable of, and sadly, I learned about the horrific systematic ritual abuse of children. Done in the name of Gods that most of us don't pray to, nor do we want to. This abuse is beyond imagination and is designed to "split" the child's psyche, among other things, and done to significantly increase the likelihood of the victim developing multiple personality disorders, etc. They are abused to the point that they no longer recognize themselves when they look in the mirror. On a deeper level, these spirits have been so obliterated (on purpose) that they NO LONGER RECOGNIZE THE PERSON STARING BACK AT THEM IN THE MIRROR! Sounds like an awful lot of spirit and soul murder going on here. At the very least, this is a spiritual crisis of epic proportions that goes back to the basic fundamental battle between GOOD and evil- spiritual warfare. The perpetrator is never good, well intentioned or having your best interests in mind but rather, will intentionally tear you down and then revel in the pain you're enduring in a sadistic way with little to no remorse. They watch, very pleased with themselves, as you are reduced to nearly nothing. This has evil written all over it, while quite the opposite is true of the victim. They are usually but not always children or at the very least, vulnerable, meek or where a power imbalance exists, and terribly overpowered by no fault of their own. "God's" sweet little angels, and otherwise harmless people who keep to themselves. The central nervous system and immune system can only make sense of such an opposing and insidious intrusion into itself by going into "fight or flight", which in turn begins the process of creating a pro-inflammatory environment within the immune system which then begins to attack the body. Yes, the body betrays itself. It self, as in no longer considered myself or *ourself*. SELF. THE SELF. There becomes a distinct separation in identity between the two. But the immune system is most definitely, *not confused*. It takes that corresponding message inward and starts mimicking what it's been enduring on the outside but inwardly directed at that new/ stranger that it now dislikes and maybe even despises. Probably not the first time you've heard that notion. The spirit and essence of that child or adult abuse victim has been so battered that it no longer recognizes itself as "its former and familiar self". It now becomes part self and part suspicious intruder, especially to the immune system, which now identifies this "stranger" invader, an antagonist, if you will, within us that it feels it must attack and continue a prolonged and ongoing attack until the job is done.

I believe this makes autoimmune diseases both quite the medical paradox and a living contradiction, which ties into and re-enforces the spiritual aspect. Paradox because it truly defies past traditional logic and expectations that align with that belief, based on the conventional reductionist model of Western science. A contradiction because the body contradicts itself in quite a wicked way. Betrays itself because part of it has become alien, an intruder, unrecognizable. Part something that the "whole" no longer recognizes as "same" or "part of", but different now. Part adversary that it doesn't like/want and this certainly can get much worse.

Now I have a question for you…which emotion can we usually associate with betrayal? We would most likely feel a level of sadness, bitterness, disgust, etc.., ultimately leading to the big bad emotion of ANGER. Yes, now we are on to something! Could it be that the person being beaten down begins to believe and, therefore, internalize the messages being fed to them by their perpetrator (immediate environment)? You're a terrible person, and you are worthless. If you had done that, then I wouldn't have had to do this, I wish you were never born and worse, much, much, much worse. The victim begins to internalize this constant message and starts taking on this hatred for self and begins the bitter descent into self-disgust, self-disappointment, and eventual full-blown self-hatred because I can tell you that the perpetrator WANTS YOU TO START DISTRUSTING AND HATING YOURSELF. Evil trumping good, on a spiritual level, manifesting physically. And because we are spiritual beings made of vibration, frequency, and energy, manifested as the human body, it causes malfunctions in the body. OF COURSE IT DOES! I think the real question is, "How could it not?" This all eventually manifests into the set of physical symptoms known as autoimmune diseases. They don't start out as full-blown autoimmune diseases, though. They like to creep up on you disguised as such things as Fibromyalgia, IBS, PTSD, thyroid issues, chronic fatigue syndrome, other gut/GI issues, muscle pain/stiffness, headaches and the like. As the inflammation increases in the immune system, things worsen, and disease develops.

Evil and self-serving people love nothing more than to destroy others and leave much damage in their wake and with as much personal gain as possible, mostly not truly theirs to claim. I believe most psychopaths, which are not incarcerated but out here with us, would prefer to have someone else destroy their own selves, at the hands of the psychopath's "invisible" abuse and terrorizing. Let's face it, killing can be sloppy- one can get caught, and put to their own death. A deed left up to those higher up on the psychopathy scale-ruthless extremely hateful with poor impulse control, among other things. (Sociopaths kill too!) Think about it, if "evil" personified and took the form of a human and wanted to kill someone in this 3D physical world, where there are severe penalties for murder, why should they do the physical killing themselves when they can do it with sneaky "invisible forces" and never ever get caught or thought of as guilty! ***MURDER BY PROXY,*** is what I would call that. Pretty genius on evil's part, I'd say! Oh, but we are onto you now, evil-we know how you like to work. You are being OUTED, now more than ever before and you really have nowhere to hide.

> **Luke 12:2-3**: "For there is nothing covered, that shall not
> be revealed; neither hid, that shall not be known. Therefore
> whatsoever ye have spoken in darkness shall be heard in the light;
> and that which ye have spoken in the ear in closets
> shall be proclaimed upon the housetops".

I was reading about quantum healing and how it is not just about the intentional healing of ourselves but also the intentional healing of others, collectively as a whole, our communities, cities, countries and the entire global community, using energy frequency and vibration. As I was reading, I had one of my thunderstruck epiphanies, as I have had numerous times during this journey. True downloads, I call them because I know they are not coming from me....If there is a quantum healing that exists, then doesn't it stand to reason that there would be a 180* degree opposite... a "quantum hurting" of sorts (just as things have inversions of themselves) that precedes the "need" to heal? If so, this is the area I'm interested in because that is where autoimmune diseases lie in wait and nobody talks about this area. Quantum Hurting can be explained as an act, timeframe, or place where negative and evil energy is drawn from, or where this injury takes place. This area explains how the energy/ frequency and vibration of another person's words, actions, etc. be it passive or aggressive, can absolutely change the biofield and therefore their target person's chemical metabolism, causing real dysregulation leading to inflammation in the immune system, related illnesses, and eventually autoimmune disease. This process sets off a cascade of negative effects, especially in the central nervous system, (think Vagus Nerve), the musculoskeletal system, HPA Axis, as well as mentally and spiritually. Quantum Hurting can also be seen as the cumulative physical effects of the negative energy, frequency and vibrations (either intentional or unintentional) exerted/projected by one person to another. "Quantum Hurting" has many applications!

In contrast, the idea behind "Quantum Healing", a term coined by none other than Dr. Deepak Chopra, himself, in his article, What Is Quantum Healing and How Does It Work, on the awakendandalign. com website, is that it "describes how our thoughts, beliefs and attitudes affect the way we experience illness and the health in our lives. It is grounded in the notion of interconnectedness. It operates on the principle that everything is connected in the universe, including our bodies, and is all connected at the fundamental level. This interconnectedness implies that changes in one part of the system, either purposeful, or accidental, (like our energy/biofield), can have far reaching and profound effects on the whole system and in turn, our overall health." (awakendandalign.com/article-What Is Quantum Healing and How Does It Work?)

In the book, "Quantum Healing", Dr. Deepak Chopra, MD., introduces this term as "a way to explain certain types of sudden and dramatic healing of the human body, such as the spontaneous remissions, and healing from illnesses that were thought to be incurable or a "death sentence", that are not understood by conventional/western medicine." This spontaneous healing happened to ME! Once the offending source was removed from my immediate environment (my abusive husband, sadly) and with little more that just some new found hope and peace, I was no longer testing positive for Systemic Lupus Erythematosus, nor were my inflammatory markers (SED rate and CRP) showing excessive or even moderate inflammation! I was feeling so much better! Now, at the time, I did not know that it was this removal of the offending source, new found hope and inner peace and new outlook on life that were automatically healing me without me even realizing it. That is right, it wasn't until after I started healing that I went on this enormous journey to educate myself to have an understanding of what happened to me. After discovering the newer sciences that are able to explain this process, a whole new world opened up for me!

In his book, Chopra goes on to discuss his belief- "these extraordinary, but few forms of healing are related to the understandings of quantum physics and consciousness. Just as quantum physics aims to describe physical phenomena normally hidden at the subatomic level, so quantum healing is directed to healing at that level as well."

Chopra talks about how the "quantum level is the smallest most fundamental scale of the energy and matter in the entire universe." So it is at this level that Deepak postulates shifts and alterations can be made, which heal the body. In other words, "this concept suggests that purposeful alterations in our energy field (biofield) can directly influence our physical, mental, and spiritual well-being."

This fact allows me to validate and make a solid case for the existence of the opposite—" quantum hurting"—the negative energy/freq/vibe, place, act of, process, and cumulative effect of it. Simply put, if there are positive energies/freq/vibes out there and they can create positive effects and, therefore, outcomes, then the same would be true of the negative energies out there.

After I had this little (big?!?) epiphany/download, I had another quick download that told me to "trademark the term, "Quantum

Hurting" and secure the domain name", as well as copyright my work, so I did! The universe knows what it's doing...✨

Sources:

Chopra, D. (2023). Quantum Body. Harmony Publishing.

Pollard KM, Cauvi DM, Toomey CB, Hultman P, Kono DH.(2019). Mercury-induced inflammation and autoimmunity. Biochim Biophys Acta Gen Subj. https://pmc.ncbi.nlm.nih.gov/articles/PMC6689266/

Kısaoğlu H, Baba Ö, Kalyoncu M. (2023). Mercury exposure mimicking systemic lupus erythematosus in a thirteen-year-old girl. Turk J Pediatr. https://pubmed.ncbi.nlm.nih.gov/36867000/

Refai RH, Hussein MF, Abdou MH, Abou-Raya AN.(2023). Environmental Risk Factors of Systemic Lupus Erythematosus: A Case-Control Study. Sci Rep. https://pmc.ncbi.nlm.nih.gov/articles/PMC10290049/

~~~~~~~
~~~~~~~

`THE CHAIN OF EVENTS-FROM QUANTUM FIELD TO AUTOIMMUNE DISEASE

Quantum Field > Biofield > Interoception > Metabolism/Chemical > Inflammation > Autoimmune Disease

Source:

Jones, J. (2024). The Chain of Events- From the Quantum Field to Autoimmune Disease. Quantum Hurting.com. (IAMTHESTORMWARRIOR.COM). https://iamthestormwarrior.com/elementor-3652/

~~~~~~~
~~~~~~~

THE QUANTUM FIELD

"Spukhafte fernwirkung — spooky action at a distance"
is what Einstein called this invisible field and its related
phenomena nearly 80 years ago, as he was quite skeptical
of such mysterious and unnerving events.

I have spent enough time researching spirituality, religion and science to come to the realization that each has its own "proprietary" names and terms for what they call the "quantum field" and "spooky" related topics. The commonalities are more so than just coincidental parallels but more like sameness, and each acknowledges and makes reference to an invisible place, field, or wave, where we are all connected. Unified at a higher level that cannot be seen.

Experts in the field believe that the quantum field provides a variety of possible outcomes for any given situation, according to the "observer effect." This allows us to "control our own destiny" and manifest our realities, at least tom a certain extent. Especially if we can improve our mindfulness, which leads to better meditation, which in turn leads to a state many, including athletes refer to as being in the flow state, being in the flow, and being in the zone. This full body state can occur during a variety of tasks and behaviors such as in sports or that at least involve focused participation or learning something new. This can be either cognitively or physically, such as in the case with the math prodigy and the violinist playing a solo in front of a large audience. In order to achieve that flow state or get in the zone, both sides of your brain need to be fully engaged and many say this is when your pineal gland is utilized to access not just our higher and best selves but also that constant flow of energy and information that is beyond our own, that is the quantum field. This highly focused state is interestingly more common when the body is in a state of hyperarousal or excitement, as is evident with the Olympic champion or even champion chess player. May be calm on the outside but aroused at least to a degree on the inside, at the anticipation of either winning or the threat of losing. These ultra motivation factors (perceived by the person) allow the person to engage at a level that can only be seen by those engrossed in something they are absolutely passionate about and deeply involved with. So, the college student sitting on the sofa, getting high, eating hot Cheetos and being forced to write an essay for his art history class probably isn't going to achieve being in "the zone". Well, maybe the Twilight Zone...

~~~~~~~
~~~~~~~

QUANTUM ENTANGLEMENT

"Science calls it *quantum entanglement*, spiritualists call it *manifestation* or *law of attraction*, religion calls it answered prayers and God, and atheists refer to it as the *"placebo effect."*

Regardless of the belief system and the underlying principles that drive those beliefs, they all agree "it" exists and just have a different name for "it". Still the same, "it", though! This spiritual interconnectedness they are referring to is known as '"quantum entanglement". Quantum entanglement is when two or more particles become linked together, by way of the very real laws that govern quantum physics, so that the state of one, instantaneously influences the state of the others. These entangled particles are dependent upon the aspects and behavioral qualities of one another. Neither distance nor time matters. This is a quality of the quantum field, which operates by a different set of principles than does classical science and its reductionist theory. This is further proof that the supernatural realm and sacred dimension(s) really do exist, even if we cannot see and identify it with our eyes and other traditional senses. Quantum entanglement not only allows us to have a small peek into the quantum world but it also serves as confirmation and as a stepping stone towards the discovery of a world or realm out there that needs to be further explored because it holds the answers to many of our unanswered questions and can fill the gaps and disconnects that we see in the traditional sciences.

Quantum entanglement is a very important discovery, as it tells us that there is, in fact, a fundamental "fabric" of interconnectedness which exists throughout the universe, and therefore validates what religion, science and spirituality have maintained all along. The interconnectedness of all living things as well as the entire universe...acknowledgement and observance of this state allows an individual to experience greater levels of compassion, empathy, and responsibility for the goodness and well-being of all living things at all levels, visible to the naked eye, or not. Also helping us to better perceive, understand and trust in that fabric of oneness we are all woven tightly into like Gramma's best Christmas quilt. When we understand that everything is connected, it allows us the ability to have a deeper understanding of how our words, actions and behaviors impact others and the world we live in. Trying to and eventually obtaining the ability to be able to "plug in" to your higher self, by way of the quantum field, ensures you will be your best self and that will reflect in your thoughts, actions and behaviors. This state also keeps us in physical homeostasis or close to it. This harmonious state allows for both core values and beliefs to be truly aligned with our everyday behaviors and actions. When this happens, we can begin to develop and hone a more profound sense of harmony as well as unity. Biologically and chemically speaking, when our behaviors do not align with our inner core beliefs and values, inner conflict and turmoil against the self, arises and the frustration, anger, sadness, etc that are felt, cause an increase in inflammation within the immune system and other parts of the body.

Another important process that happens at the quantum level is the recent discovery of "macroscopic entanglement", which is considered to be a quantum process but at the relatively larger macro level. This means multiple objects can exist in the same quantum state and are therefore linked together. In this breakthrough discovery, for example, in 2021, two separate research groups, one from Australia and Finland, and the other from the U.S. National Institute for Standards and Technology (NIST) in Colorado, were both able to create quantum entanglement between two macroscopic vibrating drumheads. According to the team from Australia/Finland, they achieved this by "measuring a specifically chosen resonant frequency between a pair of vibrating membranes- the drumheads (each about 10 micron across) in two separate microwave cavities, such that the quantum backaction (the measuring of the state of a system without disturbing it), was not visible in the signal", explains Mika Sillanpää, of Aalto University in Finland, who led the research. For the group at The U.S. National Institute for Standards and Technology (NIST) in Colorado, they created entangled states between two 10 micron-scale membrane resonators in one cavity by simultaneously applying pulses of two different microwave frequencies." This discovery is crucial for being able to observe quantum phenomena on a larger, more classical scale, where we can "see" it and therefore, better study and understand it.

People have known for ages that this energy can be manipulated for specific outcomes on a grand scale or cellular level. From the National Institute of Health study, "Biofield Quantum Body," we know that "EEGs and EKGs measure biofields. EMFs of very high intensity are given off by every living cell (around 10 to the 7th degree V/M) through rather low voltage...one of the basic features of life."

Thanks to the fields of biology, biophysics, neuroscience, functional genomics, psychology, psychoneuroimmunology, and other related fields, there appears to be a subtle electromagnetic field (biofield), which helps to organize the biological processes at the subatomic, atomic, molecular, cellular and organismic to the interpersonal and outwardly to the cosmic levels. These related sciences are slowly revealing what is hiding behind this invisible veil.

There is also a phenomenon known as "the observer effect", in quantum physics that states, the very act of observing a tiny particle can affect its behavior. This is crucial because it means we can influence the world around us and our daily lives by our thoughts, focuses and intentions. This means that perspective matters! The famous double slit experiment demonstrates the observer effect and how it works. In this experiment, both particles and waves were measured. At the point or moment of acknowledgement or observation, these particles collapse into a single unified state, behaving as either wave or particle, which implies that our consciousness and observation play a vital role in shaping the events in our lives.

Another crucial discovery in quantum physics is "quantum supposition". This fascinating concept states that particles can exist in multiple states simultaneously until they are observed or measured by an observer. This means that particles can exist in multiple states, UNTIL they are observed by an observer. This translates into the possibility that when we direct our energy, focus and intent, we are capable or potentially capable of shaping specific outcomes in our lives, or at least set us in the right directions towards an intended goal, as if it were a malleable experience to be shaped and manifested. Now with this in mind, quantum physics tells us that energy frequency and vibration are created not just by thoughts but by the words we speak out loud. Each of these particles emitted from a person's voice, vibrates so profoundly and powerfully, that even in the middle of the Sahara Desert or....the person right next to them being spoken to.....is immediately affected by it. Faster than the speed of light. Instantaneous. Some believe it is because our world is set up like a holograph because of this but that is a topic for another time.

So, let's further explore what type of effect positive versus negative spoken words have on someone. If the words are negative and toxic, it would send negative vibration/energy to the target, which is then picked up and absorbed (if accepted) by their target's biofield. Once this negativity enters a person's biofield, it can either be deflected/blocked, or absorbed and even internalized, and it is at this point where it begins affecting the body at the chemical level, creating massive inflammation within the immune system and spiraling other systems out of control and a storm begins to brew.

Not only do the above three phenomena of quantum entanglement, the observer effect, and quantum superposition help us to better understand this newer field of "invisible" science, but also help explain spirituality, and by this, we have succeeded in determining at least a few compatible components that connect the two together. We have come to a time and place where we need to understand and accept that one does not negate the other; the truth is they actually consistently ***intimately interplay*** with each other…

Modern neuroscience has given us the ability to see that the same "divine" state as described in the religious context of spirituality, can also be achieved by non-religious beliefs and practices as well. Many notable geniuses throughout history have felt that higher state of presence or being, when having a major breakthrough, discovery or revelation. For example, Albert Einstein reported having such spiritual type experiences and heightened states of awareness, just before or during his major breakthroughs, as well as the famous Indian mathematician, Srinivasa

Ramanujan, who was quoted as saying, "While asleep, I had an unusual experience. There was a red "screen" formed by flowing blood, as it were. I was observing it. Suddenly a hand began to write on the screen. I became all attention. That hand wrote a number of elliptical integrals. They stuck in my mind. As soon as I woke up, I committed them to writing." He also said he had experienced visions of scrolls with complex mathematical content unfolding right before his very eyes. Srinivasa/'s commitment and belief in a higher power and intelligent source, led him to his belief that "An equation for me has no meaning unless it expresses a thought of God." Now that's deep.

According to recent findings, being in the flow, where these rare "epiphanies" can be more common and actually created in our everyday lives. Neuroscientist, Tal Dotan Ben-Soussan, who studies the way spiritual states are reflected in the brain, has determined that "spiritual practices have been closely linked to self-awareness, a sense of connectedness, and empathy, all of which can be correlated with the frequency of brainwaves as measured by electroencephalogram (EEG). Studies using EEG have demonstrated how fragmented or out of step our whole brain activity can be much of the time, suggestive of conflicts between our behavior, thinking, feeling, and communication. On the other hand, expert meditators demonstrate more harmonious brain waves, which could be indicative of greater synchrony or connectivity within and across different neural areas. In short, spirituality, similar to LOVE, has physiological effects in the brain and body, and EEG provides a window on these changes." This is profoundly important because it shows us that when the person is in a positive spiritual state, filled with gratitude, empathy, self-awareness and love as well as a sense of connectedness, it produces positive brain wave activity and frequency. This further affects the physiology in a favorable way to help maintain homeostasis. Now the critical part for this book and for the point I am trying to make, negativity, either from the self or external forces, causes fractured and fragmented brain activity and therefore real physiological discord within the body, which causes it to fall out of homeostasis and into illness. If the negativity is coming from, let's say a loved one or caretaker, one in the form of abuse, neglect or constantly causing adversity, think about the discord that would all cause at a frequency and vibrational level! Constantly being in inner conflict to the point things like cognitive dissonance and compartmentalization develop to help the person "survive" in their immediate environment. It is this particular type of toxic stress, and chronically being in the fight or flight mode and having too many corresponding chemicals in the system, that helps to create so much inflammation in the immune system that an autoimmune disease develops. Reason being, it is the profound and polarizing emotions of "love" and "hate" and the inner conflict that comes with that, which is causing so much inner turmoil. Usually you are being told bad things about yourself and treated poorly so that message becomes internalized and acts as invisible splinters invading your body and if not dealt with, just like a virus, bacteria or real physical glass or wood splinter, it would begin to cause problems with your body at the chemical level. And this my friend, is how autoimmune disease develops. The quantum field, where all that energy, frequency and vibration is created and held, is where autoimmune diseases lie in wait…

Sources:

Pritam, S. (2023). The Interconnected Worlds of Quantum Physics and Spirituality". https://www.linkedin.com/pulse/interconnected-worlds-quantum-physics-spirituality-pritam-kumar-sinha/

Wogan, T. (2021). Vibrating drumheads are entangled quantum mechanically. Physics Worl. https://physicsworld.com/a/vibrating-drumheads-are-entangled-quantum-mechanically/

Ben-Soussan. (2021). Spirituality is a Brain State We Can All Reach, Religious or Not. Threshold of Transformation. Aeon Reads. https://psyche.co/ideas/spirituality-is-a-brain-state-we-can-all-reach-religious-or-not

Rohan, Shlok. (2020). Decoding the Mystery of Ramanujan. Wordpress-TEDxPICT Blog. https://tedxpictblogs.wordpress.com/2020/11/21/492/

~~~~~~~~
~~~~~~~~

HOW SPIRITUALITY AND THE QUANTUM FIELD ARE RELATED

The term "spirituality" has been around for a very long time and has evolved over the centuries. It started out as a religious based process of the attempts to re-configure the image of man to his original "better self", which of course was in the "image of God". Most of which can be found in various "sacred texts" relating to the early religions of the world and its various notable founders. Very early Christianity then went on to modify the term even more in the Late Middle ages, to direct the focus more towards living a life reflective of the "Holy Spirit"- to direct the focus more towards striping away the current *tarnished* self and rebuilding it to its highest self.

Following this, the term spirituality began to incorporate more mental aspects of life such as mindfulness and meditation. It was then eventually further broadened to include various religious and esoteric type practices and traditions, such as more expansive types and degrees of meditation, rhythmic movement rituals, which include dancing, chanting, etc., and prayer or any combination of the 3 but not limited to them. Rhythmic movement allows a person to focus inwardly and be mindful, which allows for the practice of meditation. Meditation is very necessary for healing. I suspect the exact time frames and the specifics are all a bit arguable to a degree.

Anyway, when someone has been traumatized, their central nervous system and vagus nerve are dysregulated and need to be calmed and re-regulated and moving in such a way helps slow down both and allows your CNS to move out of fight/flight or freeze or hyperactive state to one that is closer in sync with homeostasis. It wasn't until 1902 when the father of Western psychology, William James, specifically defined spiritual experiences as higher states of consciousness brought on by the innate need to understand better our deepest self and how we relate to the world around us as well as the true underpinnings of how that world works behind the scenes. He believed that, "individual goals can truly be realized only in the context of the whole (where all things are considered)-one's relationship to the world and to others." Modern day definitions of spirituality also now include a person's subjective experience of a "supernatural realm", alternate "sacred" dimension, within its own separate context from religion. Apparently, it has also been further modernized by adding the search for the "deepest meanings of life" and consistently observing and practicing those corresponding values. This can be accomplished by such practices as yoga, prayer, energy healing, manifestation, taking psychedelics, and rhythmic rituals, etc. The fundamental tenet in most of these spiritual principles, practices, and traditions worldwide is "interconnectedness." These beliefs are founded on the principle that all living things, including the entire universe we live in, are profoundly and fundamentally connected. This not only feeds but confirms the concept of unity and oneness at even the most fundamental subatomic level. This most fundamental level where the universe's tiniest particles are measured and studied, which also happens to align very well with spirituality.

Source:

Wikipedia. https://en.wikipedia.org/wiki/Spirituality

<p style="text-align:center">~~~~~~~</p>

"BEING IN THE FLOW"
Optimal Conscious Functioning

The place we tap into to reach our best, most creative, intelligent and productive selves. Many say we are also tapping into that higher level of information and deeper knowing that connects us all. The "universal consciousness"- The place epiphanies, thunderstruck ideas, great mathematical and breakthroughs come from. The realm, invisible fabric, etc., that monumental discoveries, and incredible physical feats as well performances come from. It's where athletes find their "A+ Game."

The first time I ever experienced such a profound state of being "in the flow" and tapping into that higher power and information was when I hit a two-run triple in the NCAA DIVISION I NATIONAL CHAMPIONSHIP softball game in 1991 against our rivals, UCLA, to put us in the lead.

It was my senior year and I told myself, "OK, this is it. This is your big moment. All the years of hard work, sacrifice and dedication all lead up to this moment. THIS ONE MOMENT IN TIME. BELIEVE! As I opened my eyes, I felt like I had the perspective of someone 7 feet tall and my vision was extra lucid, vibrant and sharp.. I could tell immediately what state I was in, I recognized it from a few times before- I was in the flow….. I looked over to my coach at 3rd base and nodded "yes" to him with some weird extreme confidence I suddenly felt, to let him know that I am going to score at least one of my teammates standing out there on the bases. Moments later I stepped into the left handed batter's box with runners on 1st and 2nd bases, and I took that first pitch over the right fielder's head with one out in the 3rd or 4th inning (I don't remember now), for a triple and 2 RBI's! It was mid game by then but the score was still 0-0. The score was now 2-0 and we added a couple more runs and maintained the lead to win the NCAA Division I National Championship that year. It was that defining moment for me that told me without a doubt that

I am a part of something much bigger than myself and am able to tap into it to access "my highest and best self." I had had those "flow states" before in clutch situations growing up in sports and it allowed me to come through in those big moments for my teams. I have since learned how to intentionally enter a flow state and sometimes even enter one when I am not trying to but get so wrapped up in and absorbed by my work that I fall into a flow state, and lose track of time. For example, I can work for let's say 3 hours straight on a topic sitting at my computer, etc. but to me it only feels like about 45 minutes have passed. (I just had a realization as I was writing this-depending on how this piece of work is received, I can say this book was a product of being in the flow. A *guided* product of my highest and best self. Stay tuned!)

Some ways to tell if you have achieved the flow state:

*Extreme mental clarity and deeper understanding about the topic you are working on.

*You feel like you may be having "downloads" or "waves of information", coming to you. (It's a feeling of, "Hey, how do I know this information all of a sudden?!?", in an enlighted and deep knowing, king of way.

*Task Immersion-you find yourself completely engrossed in and engaged in the subject matter.

*You feel deep inner satisfaction and peace while working on your task.

*Time distortion-lose track of time or don't realize how much time has passed.

*You feel highly motivated from the inside out. You don't require external motivation to do the task, etc. You feel yourself internally compelled and drawn to the activity or task.

*You lose inhibitions during the task, such as caring about what people think.

*You have chosen behaviors that are intentional and align with your goal.

*You are neither in the future nor the past but in the present moment. Acutely aware as one moment unfolds into the next.

*You're not interrupted by intrusive or erroneous thoughts as you normally are and can maintain excellent focus for longer than normal periods of time.

Flow states don't typically happen when we are in a relaxed comfort zone. No, the best flow states occur when we are stressed a bit in a way that moves us out of our comfort zone and challenges us to create and produce. When we are being called upon to stretch ourselves farther than what we are used to or are comfortable with!

Sources:

Cooks-Campbell, A. (2022). Achieving a Flow State: 7 Ways to Get in the Zone. Better Up Blog. https://www.betterup.com/blog/flow-state

Villines, Z. (2022). What a Flow State is and How to Achieve It. Medical News Today. https://www.medicalnewstoday.com/articles/flow-state

~~~~~~~
~~~~~~~

THE BIOFIELD

The term, BIOFIELD, is a relatively new one, compared to what it has also been known as, for what is most likely centuries-the AURA. The article below states, "The term was coined in 1994 by a panel on manual medicine modalities convened at the National Institute of Health (NIH) to discuss complementary and alternative medicine."

People from all walks of life, and not just scientists and researchers, have known for centuries about this invisible electromagnetic field that at the very least, surrounds us, and at the most, envelops and permeates our entire existence and universe. Not because they were formally educated about it but because most likely they have felt it and had their own experiences with it.

In more technical terms, Deepak Chopra, in his article The Interconnected Worlds of Quantum Physics and Spirituality, on the Chopra Foundation website, is the biofield can be described as "a field of energy and information, both putative (commonly believed or purported) and subtle, that regulates the homeodynamic function of living organisms and may play a role in understanding and guiding health processes." An even more in depth definition also states that the biofield is "an organizing principle for the dynamic information flow that regulates biological function and homeostasis. Biofield interactions can organize spatiotemporal biological processes (the understanding of how organisms measure and respond to time and space at both the physical and chemical level), across hierarchical levels; from the subatomic, atomic, molecular, cellular, organismic, to the interpersonal and cosmic levels."

To help make a case for the existence of a biofield, I found an excellent academic article from 2023, which reviews the hypothesis for the existence of the biofield and the corresponding scientific literature that backs it up. The article; "Biofield Science: Current Physics Perspectives"

Choprafoundation.org, begins by acknowledging the fact that conventional biology and its traditional reductionist theory framework fails to formally acknowledge certain "holistic", comprehensive, and integrative processes and, in particular certain anomalous yet consistent phenomena, which would require careful and complete consideration of the whole organism as one entire and fully integrated comprehensive unit. This anomalous yet consistent patterned phenomena and manifestation include plant photosynthesis, regeneration, olfactory reception, avian navigation microtubule interactions, and brain dynamics. Take plant photosynthesis, for example, being that it is a non-linear process (a process that does not progress smoothly from one stage to the next), involves a strong feedback regulation effect, requires an explanation that goes beyond the classical reduction theory, and makes it incompatible with the direct cause-effect approach and explanation that is traditional. The determination of when photosynthesis will commence/begin depends on the biophysics event, which is related to the light trapping and charge separation in the photosystems. Both of these take place at the organelle level. The timescale of events happens anywhere from milliseconds to several minutes. It is not until later in the process that the traditional reductionist stage even begins, and the plant will be able to convert sunlight into chemical energy, which in turn helps sustain and support the survival and well-being of nearly all higher forms of life. This process also includes light harvest, oxygen evolution, electron transport, and CO_2 assimilation, to be able to build up entire ecosystems with enormous forests and the like. The entire process, from beginning to end, should demand modern science to consider and incorporate not just quantum mechanics but also biophysics, biochemistry, and physiology, just to name a few.

In the case of regeneration and rejuvenation, they are both highly dependent on quantum coherence (the fact that the rules and characteristics that govern quantum physics and quantum field, continue to remain intact), as well as quantum metabolism. The "decoherence of quantum systems" means the loss of quantum coherence, which is the rapid loss/disappearance of the rules and specific properties which govern quantum physics and the quantum field—going from the rules of the microcosm to the rules that govern the macrocosm of the classical sciences, basically. In this case, a process related to the body's capability to allow photons (a component of the microcosmic quantum field), to work in a synergistic and collaborative way, to systematically and intelligently organize crucial biological processes within the body. And with the emergence of newer and deeper understandings such as with the process of plant photosynthesis and regeneration/rejuvenation, it has been hypothesized that "biology could ultimately be built from more fundamental underlying and elusive quantum physics and if biology is truly derived from physics, then biology should be an extension of quantum physics, the most accurate and fundamental theory at our disposal." "Because quantum physics underlies all electromagnetic theories and thus biochemistry and neurobiology, quantum mechanical processes, the role of the vacuum and the interpretations concerning the role of the mind itself, are all important aspects to consider", according to the above article. In fact, the authors of the article are challenging that genetics is NOT the only discipline that can explain the evolution process and how we really evolved. They strongly believe that, at the least, integrative biophysics certainly challenges it. "Integrative biophysics, in particular, a term coined by Popp and Beloussov, which refers to different aspects of nonconventional biophysics and biology. Specifically , the term indicates a departure from equilibrium thermodynamics, the foundation of classical physics and chemistry on which most of biology is based."

People have known for ages that this energy can be manipulated for specific outcomes, either on a grand scale or cellular level. From the National Institute of Health study, "Biofield Quantum Body", we know that "EEG's & EKG's measure biofields. EMF's of very high intensity are given off by every living cell (around 10 to the 7th degree V/M), through rather low voltage...one of the basic features of life."

Thanks to the fields of biology, biophysics, neuroscience, functional genomics, psychology, psychoneuroimmunology, and other related fields, there appears to be a subtle electromagnetic field (biofield), which helps to organize the biological process molecular, cellular, and organismic to the interpersonal and outwardly to the cosmic levels.

From the article, "The Biofield": Missing Link; Dr. Shamani Jain, the founder and CEO of the Consciousness and Healing Initiative, a non-profit collaborative that leads humanity to heal ourselves. Shamani is an Ivy League-trained clinical psychologist and an award-winning scientist in the field of psychoneuroimmunology and Integrative Medicine. She is also a sought-after speaker and teacher in mind, body, and spirit healing. Shamani is releasing a new book with, Soealth." Dr. Jain, believes that "if consciousness is limitless awareness that has no true physical form, then the big collective (not individual), could simply be the energy that manifests that consciousness into form. One that can be quantified and measured. This is called the BIOFIELD. Dr. Jain describes it as "a set of interacting and interpenetrating fields of energy and information that guide our health." She also notes that it is connected to consciousness and aligns with the Vedic Concepts, and when viewing the biofield through the scientific lense, we see that every part of us has a biofield. Cells have them and are seen communicating electromagnetically and it is all measurable and can even be manipulated."

Sources:

Jain, S. (2017). https://www.resources.soundstrue.com/podcast/shamini-jain-the-missing-link-between-consciousness-and-healing/

Chopra, D.(2015). Biofield Science: Current Physics Perspectives. The Interconnected Worlds of Quantum Physics and Spirituality. https://choprafoundation.org/wp-content/uploads/2023/03/gahmj.2015.011.suppl_.pdf

~~~~~~~
~~~~~~~

CONSCIOUSNESS

From THE CONVERSATION, article "Spiritual science: how a new perspective on consciousness could help us understand ourselves."

The science community up until recently has assumed that consciousness was a product of our brain, that it originated there, or the brain produces it. As research progressed, there were several issues and disconnects between consciousness and brain activity such as-.

1.) Why does the brain fire its brain cells as much during varied degrees of unconsciousness as it does when we are awake and lucid?

2.) Why does the brain show low-level brain activity during near-death experiences and even comas? If consciousness originated in the brain, why does the activity continue after brain death, with an increase in activity in some cases?

3.) How can our incredibly rich, vivid, and in-depth human experiences come from the clump of grey matter that is our brain?

4.) How directing mental attention and specific intentions can heal/repair the body. This phenomenon has been demonstrated countless times through the pain-numbing effects of hypnosis and the famous placebo effect.

Research and studies done by neuroscientists such as Giulio Tononi and Christof Koch and philosophers such as Thomas Nagel and David Chalmers, were able to show something different. They believed that consciousness is a fundamental component of the universe and the brain is the receiver, like a radio. It picks up and tunes into that fundamental consciousness that connects us all. It then transmits the information into the being/body as well as outwardly in our environment and towards others. There isn't just one channel available on this radio, however, there are a multitude of different frequencies to be tuned into. You can tune into the positive ones or you can choose to tune into the negative ones. (Notice I said, *choose?*)

The state and acts of altruism (at least towards those we know and love), have also been very difficult to pin down in regards to originating in the brain, so this was also studied. The belief is that since we all have a shared consciousness, we are in fact able to sense if someone is suffering. If so, we can then respond with altruistic (unselfish concern for the well being of others) and caring behaviors towards them. Because of the nature of altruism, it is actually related to empathy, and this absolutely makes sense from a spiritual perspective.

One particular area of interest for the author of this article, Steve Taylor, Senior Lecturer of Psychology for Leeds Beckett University, in England, involving consciousness, is the "awakening experience". When people first begin to become aware and that awareness greatly increases, they have a deep *knowing* that they are a part of that fundamental oneness. He believes the awakening experience is a direct encounter with this consciousness. If our awareness of this originated from the brain itself, how can it influence the function and form of the body? It's because consciousness is more fundamental than even the body itself and therefore more powerful and has unlimited resources to pull from. He also believes that the best and most productive way to understand the bigger picture and how we harmoniously fit into that picture, is to use both science and spirituality hand in hand.

I found a very recent article about an exciting new study from Shanghai University, which used mathematical models to discover the possibility of quantum type components in the brain. Specifically, certain fatty structures that make up the sheath of the nerve cell's axon have the ability to produce quantum entangled biphoton pairs. This is significant because it could potentially help synchronize neurons.

According to the article, the brain has long since been thought of as too hot of a mess for any kind of quantum anything to be going on in that spongy grey matter. The typical comparison has been to compare the brain to a traditional computer but comparatively speaking, the brain is ultra-efficient, capable of amazing computational feats many computers are not, and has a built in source of renewable energy. These facts make the human brain far superior to any laptop or supercomputer. Reason being, these computers only run on classical physics, so their abilities are limited.

Thanks to the Shanghai University study, which was recently published in the journal Physics Review E., we now know the human brain is much more like a quantum computer. The study found one specific process in the human brain that is very similar to quantum entanglement. It found that the myelin which encases the nerve cell's axon (the fiber which transmits electrical impulses to other nerves as well body tissues) actually provides an environment that is conducive to the entanglement of photons. This means we can finally explain the synchronization process, which allows for rapid responses and information processing.

The article goes on to say that, "Consciousness within the brain hinges on the synchronized activities of millions of neurons, but the mechanism responsible for orchestrating such a synchronization remains elusive. The results indicate that the cylindrical cavity formed by the myelin sheath can facilitate spontaneous photon emission from the vibrational modes and generate a significant number of entangled photon pairs."

The mathematical models the team from this study built were able to demonstrate how "infrared photons could impact energy to chemical bonds-specifically, carbon-hydrogen bonds embedded in this fatty tissue. This, in turn, could spur biphoton generation with many paris exhibiting entanglement, and serve as a type of quantum communication resource, within the nervous system." according to the study itself.

Sources:

Taylor, S. (2019). Spiritual Science: How a New Perspective on Consciousness Could Help Us Understand Ourselves. https://theconversation.com/spiritual-science-how-a-new-perspective-on-consciousness-could-help-us-understand-ourselves-116451

Swayne, M. (2024). Researchers Explore Quantum Entanglement's Potential Role in Neural Synchronization. https://thequantuminsider.com/2024/08/03/researchers-explore-quantum-entanglements-potential-role-in-neural-synchronization/

Taylor, S. (2019). Spiritual science: How a New Perspective on Consciousness Could Help Us Understand Ourselves. https://theconversation.com/spiritual-science-how-a-new-perspective-on-consciousness-could-help-us-understand-ourselves-116451

~~~~~~~
~~~~~~~

✦ <u>INTEROCEPTION...Our 8th Sense?!?</u> ✦

What happens to all that energetic information
that bombards our biofield on a daily basis?

It wasn't too long ago that the term "interoception" had little traction in the medical world and was often misunderstood. It was just a word that when I would say it, people would think, and still do, that I am mispronouncing another similar-sounding word or meant to say another word altogether. Now we know better...Traditionally, we have been taught that we have five senses: sight, smell, touch, taste, and sound. As the sciences have progressed, we have come to know at least three more-vestibular, proprioception, and interoception. So far! These terms are much more complicated than just "smell" and "touch," so let's explore them. Vestibular basically refers to our ability to balance our bodies. It helps the proprioceptive process keep us in balance and allows us a sense of body position in relation to space. Also, our surroundings contribute to muscle tone, equilibrium, and coordination. Proprioception, aka. Kinesthesia is related to muscle, ligament, tendon, and joint receptor communication systems. It means body awareness, as in knowing where exactly your arms, legs, etc, are at any given time in space. Proprioception allows us to know and feel where our body and body parts are, not just in relation to our surroundings but in relation to each other and the body itself.

Interoception can simply be described as the feeling of knowing what is happening *inside* your body, and according to good 'ol Wikipedia, "Interoception is the collection of senses providing information to the organism about the internal state of the body. Interoception refers to the processing of visceral-afferent neural signals by the central nervous system, which can finally result in the conscious perception of bodily processes." According to a study done on Interoception and stress, by a group of researchers, which is posted in the National Library of Medicine, "Interoception, refers to the processing of visceral-afferent neural signals (neural impulses/information, which travel from sensory organs/ receptors to the central nervous system), by the central nervous system, which can finally result in the conscious perception, of bodily processes." The sensory organs are considered to be, the skin, eyes, ears, nose, and tongue. They provide us with a way to learn about and "take the temperature" of the outside world and our immediate surroundings and incorporate that as being into the senses within us. The study goes on to explain that interoception can, therefore, be described as a "prominent example of information processing on the ascending branch of the brain–body axis. This can be both conscious and subconscious." Our interoceptive system allows us the ability to know what the sensations of hunger, thirst and sadness feel like, so we can easily identify them when those internal feelings arise."

Our biofield feeds interoception, and it in turn, affects our proprioception. Not just the general location of those body parts but in relation to the other body parts as well. Athletes, with all of their finely tuned and timed physical feats, have extremely good proprioception, as you can imagine. Think about those gymnasts who flip around on and high above the 4-inch balance beam. Do you think they have a keen awareness of where their arms and legs are, not just in relation to the rest of their body parts but in relation to that 4 inches of horizontal flat surface they have to land their feet securely on, *or else*! SIMONE BILES… Her kinaesthetic sense and body awareness are unbelievable! I can't even imagine the level of proprioception she must have to first "invent" without seriously injuring herself and then consistently nail the new move! Or, how about the 2024 Olympian supreme situationist pommel horse whisperer, Stephen Nedoroscik? I saw in a post-performance interview that he said his vision is quite poor, with terrible depth perception, and goes by the feel of his hands. So, his hands literally ***felt their way*** to a bronze medal! Do you think he was "in the flow" and "in the zone" when he gave his bronze medal performance? Most certainly so!

Interoception is the foundation of, feeds and creates our specific emotions and it is these emotions that cause the chemical/metabolic reactions in our systems, as well as our thoughts, and memories (as is the case with PTSD), which dictate our actions and behaviors in such a way that are reflected either positively or negatively in our lives..Current concepts of the term describes it as "a sense of the physiological condition over the body, which includes a much wider range of physiological sensations, including, for example, muscular effort, tickling, or vasomotor sensations. These sensations are triggered by stimulation of unmyelinated sensory nerve endings (free nerve endings) that project to the insular cortex rather than to the primary somatosensory cortex which is usually considered as the main target of proprioceptive sensations"(Berlucchi & Anglioti 21010).

The above article goes on to say that "Feelings from these sensations not only have a sensory, but also an affective, motivational aspect and are always related to the homeostatic needs of the body. They are associated with behavioral motivations that are essential for the maintenance of physiological body integrity."

The article continues, "Interoception is generally described as a perceptual process through which sensations coming from inside the body are perceived and integrated. (Craig 2003). Specifically, interoception is a process that gathers information form various bodily systems, such as gastrointestinal, visceral motor, cardiovascular, respiratory, genitourinary, thermoregulatory, chemosensory, and autonomic nervous systems (Khalsa et al., 2018: Vaitl, 1996). The main purpose of conceived as a conveyor of perceptual information related to the body's physiological state, is to monitor the functional states of visceral organs and guide behavior towards satisfaction of basic needs (Craig, 2003: Dunn rt l., 2010:Tsakiris and Critchley, 2016). Interoception also plays a very important regulatory role in which bodily sensations continuously interact with top down expectations related to prior knowledge and appraisal processes to adjust behaviors (Craig 2009: Sennesh et al., 2022). The regulatory nature of interoception has been associated with an evolutionary advantage in maintaining homeostasis and supporting emotional balance (Craig 2013: Herbert and Pollatos, 2012: Seth, 2013). From the neuroanatomical point of view, there are several neural pathways known to be involved in interoception located in both the peripheral and central nervous systems (Critchley et al., 2004). The peripheral nervous system with its afferent and efferent pathways, is essential in conveying information from different bodily parts to the central nervous system and in controlling peripheral organ functions (heart rhythm, gastric motility, blood pressure) through the spinal cord for cranial nerves. The cerebral region primarily involved in processing the state of the interoception system and its perceptual information is the insular cortex (Craig, 2003: Wang et al.,). In this region, bodily information is gathered, processed, and then integrated with exteroceptive information (Gogolla, 2017: Zu Eulenburg et al., 2013). The insular cortex is widely connected to different frontal and medial regions involved in attentional processes, modulation of the reward system, affective evaluation, and decision making. These regions include dorsolateral prefrontal cortex, anterior cingulate cortex, orbital frontal cortex and amygdala (Shura et al., 2014). These interconnected regions constitute the interoceptive network. Considering the localization of the insular cortex and its complex connectivity pattern with regions involved in a large variety of functions, it is considered the brain **location** where internal states are integrated and joined with other perceptual information to provide a coherent experience of the internal and exterior external world at the same time (Kurth et al., 2010: Zu Eulenburg et al., 2013). Studies on neuroanatomical pathways and cortical regions associated with interception suggest that perceptual sensations arising from the internal environment of the body primary dedicated cortex receive signals from the peripheral nervous system through neuroanatomical pathways and a wide range of connections in associative and frontal regions. This neuroanatomical structure is similar to that which underlies the classical 5 senses that convey information to the brain from the exterior-vision, hearing, taste, touch and smell, namely, exteroception." (Critchley the and Harrison, 2013)

The vagus nerve, a component of the parasympathetic division of the autonomic nervous system, plays a crucial role in the interoceptive process and in regulating and maintaining metabolic homeostasis. It controls gastrointestinal motility and secretion, heart rate, pancreatic endocrine and exocrine secretion as well as other visceral functions. It also is a major component/part of a neural reflex mechanism known as the inflammatory reflex, which regulates the enormity and immensity of our innate immune responses.

The reason the above processes is so crucial here, is because according to an extremely insightful study titled: "The Vagus Nerve and the Inflammatory Reflex-Linking Immunity and Metabolism"(link; https://www.ncbi.nlm.nih.gov/pmc/articles/PMC4082307/), "the innate immune responses are activated by pathogen-associated and *danger*-associated molecular patterns that are recognized by sensors on the immune cell surface or in intracellular compartments. These cellular sensors include Toll-like receptors (TLRs), nucleotide-binding oligomerization domain-like receptors (NLRs) and other pattern-recognition receptors ([Figure 1](#)).[4-6] Activation of signalling cascades downstream of TLRs results in increased production and release of tumour necrosis factor (TNF), IL-6 and other proinflammatory cytokines.[1,7] In addition, activation of NLRs is associated with the formation of multimeric protein complexes, termed inflammasomes, which regulate maturation and release of the proinflammatory cytokines IL-1β and IL-18.[5] Proinflammatory cytokines, along with chemo-kines, reactive oxygen species, nitrogen intermediates and other inflammatory molecules, are critically implicated in extracellular pathogen clearance, vasodilatation, neutrophil recruitment, increased vascular permeability and induction of acute-phase proteins, such as C-reactive protein (CRP), and coagulation molecules.[1,5,7] Proinflammatory progression is balanced by the release of IL-10, TGF-β, soluble cytokine receptors and other anti-inflammatory molecules."

The inflammatory reflex works in a way that allows the afferent arm (the sensory arm) to sense, receive, and convey visceral information regarding the status of the immune system upwards to the brain. These specific afferents express cytokine-binding sites. Also, antigen-presenting cells accumulate around areas of inflammation, receive information, and then relay it through visceral afferents using cytokine-dependent and independent mechanisms. According to another academic article from the NCBI website, "Interoception and Inflammation in Psychiatric Disorders".

Once an emotional response is registered, especially an extreme one, it will either going to have a positive or detrimental effect on the immune system, depending on the duration and specific context of the emotion being experienced. These strong emotions have the ability to modulate cytokine production and cellular responses in many immune stimuli.

Anger, for example, produces a specific response when the response happens within the context of a marital dispute between husband and wife. (could be any close interpersonal relationship) Studies have shown that a marital argument causes "an increase in the production of the inflammatory cytokine Interleukin-6 (IL-6) and circulating levels of C-reactive protein. CRP, is a liver-derived acute-phase response protein.

Interestingly, the effects of anger were also studied amongst a group of rugby players and after 2 and 72 hours after the match, a positive relationship was determined between feelings of anger, aggression and anxiety. The results also showed increased levels of IL-1B. It was also determined that the "memory" of anger-triggering events significantly increased peripheral blood monocyte production of tumor necrosis factor-a (TNF-a) and Interleukin-6 (IL-6). Interleukin-6 is responsible for the over production of autoantibodies in Systemic Lupus Erythematosus. It is also responsible for promoting the differentiation of naive CD-4+ T cells into Th17 cells by activating the STAT3 pathway, but IL-6 also contributes to SLE by mediating the Th17/Treg imbalance, which is involved in the development of many autoimmune diseases as well. It also increases the production of interferon (INF)

These findings show us how anger, in the proper context, can be useful. Think about how our distant ancestors utilized anger from an evolutionary perspective. It usually involved some type of violent act resulting in a degree of physical injury. A highly reactionary immune system, conjuring up all these warrior proinflammatory cytokines, TNFs, etc., was most likely very beneficial for efficient wound healing once upon a time when man was getting mauled by velociraptors and running from erupting volcano lava on the regular; however, when the immune system is hyperactive and continuously in this mode, it becomes detrimental. A quick and aggressive immune response was probably necessary if the fight for resources was constant and caused some gruesome bodily injuries. This continuous state, also known as "fight or flight" and sometimes freeze, is how immune system imbalance, dysregulation, and, therefore inflammation, begins.

Context matters. The above studies demonstrated that the effects of anger, not just on the immune system specifically but many other systems of the body as well, are much more toxic and damaging from interpersonal traumas/adversities than in other contexts, especially where the feelings of anger and aggression were associated with a positive outcome or goal, such as winning a sporting event or important title.

The emotion of anger doesn't just cover the emotion of "anger," however. Often, anger is a secondary emotion, meaning another emotion or combination of emotions is causing the anger along with varying degrees of emotion, such as fury, irritability, hostility, outrage, wrath, and resentment, other preceding emotions like sadness, encompassing gloom, melancholy, grief, sorrow, despair, depression, and loneliness. The other big contributor to anger is the emotion of fear. This includes anything from apprehension, nervousness, anxiety, panic, dread and the like. If you have ever gotten into a severe argument or even fight with your significant other, then you know that you feel a mixture of and varying degrees of many of the above emotions, all funneling into the big bad volatile immune destroyer known as anger! A person or athlete during competition is also unlikely to experience the emotions of loneliness, sorrow, or melancholy as a result of a sporting match or game, which would also be another reason interpersonal injuries are more damaging to the immune system.

The many studies that have been conducted on adults and kids that have had "adverse childhood experiences", have also demonstrated that abuse not only causes inflammation in the immune system but is causing autoimmune diseases later in life. The effects for children experiencing these types of interpersonal adversities, is much worse on the body and psyche than adults facing these issues, as it is happening within the context of their developing bodies and minds. In one study, adults who had maltreatment experiences within the first ten years of life, showed a graded and significant elevation in all three of the clinically relevant inflammatory biomarkers, which were fibrogen, C-reactive protein (CRP) and white blood cell count.

The damaging effects of childhood maltreatment/interpersonal adversities, does not wait until adulthood to manifest its symptoms, however. Inflammation within the immune system has already been detected in young children in many studies geared to assess such effects on the immune system.

The illustration below shows how severe
emotional trauma can trigger inflammation.

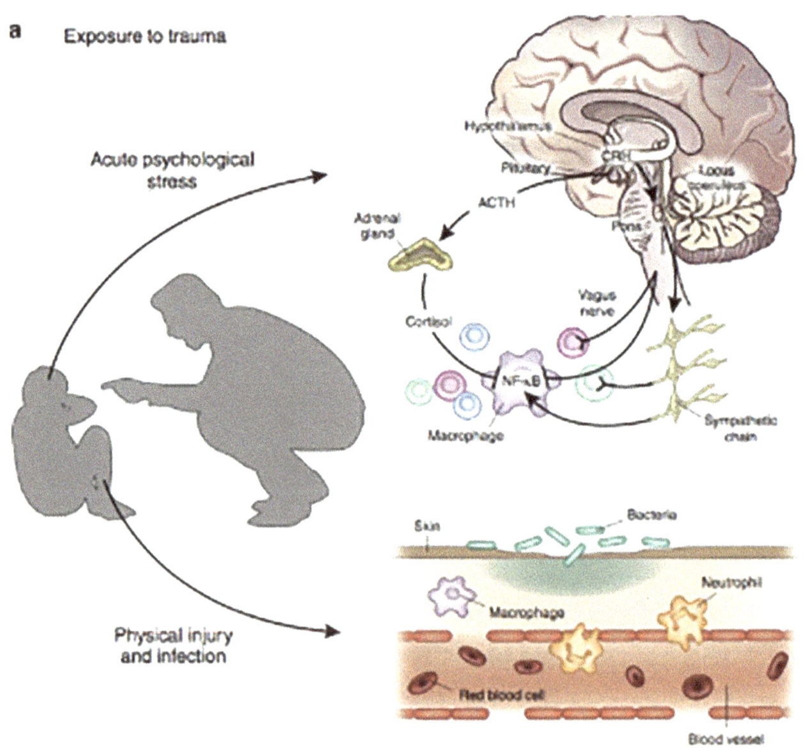

Pavlov VA, Tracey KJ. The Vagus Nerve and the Inflammatory Reflex-Linking Immunity and Metabolism. Nat Rev Endocrinol. (2012 Dec;8) (12):743-54. doi: 10.1038/nrendo.2012.189. PMID: 23169440; PMCID: PMC4082307. https://www.ncbi.nlm.nih.gov/pmc/articles/PMC4082307/

Kano, M. (2024). Gut–Brain Interactions. https://www.sciencedirect.com/science/article/abs/pii/B978012820480100036X

Schulz A, Vögele C. (2015).Interoception and Stress. https://pmc.ncbi.nlm.nih.gov/articles/PMC4507149/#:~:text=Interoception%20refers%20to%20the%20processing,of%20the%20brain%E2%80%93body%20axis.

Brod S, Rattazzi L, Piras G, D'Acquisto F. (2014). As Above, So Below-examining the interplay between emotion and the immune system. https://pubmed.ncbi.nlm.nih.gov/24943894/

Savitz J, Harrison NA. (2018). Interoception and Inflammation in Psychiatric Disorders. https://pmc.ncbi.nlm.nih.gov/articles/PMC5995132/

~~~~~~~
~~~~~~~

THE NEUROCHEMISTRY OF EMOTIONS....

Emotions occur as neurochemical reactions in our bodies which are felt as abstract internal sensations. Our "8th sense", interoception, actually determines which state or "feeling"we will experience and is the seat of our emotions. These sensations then direct us or motivate us in a specific way. Especially in higher order animals, such as, well, *"us"*, this internal emotional signaling serves as a prompt and cue to modify behavior to benefit the survival and "thrival" of the person. A simple example of this would be fleeing when you sense a dangerous person or situation nearby. (or a bear or man in the woods, which seems to have social media perplexed right now as to which is scarier. I think the scariest thing about this is that women cannot actually decide.) This tells us that emotions are a crucial component and contributor in learning, decision making and future behaviors, by appropriately categorizing them as either positive or negative and then modifying and adjusting our beliefs and behaviors accordingly.

Humans, specifically, have developed a higher rational ability alongside our emotional range, complexity, and depth. This gives us the ability to be mindful, self-reflect, and contextually evaluate our emotions and those in relation to the situation. It allows us to modify them in a beneficial way.

Although there is still much to learn about how emotions work entirely, we do know that the specific method of how neurons fire to create an emotion is a result of several processes;

1.) Neurotransmitters, which are chemical messenger molecules, are produced by neurons to electromagnetically deliver a message across a synapse- which allows neurons to deliver chemical messages or signals to other neurons and also serves a junction where both the delivery and processing of the specific information occurs. These messages are delivered to the target cell. Synapses also allow neurons to form specific circuits that work together to perform movement tasks or complex thought processes.

"When a person experiences what is known as a "sensual" (external) or "conceptual" (internal) stimulus or situation, the biological reaction, which consists of nerve impulses and chemical changes happening within the brain and body, informs the cells of the body on how to react-either positively or negatively. This is part of the process known as, "interoception". This process is heavily reliant on the movement of Ca2 (calcium ions), which works synergistically with magnesium and ATP (the energy molecule), to increase the electrical (energy) potential of the cell. This causes stored transmitters to move to the neuron's membrane and be expelled across the synapse. The electrical potential gradient generated with calcium and ATP moves across to the next neuron to open up neurotransmitter receptors and is continuous to form nerve transmission. Neurotransmitters that are not absorbed by the next neuron as a result of closed receptors (each of which are specific to the molecule in question) are either recycled or degraded."

Neurotransmitters are associated with cognition, maintaining states of perception and perspective, awareness, and various physical processes. They allow us to engage in complex functioning that goes beyond emotions and behaviors.

There are 3 basic neurotransmitters, each associated with the 3 basic emotional states. Any combination of these can cause different types of emotions and degrees of emotion. The emotional outcome is dictated by the brain areas they engage with and the functionality of receptors.

1.) Serotonin, also known as 5-hydroxytryptamine (5-HT), is associated with punishment, dislike, and sadness. These responses are a result of a decreased level of the serotonin precursor tryptophan. Serotonin is also a big component in the decision-making process, not just in one's personal life but also in social settings and engagements, where other perspectives and points of view must be considered.

2.) Dopamine, a monoamine neurotransmitter that can also act as a hormone, is associated with pleasure, reward, and joy. It plays a role in reward-seeking pathways and reward centers and affects motivation, memory, movement, attention, and more.

3.) Adrenaline and noradrenaline- are associated with surprise, arousal, fear, and anger.

Interestingly, hormones also contribute to producing hormones in a way similar to neurotransmitters , modulating the function and expression of neurons. Unlike neurotransmitters, hormones do not interact at neuronal synapses and are found in the bloodstream. The brain, for example, produces hormones that often lead to the release of other hormones in distant body sites. For example, cortisol releasing hormones stimulates the adrenal glands to produce cortisol. The blood levels of cortisol then affect brain function by binding on neuronal receptors. Adrenal and reproductive hormones and the thyroidal hormones are the main influences that affect the brain and their levels are also associated with different emotional states.

Recent research findings confirm that immune cell signaling molecules, such as interleukins and other cytokines, can modulate the neuro-anatomical components of the above-described circuits and contribute to producing an emotional state of being. Thus, our state of health and immune function also modulates mood and our emotional state of reactivity.

Hormone activity and their release as well as some neurotransmitters, is highly dependent on our daily and nightly rhythms. This means that our emotional state of being is, as well. The sleep-wake cycle that sets the body's daily biorhythms is operated by the sympathetic nervous system and the primordial circuitry of the brain that governs our state of arousal.

In the average person, cortisol peaks first thing in the morning in tandem with a few other hormones,, such as testosterone and growth hormone, signaling for the body to wake up and be alert. This is why many feel at their most energized in the morning and become progressively more tired as the day wears on. (3:00 p.m. coffee, anyone?!?) Interfering with the sleep-wake cycle can make the body release hormones and neurotransmitters at the wrong time and different from what is "normal", potentially interfering with a person's emotional state, regulation and control of those emotions.

Nervous System Circuitry-

"The brain operates through neuronal communication in which neurons from unique brain compartments connect to one another. The constant back and forth creates observable nervous system feedback loops between brain areas, which are paramount to overarching brain function. Emotion arises from this same basic neural-circuitry and is suggested to modify behavior in such a way that is conducive to the survival of the organism. Interestingly, the majority of brain circuitry involved in generating either positive or negative feelings is virtually the same with some minor variances. Either ends of the emotional spectrum are brought into being through two overarching circuits that are joined at central brain areas associated with emotional processing and learning. These circuits fall within the limbic system in the brain, comprising some forebrain areas, the cingulate cortex, the amygdala, the hippocampus, the habenula and various other brain regions, such as specific parts of the grey matter.

The one circuit or network is associated with generating emotional reactions that elicit behavior most likely to help the organism avoid undesirable circumstances (misery fleeing), while the other is associated with behavior that seeks out desirable ones (reward seeking). The precise way in which these circuits fire, with their respective neurotransmitter ratios and other chemical components, is ultimately what is responsible for producing a negative or positive emotional reaction.

The two circuits integrate and are connected to primordial (since the beginning/inception) brain networks, including the hypothalamus and brainstem, which regulate body function and contribute to the physical sensations brought about by emotional states of being. These primordial areas are responsible for receiving physical motor and sensory feedback from the body in order to generate our basic physical experience of the five senses (sight, taste, touch, sound and smell). Now we know we have 3 more legitimate senses- vestibular, proprioception, and interoception.

When we experience an emotion, these areas send feedback toward the rest of the body that alters cellular function and in turn our physical experience. Classically this is achieved through central nervous system communication with the autonomic nervous system; inducing either a sympathetic (stressed) or parasympathetic (relaxed) nervous response. These responses constitute the experiential (based on experience and/or observation.) physicality behind an emotional state of being. Meaning the behaviors one exhibits, which align with the emotional state such as: Examples include shock-induced labored breathing, an excitement-induced increase in heart rate and trust-induced muscle relaxation."

Other components that play a chemical role in emotions are neuroplasticity and neurogenesis. These both actively take place during the person's lifespan. Neuroplasticity, also known as brain plasticity, is the ability of neural networks in the brain to change through growth, pruning, and reorganization, as we grow and develop throughout our lifetime. It was previously thought this process only happened during the developmental stages of childhood but that has been proven to be untrue. This takes place when the brain is rewired by functioning in a way that is not typical or different than what it is accustomed to. This continued "new" behavior encourages these specific neurons being fired, to become wired in a way that is more robust and powerful within the brain. "Have you ever heard the saying, "neurons that fire together, wire together"? That is describing neuroplasticity, which is specifically strong with activities such as positive growth, learning new information or skills, with positive reinforcement, outcomes or reward. Other factors that have an effect on neuroplasticity are, nutrition (food type and caloric intake and quality of), level and quality of physical activity, and the type and severity of stress.

Not all these circuits are firing at the same time and neurons do have the ability to jump ship from their current neural circuit and connect to another circuit, if and when adjustments need to be made during the neuroplasticity process, (or maybe if it suspects the *neural grass* is greener on another circuit, where it feels it might be more "wanted and appreciated"?!?.) Those neural circuits and neurons not used often or at all tend to atrophy to the point they no longer thrive or are functioning and eventually die. Some die quicker than others. Neuroplasticity and neurogenesis give the brain the ability to house many neuronal circuits efficiently as well as give us some understanding and insight as to why and how sudden flashbacks of a traumatic memory and mood swings are manifested. They have also been associated with emotional control and therefore affect the perception of and emotional reaction to situations, etc. A process that also allows neural stem cells to produce new neurons and nervous system cells, in the brain. It also allows the nervous system to store a reservoir of neuronal stem cells which are used in the neurogenesis process.

Neurogenesis is a multistage process of neural stem cells producing new neurons or nervous system cells, in the brain. These new neurons are necessary when learning a completely new skill or task and will be recruited to participate in the new neural circuit being created. Sometimes it is only necessary to switch to another circuit. When neuroplasticity and neurogenesis become out of balance and faulty, emotional volatility and loss of control can manifest, as in such neurodegenerative disorders like dementia, where other emotional related symptoms are apparent, as well.

There are 5 basic emotions that have been studied to some extent. They are happiness, fear, anger, love, and sadness.

HAPPINESS, which can mean different things to different people and is undoubtedly subjective, can ultimately be seen as the absence of negative emotions and fear as well as the ongoing process of desiring, reward-seeking, and experiencing pleasure. That's a pretty odd way to think about happiness!

The actual chemicals, hormones, and neurotransmitters that come into play when a state of happiness is obtained, are oxytocin, dopamine, serotonin, GABA, and endorphins.

Oxytocin, sometimes referred to as the "love hormone", is a peptide hormone (has a shorter amino acid chain than protein hormones), is created in the hypothalamus and released into the bloodstream when engaging in friendly, loving , and bonding type activities and behaviors such as hugging and kissing. It can also be released through music and exercise. Oxytocin allows for increased empathy and trust, which helps to facilitate deeper and more long lasting relationships, both platonic as well as intimate. This hormone also creates a calmness within the nervous system and helps to lower stress and anxiety.

Dopamine, often referred to as the "pleasure hormone" is a big driver of happiness from a pleasure, motivation, and reinforcement perspective. Meaning, happiness can be achieved by way of those 3 components. When there is a deficiency, or when it is inhibited, let's say for example, by serotonin, it can lead to negative emotional states. Serotonin must regulate as well as inhibit dopamine to an extent in order to ensure addictive behaviors don't develop since much dopamine is derived from such things as, sex, spending money, smelling and tasting good food and the like.

Serotonin, discussed earlier in the article, helps regulate several emotions, including promoting feelings of contentment, confidence, and positive self-esteem. Estrogen hormones have also been shown to increase serotonin formation.

GABA (Gamma Amino Butyric Acid), is the largest contributor in achieving and maintaining a calm state within the nervous system. This is crucial because the nervous system seems to favor being in a more alert state. This makes sense and is probably a good thing because it causes behavior that is favorable to the person avoiding danger, and unsafe situations, circumstances and people. When the nervous system does become overactive, it manifests as more stressful and negative emotions.

Similarly, the hormone progesterone has the same effect as GABA, in terms of relaxing the nervous system.

Endorphins, are peptide hormones (short chain amino acids), are correlated with pleasurable emotional states and pain relief. Engaging in activities like laughing, exercising, playful activities, being in love, eating chocolate (and supposedly oysters), all release endorphins into the system.

(We are approaching inflammation and
possible autoimmune disease territory.....)

LOVE is a very complex emotion, as it involves many compatible and conflicting feelings and states combined, which makes it a bit of a paradoxical emotional state. The quick and simple explanation is that love can be seen as mainly a combination of pleasure, joy, reward (components of happiness), attachment, bonding, and stress. It also connects the stress centers of the brain to the reward-seeking circuits. No wonder it causes people to go crazy!

Once we have identified someone specific that makes our "Spidey senses" tingle, hee hee, and an attraction begins, our stress response is activated to a degree and we are in a stress state. When love is unrequited, (loving someone who doesn't love you back), it usually results in a degree of anger or frustration, then sadness. The reason is because when we first realize that the other person (our reward) is not interested, anger/frustration arises because your "reward" has been blocked. BOO!!! After processing some of this, we can move into sadness because we become disheartened and discouraged. We can also turn to self- criticizing and punishment as well, which is one of those super fun activities we like to engage in with ourselves when alone. (I am not good enough, pretty enough, smart enough, etc.) You know, the usual self- beat-downs…

Studies have shown time and time again that love begins as more of a stress response than anything else. (GO FIGURE…) As I sat here and thought about the very few times I thought I was "in love", it sure felt stressful. YEOWW! It all makes sense now! This doesn't sound like a good thing because it involves the word "stress", but this *is* a good thing as it motivates us to behave in a way that encourages us to spend time with this person and build a bond and relationship. This also facilitates the anticipation of reward. The more we spend time with this special person, the initial stress response relaxes because the familiarity, comfortability, and trust increases with time. The stress response to love is actually a pleasant one, as the specific neurotransmitters involved in stress are being constantly moderated by ones that promote security and trust. Many studies have shown that when someone suffers from heart ache, a broken heart, or the like, it sets off a cytokine storm in the immune system. This, of course, results in not only massive inflammation within the heart muscle itself but the heart sends out these inflammatory signals throughout the body. Studies have also shown that this specific type of emotional upheaval actually suppresses parts of the immune system. So, not only is massive inflammation circulating around the body and heart, but this state also keeps part of the immune system from helping out and doing its job to its fullest capability. A study done by Ohio State University, showed that people who recently got divorced were more likely to contract and fall ill from viruses such as the Epstein Barr virus. They were also shown to produce less natural killer cells, which are crucial for fighting diseases. We are definitely headed into "pre-autoimmune" disease and autoimmune disease territory here. When any type of prolonged abuse happens between loved ones, such as psychological and emotional, (assaults on the soul and spirit vs. the physical body), child or adult, the intense polarizing emotions of love and hate (the alternating hatred experienced, either for the person or the acts committed), causes massive amounts of inflammation that will eventually manifests physically.

FEAR (which includes anxiety) happens when we are faced with either a real or perceived specific threat that will require us to either "fight" or "flee", and sometimes "freeze", and is a sympathetic nervous response. A swift response is necessary here!

Anxiety, on the other hand, can be described as more of a generalized feeling (in the absence of an external provocation), which usually comes from an internal place of being worried/concerned about a future event and feeds "catastrophizing", where a person ruminates about the worst possible outcome regardless of how small the probability of it occurring, statistically speaking. Sometimes it happens for no apparent reason. It is for this reason that anxiety is thought to be a product of "fear- based learning". This means it helps us prepare for possible future negative events by using the brunt of our energy to think about (in this case, ruminating) how we need to modify or adapt to prepare. When this becomes worse in frequency and depth, anxiety disorders begin to manifest.

It appears that through evolution and facing the profound dangers our ancestors had to face on the daily, our waking hours are controlled by the stress hormones. Some level of stress chemicals and hormones are necessary for all emotions. What they do is provide the necessary energy to increase it from its baseline level, in order to motivate the body into taking action. Disproportionately low levels can lead to such feelings as lethargy, boredom, and restlessness. Obviously the opposite happens when there are too many stress chemicals surging throughout the body, it causes stress symptoms and volatile emotional levels.

Whether or not a person interprets an external stimulus as a threat, has much to do with the amygdala. (The amygdala that cried wolf?). The amygdala plays a salient role in identifying the threat and the degree of threat. Based on the type of threat, the nervous system will respond accordingly. For example, when faced with what is perceived to be an inescapable threat, the nervous system will typically go into the "freeze" state. When someone is faced with what they perceive to be an escapable and lower level threat, it may provoke their anger and they go into the "fight" response, to fend off the threat.

The neurochemicals that drive fear are mainly adrenaline, noradrenaline, cortisol, serotonin, and GABA.

Adrenaline and noradrenaline—in this case, these hormones are the main driver behind the "fight-flight" response and activate the corresponding coping mechanism.

Cortisol is the adrenal hormone that controls our state of arousal. It increases when a person perceives danger, triggering the fear response.

Serotonin, in context to the fear response, can promote fear in certain parts of the brain while actually inhibiting it in other areas. Serotonin's role in fear is a regulatory and facilitative one and is partially responsible for the feelings of dislike, avoidance and even disgust, when faced with something perceived as off-putting.

GABA is a neurotransmitter that helps calm and stifle the fear response. If there is too little, it can cause an ongoing feeling of fear and anxiety.

(Now we are really getting close to
inflammation and autoimmune diseases!)

ANGER (including the lesser forms of frustration and irritation), is an emotion that can be a real trouble maker! It can be described as a combination of stress, hostility and usually but not always, aggression. Common associated feelings are disgust, dislike, judgment, dislike, and criticism.

Since the sympathetic stress response is the most studied component of the emotion of anger, we know it has its neurochemical origins from fear. Because fear is seen as a product of "fear-based learning", anger is taking that one step further, as "an adaptive survival mechanism", which prompts the person to motivate to defend itself. Because humans have a more advanced nervous system than animals, it allows us the ability to experience anger, process it and dissipate it in a way that does not always lead to physical aggression. The frontal lobes of humans allow us to reason things out and come up with better solutions than aggression.

People can have various things that cause them anger, but most people become angry when faced with some type of personal or social injustice, bullying, or when their dreams, goals, etc. are blocked, stifled, or redirected.

When the emotional brain and limbic system are caught in the anger response, our conscious brain has little to no control over it and this can lead to explosive bouts of physical aggression and violence without the person even realizing and feelings of remorse, afterward. Anger usually will dissipate on it's own by itself but when a person is in this state, their cognitive functions go offline to varying degrees and their mental processing becomes much faster, which allows a person to do a couple of things, either find more reasons to be angry within the situation, (often times with a skewed angry perspective and point of view), especially as it unfolds and the situation progresses. Regardless, the high speed cognitive processing can also allow us to work towards other options besides physical aggression, such as, verbal arguments, and the use of negotiation tactics and strategies. The prefrontal lobes, specifically, allow for a timely intervention of the primordial fear pathway, precisely, to modulate and decrease the effects and allow for reasoning.

A common component of anger, but not always, is aggression. It appears to result from low emotional control and an increase in the perception of threat coming from the prefrontal lobe and emotional centers of the brain. The prefrontal lobes allow a person to engage in reflection and re-evaluation of the situation, which allows for real-time behavior modifications and adjustments. If the threat is perceived to be severe enough, however, those emotional control centers in the brain will likely generate the "fight response".

Frustration and irritation are lesser degrees of anger. Frustration is seen as failed reward-seeking attempts usually, and irritation is experienced as a generalized version of anger (as anxiety is to fear) and can occur with little to no external provocation. Someone can merely "wake up" irritated, possibly from a bad dream or from holding over thoughts of negative events.

The neurochemicals involved in anger are mainly, serotonin, dopamine, adrenaline, noradrenaline,

Serotonin-a deficiency in this neurotransmitter, has been proven to be a main component of anger, especially aggression involving anger.CLAR-IFY!!! CONFUSED

Dopamine has a role in anger, particularly when the anger is a result of an anticipated reward or goal not being met. This causes a drop in dopamine in relation to serotonin, and when that happens, feelings of frustration, anger and worse can develop.

SADNESS-the simple definition is that emotional reaction to some type of real or perceived "loss" in their life. There is nothing simple about this emotional state, however, as the exact neurochemistry is still being debated upon. The main reason appears to be because sadness can be in relation to varying things like distress, anguish and fear. When faced with a loss of such things as goals, dreams, a career, or a person, it caus-es a neurological reaction that not only interrupts the reward seeking pathways, but also inhibits feelings such as creating and appreciating humor and engaging in laughter and happiness. Because it has been found to inhibit the reward seeking pathways, it has been theorized that sadness has an evolutionary benefit of making the person remove focus from "not being able to receive that future reward". This is known as the "sadness theory".

Interestingly, even though sadness can be linked to other emotional states, it has a distinctive connection to anger, neurologically speaking. Sadness inherently promotes a strong sense of punishment, usually en-couraging a strong sense of penalizing and punishment. Mainly self-di-rected, which overlaps with anger, mainly experienced as frustration, in brain regions that sadness shares with anger.

Now, if sadness is also experienced with a profound surprise, such as the common death of a loved one, it can easily send a person into "fight or flight", which can end up being prolonged and therefore caus-ing increased and ongoing inflammation in the immune system. Intense sadness even modulates the brain in a way that it sends the body a signal to produce real physical pain. This would be why we feel real physical pain, usually in the heart and chest area, when experiencing the sudden loss of a loved one. It can also happen after divorce from a long marriage. Think of it like this, even though we are having these experiences in a physical 3D world, it is the soul and spirit that are profoundly affected here, so of course it is going to manifest as physical symptoms, here in this physical world. An autoimmune disease percolating, no doubt....

There is still much research to be done to figure out exactly which chemicals are doing what, but they have identified the following, serotonin, dopamine, adrenaline, and noradrenaline.

Serotonin, in this case, when elevated, promotes punishment type mentality, dislike, and behaviors that align with antagonizing the reward pathways.

Dopamine, in this case is low, which results in the reward pathway being inhibited.

Adrenaline and noradrenaline could be elevated or decreased, depending on whether the fear is coupled with surprise or shock. In this combination, the fight or flight will be set off to varying degrees for varying lengths of time, depending on several factors.

Sources:

Mya Care Editorial Team.(2017). FEELINGS & THE NEURO-CHEMISTRY OF EMOTION.https://myacare.com/blog/feelings-the-neuro-chemistry-of-emotion

~~~~~~~
~~~~~~~

✻ THE FREQUENCIES OF DIFFERENT EMOTIONS ✻

I think many of us know by now and many more are not far behind in learning that every single one of us is a vibrating being. We are always vibrating at a very subtle hertz frequency rate. Each individual has what is referred to as a base metabolic rate when at rest. Everyone is slightly different when the body is in homeostasis, but when we are met with stressors and events start happening in our lives, the corresponding emotions become engaged at various degrees, depending on the stressor so our vibrational rate changes rapidly and often dramatically.

We spend our entire lifetimes experiencing and collecting both positive and negative emotions along the way. It is mainly the negative emotions that become stored in our bodies in various places such as in the fascia and muscles. These stored negative emotions can and do also affect our bodily systems and areas such as the amygdala, frontal lobes, and emotional brain and more. If these volatile situations or environments continue, we become stuck in a negative feedback loop. This keeps us in a negative mindset where our first instinct is to have a negative reaction even when a positive or neutral one would have been better suited.

If you look at the frequencies of the lower-level emotions, from *anger* on down, there is an enormous difference between them and the higher, more positive ones. The lower the frequency, the lower the vibration. The higher the frequency, the higher the vibration.

Once a person is stuck in this negative down spiral, they draw more negativity into their lives and soon anything or anyone around them gets sucked into their "vortex of negativity", as I call it. It's the equivalent of always having to look at life through muddled lenses that only allow you to see things from the negative perspective, which includes the worst case scenario, even when statistically speaking, the odds of that "thing or event" ever happening are extremely low. "Catastrophizing" is what it's called and the "Eyeores" of the world do it all the time. Always the worst case scenario. Think about the negative energy these people wallow in… and…want you to wallow in. Misery loves company. That vibe is contagious if we are not careful to identify and protect ourselves from it.

I would like to note that *anger* is mainly a secondary emotion which is fed by the emotions below it. It is 150 on the scale, so energetically speaking, it is still high enough to cause much physical motivation and volatility not just within the body but outwardly as well. The emotions below anger are much more passive ones. Many studies have now confirmed that the emotion of anger (can be the collection and sum effect of multiple other underlying emotions) is a main component in not just auto-immune disease (anger ='s inflammation within the body), but other pre-autoimmune disease such as, fibromyalgia, chronic fatigue syndrome and more. Not just your garden variety anger but a special and most insidious kind of self-directed anger that was created and cultivated by someone or something else in their immediate environment giving them the message that they are deficient, not worthy, or a bad person, etc. Being stuck in a chronically negative, oppressive or threatening environment will also cause this as well.

$\sim\sim\sim\sim\sim\sim\sim$

The Emotional Vibration
Analysis Frequency Chart, in Stress.

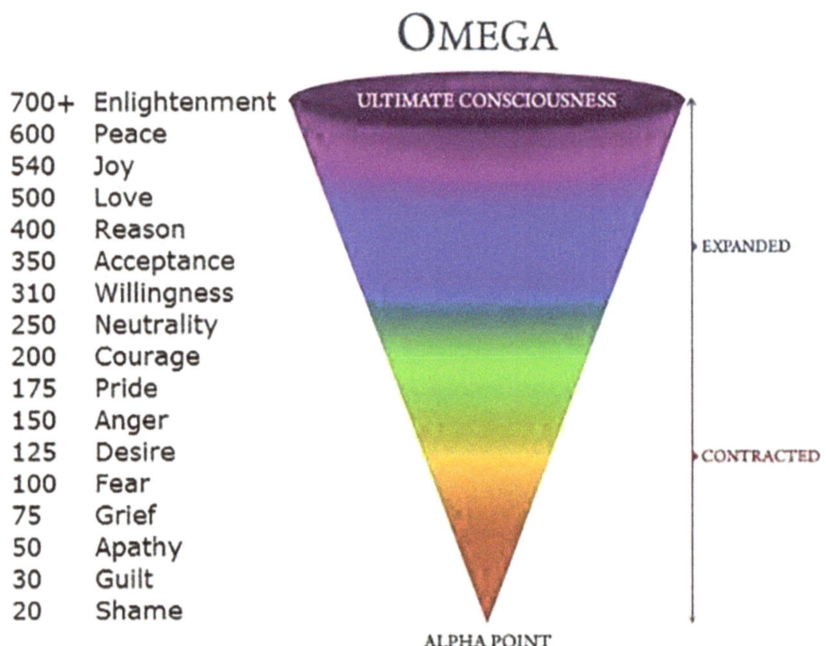

Chart Provided by -Blisspot.com.

Sources:

Smith, J. (2024). The Emotional Vibration Analysis Frequency Chart, in Stress. https://blisspot.com/blogs/the-emotional-vibration-analysis-frequency-chart/

~~~~~~~
~~~~~~~

SHAMAN PERSPECTIVE ON AUTOIMMUNE DISEASES

If you happen to ask your local Shaman (a traditional medicine man) what causes autoimmune diseases they may very well tell you there are 3 things that cause them because their beliefs say that in order for true healing to take place, the root cause must be addressed instead of using medicine etc. to treat it. What I have found is that Shaman believes that most, if not all illnesses come from the invisible and esoteric realm and not from the traditional bacteria, viruses or microbes. That place where science, religion, spirituality and maybe even atheism all agree exists but just can't agree on what to call it. They believe that illnesses come from one of three places, which are negative internal states that develop within the person as a result of traumatic, negative or adverse experiences can create. They are **disharmony,** *fear*, and the worst most damaging of all, is **soul loss.**

1.) DISHARMONY-This happens when we suddenly and swiftly lose a connection to life which is important to us or when it loses its meaning for us in some way. A classic example of this would be an elderly couple who have been married forever and one of them suddenly passes and this passing causes the spouse who's left behind to quickly spiral into a crisis situation that causes their physical health to seriously and rapidly decline and soon after, comes death. Suffering such a tremendous loss, not just of our "person", but of a source of power, comfort, familiarity, and so on, for us.

2.) FEAR-When someone is going through life being in varying degrees of "fight or flight" mode, the corresponding chemical activity in the body is going to cause dysregulation and imbalances. Being in fight or flight, filled with anxiety and restlessness, quickly diminishes our ability to feel safe and grounded in our world. Not to mention, fear feeds the powerful and volatile emotion of anger, and we've already learned what anger can do to our immune systems!

3.) SOUL LOSS-This is the "big bad one", and usually happens as a result of trauma and mostly of the interpersonal type. When the trauma is severe enough and/or lost standing, a person feels as if they've lost their very essence and spirit. Their soul can feel anywhere from fragmented to completely obliterated to the point it becomes shattered or shut down completely. The most common and primary symptom of soul loss is depression. Depression is your body going into the "freeze" state of the "fight, flight or freeze" states. It is the immobilization state where it feels it can neither fight nor flee the danger, perceived or real, so it shuts down.

Some symptoms of soul loss;

*A blocked, fragmented or lack of memory or pieces of long term memory.
*Feeling a disconnect from yourself and who you are or were.

*Emotionally distant-not feeling or feeling very little, especially positive emotions. Increased apathy and flattened or subdued mood.

*Inability to give and feel any degree of love or positive emotion to someone else.

*Lack of enthusiasm and failure to thrive.

*Develop an "I don't care" attitude towards everyone and life in geeral.

*Develop depression, chronic negativity and addictions

*Become suicidal.

Wesselman, H. (2024). 3 Causes of Spiritual. https://www.eomega.org/article/3-causes-of-spiritual-illness

~~~~~~~
~~~~~~~

Autoimmune Disease:
A Shamanic Belief of Emotional Inflammation

Shamanic belief is that the immune system is an element of the earth and therefore takes its instructions from that fundamental source of intelligence and interconnectedness that surrounds us all. In terms of the immune system, they believe 2 main things can happen. It can either become underactive, which is the case with AIDS, cancer or as a result of chemotherapy, certain medications or vaccines. The other state the immune system can fall into is hyperactivity. To a Shaman, these hyperactive states are considered "allergic type disorders/diseases" and are associated with internal emotional responses. Some examples range anywhere from eczema, allergies, hives, dermatitis, shortness of breath, etc. all the way to Multiple Sclerosis, Lupus and Rheumatoid Arthritis, Diabetes Type 1 and more. They believe that these illnesses are largely a result of not having good enough personal and other boundaries as well as a lack of discernment of sorts. Interestingly, these all result in exaggerated fear responses. This makes sense to me because not having strong boundaries means you are going to get walked on, taken advantage of, and knocked around and will therefore suffer many negative spiritual attacks and much distress, as a result. These types of injuries cause emotional heat and inflammation and the final steak in the heart is when the person finally disconnects from their self or spirit. It's a zombie-like detachment. These tumultuous mixture of emotions cause internal conflict and much worse. They result in maladaptive coping mechanisms, negative internal talk and beliefs, self-criticism, mistaken, confused or modified morals and values which all eventually result in various degrees and layers of fear and anger. We now all have learned what anger does to our immune system. These illnesses don't start as autoimmune diseases though, they will first appear as PTSD, anxiety, depression, hypervigilance, and similar symptoms. Your subconscious is giving direct orders to your bodily systems on how to act and your immune system was specifically designed to seek out and attack foreign invaders. This attack will continue (inflammation increases) until an autoimmune disease develops.

Now psychologically speaking, these issues may manifest in the personality as depression, anxiety, withdrawal, projection, over reactions, blaming, mood swings, listlessness, etc. The big picture perspective is that Shaman believe that either a spirit/soul in the body wants to actively live or die. Once the decision has been made, the subconscious kicks in and starts going to work on killing the self. This belief also would explain the real phenomena of *spontaneous healing*. This is where a sick or injured person heals without seemingly any type of real medical intervention either acute or chronic. This is what happened to me. I mysteriously started healing after my divorce from a 30 year marriage. That is actually the reason I started this entire truth finding journey...

Just as these situations and negative symptoms develop, they can also be reversed. Fortunately, I can speak from first- hand experience on this phenomena, as I experienced just this. There are things you can actively do to start and to facilitate the healing process. They are;

*Accepting and forgiving others, but mostly ourselves. This is paramount because acceptance is the precursor to LOVE, and that is what is needed in order to heal. Self-love and forgiveness of ourselves and others, when appropriate, will help release much unnecessary guilt and shame and allow us to tip the pendulum to a more healing internal environment.

*Self-care is crucial because it is an active way to love and appreciate ourselves and also induces relaxation which is what our ramped-up systems need. This can be anything from brushing your hair and getting a manicure to walking in nature, or engaging in yoga, meditation and grounding.

*Empathy and compassion are also paramount to the healing process because we must have both for ourselves, at the very least, for the body to follow suit.

*Reflection is a great one because it allows us to go back to specific situations, hopefully with a different perspective, which time is always wonderful at providing, so we can see what we could have done differently or better. This allows us to reduce much of that internal conflict we develop within ourselves because we either are not able to live our genuine authentic selves or we have to compromise our values and core beliefs for some reason.

*Allow ourselves to feel both the mental as well as the physical pain. This is important because if we are suppressing the pain, it will eventually fester and become worse. It's vital that we release these negative emotions and remove them from our bodies just as we would remove a virus, bacteria or splinter that has entered our system. *Suppression does not equal removal.*

*Zoom out a bit and look at the big picture perspective. As time progresses, information comes forth, so with this in mind, try to find the more significant meaning within the situation and learn from it. Learn either what to do or what not to do for next time.

The above ideas are not just ways to cognitively think about how to heal, they actually set off the relaxation response which allows our systems to move to homeostasis and therefore heal.

D'Onofrio, A. (2016). Emotional Inflammation; What It is and How to Heal.. https://sunnysidehealingarts.com

~~~~~~~
~~~~~~~

MITOCHONDRIA AND BIOHACKING-
An interview with Dave Asprey.

The more we study mitochondria, the more we realize how they are truly our "spiritual antennas" and frontline spiritual sensors of the outside world. According to the National Institute of Health, Mitochondria are "living, dynamic, maternally inherited, energy transforming, biosynthetic, and signaling organelles that actively transduce biological information." That is a mouth full, so let me simplify a bit- Mitochondria are double membrane-bound cell organelles that generate most of the chemical energy needed to power the cell's biochemical reactions and are referred to as "the powerhouse of the cell." they play a major role in breaking down vital nutrients. They are also responsible for generating energy-rich molecules for the cell. Numerous biochemical reactions that are a crucial part of the cellular respiration process takes part within the mitochondria.

Dave Asprey, known as the "Father of Biohacking" and a former Silicon Valley executive and CEO of eight companies, went on a personal, educational journey for many years and discusses some of what he has learned about the importance of mitochondria in sensing our external environment and relaying the corresponding message internally.

Dave, although very successful, had been unhappy for many years and was depressed and anxious. He claimed to have done all the things that were supposed to bring him joy, but those things just didn't work for him. What he discovered when he took a deep dive into the world of personal development and spiritual practice roximately 20 years ago was that *trauma is the primary programmer of our mitochondria and our nervous system.* It affects the long-term operations of the nervous system. It involves the balance between sympathetic and parasympathetic systems trauma that is stored in your body." Dave believes that unprocessed emotion that we hold onto gets stored within those mitochondrial networks and within the fascia. This will then become the lens through which we see reality. Once this perspective sets in, bad pattern matches are created where the mitochondria are looking around and trying to keep you safe and triggering us to feel anxious. Dave believes this because of an inappropriate connection between something happening in our immediate environment and an emotional response that is no longer serving us. A skewed perception of reality it becomes. Dave says that it is because of these reasons that emotional healing is a necessary part of biology. He reasons that if we are triggered and have triggers, then we are walking around with a loaded gun, so to speak, so by doing your spiritual work/biohacking, you can unload the gun so you are not so triggered. Spiritual practice allows us to go in and "edit" our operation systems settings. Dave claims FORGIVENESS is what will unload the gun that triggers us all.

The way these "spiritual antennas" contribute to autoimmune disease, specifically, is that when they become stressed, non-functioning, or damaged, they begin to release damaging substances that can cause autoimmune diseases. They not only release their own mtDNA but also modified self-antigens and danger-associated molecular patterns. (DAMPs)

According to the article Old and New Damage Associated Molecular Patterns (DAMPs) in Autoimmune Diseases, on the Wiley website, states that "The mitochondria's own DNA, the mtDNA, is released into the cell's fluid, the cytosol, which is part of the cytoplasm and surrounds the organelles. It then sends them into the bloodstream." The immune system will then detect this "new and different DNA" as foreign and dangerous and produce type 1 interferon, which can cause inflammation and autoimmunity. This process is called interferonopathy and is a prominent feature of certain autoimmune disorders and diseases. "Mitochondria contain genetic material called mtDNA. Alterations in the mtDNA copy number (CN) have been reported to be a hallmark of autoimmune and inflammatory diseases.[15] There is strong evidence that a decreased leukocyte mtDNA CN contributes to the progression and development of SLE and secretion of proinflammatory cytokines, and may contribute to the persistence of low-grade inflammation in SLE."

Modified self-antigens, known as autoantigens, are the result of the mutation of old normal protein or protein complexes, neoantigen formation, or exposure of previously hidden self-antigens. Genes producing self-proteins can mutate and create a new immunogenic protein called a neoantigen. According to the article "Autoantigens" on the website sciencedirect.com, They contribute to autoimmune diseases and conditions by triggering an immune response. Under normal circumstances, our immune system will not attack antigens; however, attacking these "newly unrecognized and foreign" antigens is a vital component in developing autoimmune diseases, disorders, autoimmunity, allergic reactions., and immuno-suppression. Antigens can be either DNA, RNA, or proteins and protein complexes and can be located on or in the cell and even extracellularly.

When someone has the above issue with antigens, the symptoms usually manifest as fatigue, low or high fever, muscular weakness/pain, weight loss, and allergy or cold-type symptoms.

Danger-associated molecular patterns, also known as DAMPs, consist of several molecules such as, ions, nucleic acids, glycan and metabolites. These can all mutate into DAMPs, if they become stressed out or subjected to injury, meaning they can change in distribution levels, concentration as well as, both chemical and physical properties to become these DAMPs. They are created and are delivered from within the cell (endogenous) but can also be caused by environmental factors such as, UV light, chemotherapy, radiation, thermal heat, trauma, toxic substances and chemicals, etc., (exogenous). These DAMPs then become detected by innate immune receptors, which then activate the immune system and cause an inflammatory response. These responses can include metabolic and adaptive pathologies as well as inflammation.

The way that DAMPs contribute to autoimmune diseases specifically, is that: "DAMPs released from injured or dying cells activate the immune system and invoke inflammatory responses in autoimmune diseases, such as rheumatoid arthritis (RA) and systemic lupus erythematosus (SLE)", according to an academic article, "Old and New

Damage-Associated Molecular Patterns (DAMPs) in Autoimmune Disease", in the Rheumatology and Autoimmunity section of the online Wiley Library www.onlinelibrary.wiley.com. This article goes on to say that, "Some reports have elucidated that DAMPs play a crucial role in aggravating the pathogenesis of autoimmune diseases, including RA, SLE, and systemic sclerosis because they are concurrently involved in the maturation of various immune pathways through a series of pro-inflammatory cytokine mediators".

Dawn, K. (2024). Dave Asprey: Beginner Biohacker's Guide to Overcoming Stress & Confronting Fear | 105 | Karena Dawn. https://www.youtube.com/watch?v=GXgRE7-HmHo

Kan, N. et al. (2022). Old and New Damage-Associated Molecular Patterns (DAMPs) in Autoimmune Diseases. https://onlinelibrary.wiley.com/doi/full/10.1002/rai2.12046

Barabas, A. & Lafreniere, R. (2005). Antigen-specific down-regulation of immunopathological events in an experimental autoimmune kidney disease. Antigen-specific down-regulation of immunopathological events in …

~~~~~~~
~~~~~~~

ALEXITHYMIA-HOW IT CAUSES IMMUNE DYSFUNCTION

Alexithymia, is a dimensional personality trait (a member of one of the 5 personality trait dimensions known as "The Big Five".) These traits are relatively stable over time that vary in intensity from person to person. According to Wikipedia, alexithymia is measured on a continuum and is defined by; (1) a difficulty identifying feelings (certain ones or all of them) and distinguishing between feelings and bodily sensations of emotional arousal (2) difficulty describing feelings to others (3) constricted imaginal process, as evidence by scarcity of fantasies."

In Greek, ***Alexithymia*** means "not having words for feelings" and it causes people to register their emotions as a physical problem/ailment rather than a sign or distinct inner feeling that signals us to the fact that something needs our attention. For example, instead of registering a feeling of anger (more specifically a degree of mental anguish never experienced before) they cannot process it at the cognitive level because it's beyond what their psyche can handle or is familiar with, so it gets experienced as a headache, indigestion or muscle pain and stiffness, or worse, according to Dr. Bessel Van Der Kolk, in his bestselling book, "The Body Keeps The Score- Brain, Mind, and Body in the Healing of Trauma."

Traumatized children and people are often alexithymic because they've learned to shut down their emotions because they were too overwhelming (during abuse, trauma, etc.) and as a result, they have lost touch between their mind and body and can no longer identify what they're feeling. This condition causes people to use "action" instead of "language" to express what they're feeling. For example, a child that was bullied at school may not appear to be too upset about it but may spend that evening and the following days with an unexplained headache or stomach and gastrointestinal distress.

Alexithymia also causes changes in the immune system which lead to autoimmune illnesses and diseases. Below is an academic article (review) that helps explain the process, which includes increases in Tumor Necrosis Factor (TNF).

Alexithymia - Wikipedia

Van Der Kolk, B. (2014) The Body Keeps the Score-Brain, Mind , and Body in the Healing of Trauma. Penguin Books.

~~~~~~~
~~~~~~~

FROM AUTOINFLAMMATION TO AUTOIMMUNITY

During my research, I came across a fascinating academic review (of multiple studies) out of Italy that uncovered not only the differences and similarities between autoinflammation and autoimmunity, as well as the moment one switch to the other, but ***also*** *the fact that these illnesses lie on a spectrum, where they can worsen and progress to the other. For example, fibromyalgia can develop into systemic lupus erythematosus and vice versa. THIS IS HOW MY ILLNESS PROGRESSED.*

Crucial excerpts below taken directly from the academic review. (For the review in its entirety, as well as references, please click the link below)

- The term autoimmunity used to be referred to as a condition associated with the dysregulation of adaptive immunity alone, whereas autoinflammatory was initially defined solely as a consequence of dysregulated innate immunity.
- Consequently, the pathogenetic mechanisms of autoimmune diseases (ADs) were considered to be exclusively mediated by B and T lymphocytes whose B and T cell receptors (BCRs and TCRs) recognized specific antigens, started the inflammatory response against autoantigens, and activated B cell-mediated autoantibody production whereas the autoinflammatory diseases were defined as unprovoked episodes of inflammation, without high titer of autoantibodies or antigen-specific T cells.
- This view clearly separated autoinflammation and autoimmunity as distinct immunological diseases.
- More than ten years ago, McGonagle and McDermott first theorized the existence of a ***continuum model*** of immunology, in which diseases lie on a *spectrum from autoimmune to autoinflammatory,* with variable contributions of both the innate and the adaptive immune responses to particular diseases.

- Autoinflammatory diseases are a group of monogenic and polygenic disorders characterized by recurrent inflammatory episodes whose heterogeneous symptoms are frequently associated with fever. The key pathogenetic moment in autoinflammatory diseases is the direct and indirect dysregulation of inflammasomes, the multiprotein cytoplasmic complexes characteristic of innate immunity and inflammatory responses.

- The main components of inflammasomes are members of the nucleotide-binding oligomerisation domain (NOD)-like receptor (NLR) family, a class of pattern recognition receptors (PRR). When induced to do so by proinflammatory triggers such as the stimuli transmitted by pathogens or damaged cells, NLRs respectively detect pathogen associated or damage-associated molecular patterns ((PAMPs or DAMPs) and begin inflammasome assembly, which generates the proteolytic activation of caspases and the conversion of pro interleukin(IL)-1β into active IL-1β, a key molecule of inflammation and innate immunity.

- Although ADs are still considered adaptive immunity-mediated disorders, there is increasing evidence that innate immunity and inflammasomes are also involved. It seems clear that despite the differences in the system primarily involved, autoinflammatory and autoimmune disease share common characteristics, such as activation against subsequent systemic inflammation, and the absence of an external causal trigger clearly identified.

- The main difference between the two pathogenetic mechanisms is that in autoinflammatory diseases, the innate immune system directly causes inflammation, while in ADs, it subsequently activates the adaptive system, which activates the inflammatory process.

- It is known that innate and adaptive immunity are strictly interconnected. In the case of innate immunity, macrophages, antigen-presenting cells (APCs) and dendritic cells (DCs) act as the first line of host defense. PAMPs and DAMPs are neutralized by NLRs and other classes of PRRs such as

Tolllike receptors (TLRs), which recognize various microbial ligands, activate inflammasomes, thus increasing the synthesis of pro-inflammatory cytokines including IL1β, IL-18, tumor necrosis factor-alpha (TNF-α) interferon(IFN)-α and IFN-β. These cytokines subsequently activate adaptive immunity.

- There is increasing evidence that the protracted or increased activation of PRRs plays a key role in autoimmune mechanisms: Leadbetter et al. have shown that the activation of rheumatoid factor-positive B cells mediated by IgG2a/chromatin immune complexes is associated with the synergistic action of the antigen receptor and a protein belonging to the TLR family.

- This link between TLRs and B cells suggests that TLRs could play a potentially key role in autoantibody responses in various ADs. For examples, TLR4 promotes B cell differentiation and leads to the production of antibodies by upregulating the expression of B cell-activating factor, a crucial factor that regulates B cell maturation, survival and function, and is upregulated in systemic lupus erythematosus (SLE).

- An important link between autoimmunity and autoinflammation is represented by IL-1ß, which is crucial in connecting the innate immune response due to NLR activation and the adaptive immune responses of T and B cells. It has been demonstrated by Chung et al. that the increased levels of IL-1 following inflammasome activation can induce T cell polarization (Th17 differentiation) and, synergized with IL-6 and IL-23, is crucial in maintaining cytokine expression in effector Th17 cells.

- IL-1 has also been implicated in the activation of IFN-γ in memory T cells, T cell proliferation (which is also mediated by IL-2 and its receptor), increased B cell proliferation, and increased antibody synthesis [30], thus connecting the inflammasome-driven responses to the adaptive immune system in response to exogenous and endogenous signals.

- The role of IL-1 has always been considered of crucial importance in autoinflammatory diseases, as demonstrated by the rapid and sustained improvement in disease severity after treatment with IL-1β drug. Other than in monogenic auto-inflammatory diseases, IL-1 β has a pivotal role in rheuma-toid arthritis (RA): it has been shown that IL-1 β induces the expression of different proteolytic enzymes, such as metallo-proteinases, collagenases and elastases, thus leading to bone erosions and cartilage destruction. However, treatment with IL-1 drug in RA is not as effective as in autoinflammatory diseases, having a modest effect in comparison with other biologic agents blocking TNF pathways.

- Another emblematic example of the link between autoimmunity and autoinflammation is represented by the role of inflammasomes, crucial components of the innate system, in a paradigmatic autoimmune disease such as systemic lupus erythematosus (SLE). Several autoinflammatory disorders, such as CAPS, FCAS, MWS and NOMID, have been linked with mutations in inflammasomes, particularly involving NLRP3 inflammasome, thus leading to increase in release of IL-1.

- These mutations have also been linked with polygenic inflammatory disorders, such as gout and pseudogout. In comparison the understanding of the role of inflammasomes in autoimmunity is less clear. In recent years there have been increasing evidence that inflammasomes, particularly NLRP3, could play a potentially key role in SLE, with various mechanisms.

- In recent years there have been increasing evidence that inflammasomes, particularly NLRP3, could play a potentially key role in SLE through various mechanisms. Immune complexes formed secondary to antibody recognition have been shown to stimulate inflammasome activation through upregulation of TLR-dependent activation of NFκB and subsequent activation of the NLRP3 inflammasome.

- Kidney biopsy findings from SLE patients have shown increased expression of inflammasome components, including NLRP3 and caspase-1 [39]. C3a, which is released during complement activation in tissues in SLE, regulates ATP secretion in inflammasome thus causing their activation and subsequent production of IL-1.

- Autoinflammatory diseases are a group of monogenic and polygenic disorders characterized by dysregulation in the innate immune system, particularly in key cytokine pathways such as the ones involving TNF and interleukin 1, including the complex of adaptor molecules known as inflammasome, as well as mutations in proteins associated with bacterial sensing. They share as clinical manifestations recurrent episodes of unprovoked inflammation, often accompanied by fever and a wide range of systemic manifestations involving cutaneous, vascular and musculoskeletal systems in the absence of auto-antibodies or antigen specific T-lymphocytes.

- The adaptive immune response is also potentially linked to innate immunity through the Th1 and Th17 cell responses mediated by the nucleotide oligomerisation domain-like receptor family, pyrin domain-containing 3/caspase-1 (NLRP3) inflammasome, mutations of which are responsible for the autoinflammatory diseases known as cryopyrinopathies (CAPS).

- Genetic variants of the major histocompatibility complex (MHC) or the human leukocyte antigen (HLA) region located on the short arm of chromosome 6 are associated with autoimmune and inflammatory diseases.]. Fernando et al. made a pooled analysis of different studies investigating the causal links between MHC variants and various autoimmune and inflammatory diseases, and found that HLA-DR2 and HLA-DR3 were alleles inducing susceptibility to SLE and multiple sclerosis (MS) among Europeans, and that several HLA-DR4 haplotypes may predispose to SLE (HLADRB1* 0401) and MS (multiple HLA-DRB1*04 alleles).

- Autoimmune diseases with distinctive autoantibody profiles and diseases seronegative for autoantibodies are respectively associated with MHC class II and class I alleles, and HLA-DR3-DQ2, HLA-B8 and HLA-A1 alleles are associated with diseases such as celiac disease, T1D and autoimmune thyroid diseases (also due to linkage within the MHC locus).

- In the case of autoimmunity both mechanisms involved in the binding between self-peptide and the MHC complex and post-translational modifications in self-peptide can be involved in the pathogenesis of autoimmune disease in subjects with an HLA risk allele. The phases linking innate and adaptive immunity provide that peptide/MHC (pMHC) class II tetramers play a predominant role in the interactions between T cells and APCs.

- DCs are APCs capable of stimulating the clonal expansion of naïve T cells, impairing tolerance of self-reactive lymphocytes, and inducing autoimmune mechanisms in ADs. DCs play a significant role in breaking tolerance of self-reactive lymphocytes and in supporting autoimmune responses.

- Impaired tolerance of self-antigens or modified selfantigens due to the non-clearance of apoptotic debris, inflammation-mediated modification of self-antigen, or cross-reactivity between non-self and self-antigens are responsible for the synthesis of autoantibodies.

- The synthesis of (mainly IgG) autoantibodies can lead to inflammation with the release of intracellular or modified self-antigens, thus determining antibody effector function and the proliferation of the autoreactive B cell clones.

- Other cells involved in the pathogenesis of autoimmunity are T cells. TCRs are heterodimers consisting of two di-sulphide-linked chains: one α and one β chain, or one γ and one δ chain.

- Glycolysis, lipid oxidation and mitochondrial processes are also essential in regulating the activation, proliferation, and differentiation of CD4+ T and memory cells. In a recent study, Yin et al. found that impaired T cell metabolism was a key factor in the pathogenesis of SLE and suggested that it might be an appropriate therapeutic target.

- Another T cell population involved in the pathogenesis of autoimmunity is that of Th17 cell, which can express transcription factor ROR$\gamma\tau$ and synthesize a number of chemokines. The IL17 axis cytokines include IL-17A-IL17F, IL-22, TNF-α and IL-6, which have pro-inflammatory activity in autoimmune and autoinflammatory diseases. e.

The dysregulation of Th17 cells is crucial for autoimmunity and inflammation.

- IL-1 stimulation during the polarization phase, strongly suppresses IL-10 and promotes IFN-γ induction, thus these two kind of Th17 cells, that possess either proinflammatory or anti-inflammatory functions, can be modulated by IL-1β. As seen before, autoinflammatory syndromes are characterized by overproduction of IL-1β caused by dysregulation of inflammasomes. Noster and colleagues have demonstrated that in the autoinflammatory disease Schnitzler syndrome, a loss of anti-inflammatory TH17 cells is present, and that physiological levels could be restored after therapeutic IL-1β inhibition.

- Tregs are critical in ADs because of their effect on immune homeostasis and the maintenance of peripheral self-tolerance. Their development and function are controlled by the Foxp3 transcription factor. Altered Treg development, function and balance are associated with the development of inflammation and autoimmune mechanisms, whereas the homeostasis of Tregs and effector T cells (Teffs) balance tolerance and effector immune responses.

- CD4+CD25+ Tregs have an immunosuppressive function and mediate immunological self-tolerance by suppressing the potential suppression of autoreactive T cells [166, 168–170], and an altered number and/or function of CD4+CD25+ Tregs has been associated with severe autoimmune diseases, including RA and SLE.

- The complement system, a key component of the innate immune system, represents another link between innate and adaptive immunity. Its main function is to recognize and eliminate pathogens by means of direct killing or to stimulate phagocytosis in modulating adaptive immunity, thus bridging innate and adaptive responses [173, 174]. When complement mechanisms are unbalanced, the complement system may cause damage by mediating tissue inflammation.

- Dysregulation of the complement system has been implicated in the pathogenesis and clinical manifestations of a number of autoimmune diseases, including RA, SLE, Sjögren's syndrome, the vasculitides, dermatomyositis, SSc, and antiphospholipid syndrome. Complement deficiencies have also been associated with an increased risk of developing autoimmune disorders.

- Autoimmune diseases are a direct effect of tissue and organ damage mediated by autoreactive immune mechanisms and, in this context, a key role is played by autoantibodies, such as rheumatoid factor or antinuclear antibodies, which are totally absent in autoinflammatory diseases.

- CONCLUSION SECTION- ADs and autoinflammatory diseases have a number of similar etiopathogenetic and clinical characteristics, including genetic predisposition and recurrent systemic inflammatory flares [6–8]. The first phase of ADs involves innate immunity: by means of TLRs, DCs recognize and internalize autoantigens arising from the process of apoptosis, which leads to IFN-α production, DC maturation, autoantigen presentation, B and T cell recruitment, and autoantibody synthesis. The second phase involves adaptive immunity, a self-sustaining process in which immune complexes containing nucleic acids and autoantibodies are internalized by DC by means of Fcγreceptors (FcγRs), thus leading to IFN-α synthesis, additional DC and T cell activation, and autoantibody production Various data indicate that innate and adaptive immunity represent two strictly interconnected phases in the development of ADs. The protracted or increased activation of PRRs plays a key role in autoimmune mechanisms, and the strict link between TLRs and B cells suggests that innate immunity may play a key role in inducing autoantibody responses. Another important link between autoimmunity and autoinflammation is IL-1ß, which is crucial in connecting the innate immune response due to NLR activation and the adaptive immune responses of T and B cells.

It has been reported that the increase in IL-1 levels following inflammasome activation induces T cell polarization (Th17 differentiation) [25]. Adaptive immune responses are potentially linked to innate immunity through the Th1 and Th17 cell responses mediated by the NLRP3 inflammasome, mutations in which are responsible for CAPS.

- The study of the connections between autoimmunity and autoinflammation represents an exciting challenge for further studies [211–214]. Recently, a study by Arakelyan and colleagues, using a comparative gene expression analysis of a large set of transcriptome data, focused on finding existing similarities and common inflammatory components in ADs and autoinflammatory diseases. The results revealed that some pathways were similarly perturbed in both diseases,, such as PI3K-Akt, Toll-like receptor, and NF-kappa β, all important signals involved in immune cell polarization, migration, growth, survival, and differentiation.

- They identified two clusters of diseases basing on specific disregulated pathways: one prevalently composed by autoimmune and the other by autoinflammatory disease. Interestingly, some diseases did not seem to belong to the cluster they classically were believed to belong to. PAPA, one of the autoinflammatory diseases discussed above, was closer to the cluster of autoimmune diseases, confirming some differences found between this disease and the others autoinflammatory syndromes, such as the poor response to IL-1 blockade.

- Furthermore, SLE, a typical autoimmune disease, seemed to belong to the cluster of autoinflammatory syndromes [215], thus apparently remarking the systemic inflammatory nature of SLE and, as discussed above, a possible role for inflammasomes in its pathogenesis. This study identified disease specific variations in activation of common pathways, thus highlighting not only the similarities but also the basic differences between the two types of diseases. The inflammatory aspects and the role of innate immunity in ADs should be further studied in order to identify their underlying autoinflamma-tory pathogenesis, thus opening up new perspectives on the link between innate and adaptive immune mechanisms. This would be a useful step towards developing the best-tailored treatment strategy.

Source:

Caso F, et al. (2018). From Autoinflammation to Autoimmunity: Old and Recent Findings. https://pubmed.ncbi.nlm.nih.gov/30014358/

~~~~~~~

As you can see from the above results and findings from my latest epiphany, the field of quantum physics holds the secrets and answers to how and why people are developing these specific illnesses from nega-tive energies as a result of interpersonal trauma. On a larger scale, it can be seen as spiritual warfare, good against evil being played out in our physical reality.

~~~~~~~

PART 2

THE OLD SCIENCE
(I wrote back in 2018)

"WE MUST PRESUME RATHER THAT THE PSYCHICAL TRAUMA, OR MORE PRECISELY THE MEMORY OF THE TRAUMA-ACTS LIKE A FOREIGN BODY WHICH LONG AFTER ITS ENTRY MUST CONTINUE TO BE REGARDED AS AN AGENT THAT IS STILL AT WORK"
~Dr. Sigmund Freud and Dr. Josef Breuer

Think about the above statement for a moment… If you can, it helps to visualize or picture big and little shards of, let's say, shards of glass piercing your mind every time you are verbally, physically, sexually, or otherwise abused and gaslighted, etc. What happens when you don't remove or treat all of those shards of glass that have entered your body? They will fester and get infected! In other words, the *"result and effects"* of these often invisible assaults on us don't just go away, they affect our psyche and bodies, especially the central nervous system and immune system, the same way a virus or bacteria (foreign invader) does.

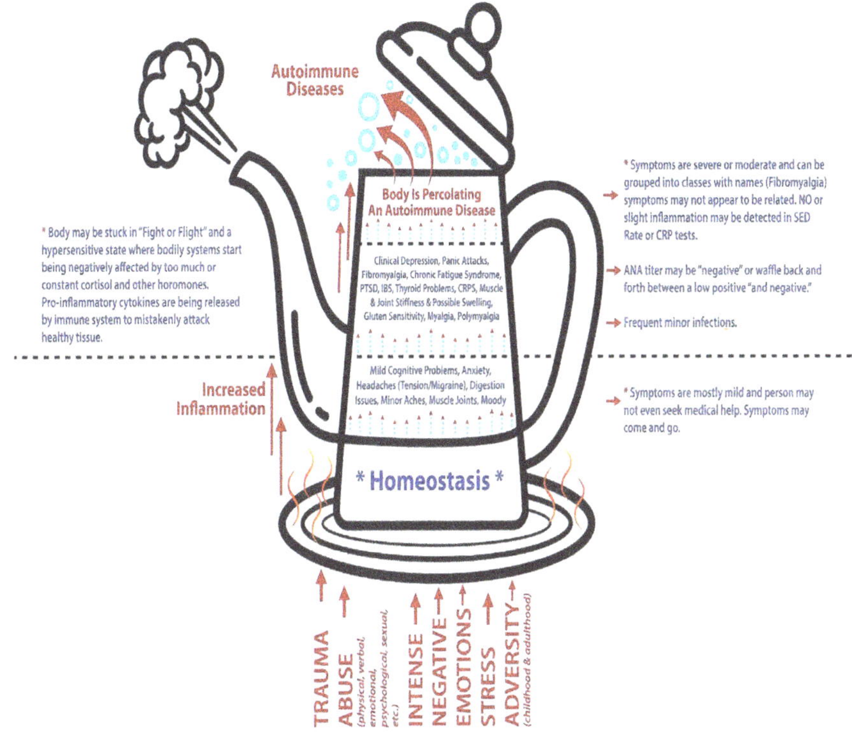

This ***PERCOLATOR* ILLUSTRATION**, which I created in 2018, represents your body, and the water in it represents the inside of your body (internal systems, organs, etc). The natural temperature of the water (room temperature) in the percolator represents our body in the internally peaceful and perfectly synced state of *"homeostasis,"* where everything is running just fine! Now, when the percolator is placed on the warm oven burner, the water begins to warm up.

The oven burner represents the STRESS, TRAUMA, ABUSE (child or domestic/intimate partner and includes physical, verbal, emotional, psychological, sexual, neglect, rejection, abandonment, and excessive yelling), and ADVERSITY (in childhood, adolescence, or adulthood), and the INTENSE NEGATIVE EMOTIONS and mental anguish that accompany all these events. These can and often do cause system malfunction, depending on factors such as type, level of emotional arousal during the event, time frame, frequencies of the traumatic event/events, and the coping abilities of the specific individual (including the level of ***alexithymia)*** at the time and their current situation and environment (peaceful and conducive to healing versus abusive) and the vulnerability of certain bodily systems in an individual. The *heat* that the burner is putting out represents "***inflammation***". The more these "external factors" (stress, trauma, abuse, rejection, neglect, etc.) are "attacking" you or have in the past, the more likely ***inflammation*** is to grow and continue. This can become chronic, where ***inflammation*** (the *heat*) continues to increase, and when it becomes severe enough, it develops into an autoimmune disease! ***INFLAMMATION IS WHAT DRIVES THESE DISEASES!***

Victims of interpersonal trauma, abuse, and adversity tend to have hyperactive and hypersensitive central nervous systems as a result of such events. Regardless if the abuse is physical, verbal, emotional, psychological, sexual, neglect, or rejection, ***THE BODY REACTS THE SAME WAY!*** These "threats" set off the "fight, flight or freeze" response, which is a survival mechanism built into our older, more primitive parts of the brain- the limbic system (also known as our "emotional brain"), specifically the amygdala. The amygdala is responsible for warning us about possible dangers we may encounter in our surroundings. When it detects danger, it activates the body's "stress response" (fight/flight/freeze) to allow us to fight or flee and sometimes freeze. These "danger" signals that the amygdala detects can be registered in all the senses, even from *our own thoughts, memories,* and nightmares. (As is the case with PTSD) When the "stress response" is activated, nerve impulses are triggered, and stress hormones are activated. These drive up heart rate, blood pressure, and oxygen intake, which create excess energy, strength, and oxygen capacity to fight or flee.

During these times of extreme emotions, the "Vagus Nerve" (formerly referred to as the "pneumogastric nerve") is activated, which communicates bi-directionally with the heart, mind, and gut (stomach/ intestines/microbiome). This nerve is crucial in the control and expression of emotions in animals and humans. Also, the very important Vagus Nerve uses "mirror neurons" to detect the safety or danger of the people and places around us, which then relays a corresponding message internally to areas such as the gut microbiome to make adjustments. When someone experiences strong negative emotions, they are not only registered in the mind, heart, and gut but are also registered viscerally (with all of our senses). Think about the pain in your gut and heart when someone you love dies. You can actually physically "feel" the pain of loss in your body. It's *horrible*, is it??? Normally, after the trauma, threat, or danger has passed, hormone levels and bodily systems return to normal. However, in a person who has been tr*aumatized*, these stress hormones take much, much longer to return to baseline levels and disproportionately and rapidly rise in response to even mildly stressful events and situations. These constantly elevated hormones (namely adrenaline and cortisol) coursing through a person's body begin to cause damage. Damage from the constant surge of stress hormones usually begins to manifest as problems with sleep, mood (irritability), concentration, memory, and attention, and the person may begin having issues with anxiety and or depression, heart flutters or palpitations, acid indigestion, nausea, stomach or intestinal issues, and muscle stiffness/pain. Symptoms during this stage may be anywhere from a "nuisance" to significantly affecting daily life. The person may or may not seek medical attention for their symptoms. The amygdala, at this point, is keeping you in "survival mode" instead of the "rest and digest' mode that we should normally be in.

The traumatized person's mind might learn to ignore or even deny these 'faulty" danger messages which are continuing to be sent from the limbic system, but the amygdala still keeps sounding the alarm bells and setting off the "stress response " throughout the body. When this continues to happen, organs and systems including the HPA Axis, and the immune system become faulty. Stress hormones start to turn your immune system into a more "pro-inflammatory state". Many studies have shown levels of pro-inflammatory cytokines (inflammation causing), such as

IFN-y, TNF-a, IL-17, IL-6, in the plasma, and increased levels of inflammatory Th17 and immune stimulatory Th1 cells in the blood. There is also a decrease in inhibitory cytokines and proinflammatory mediators, which control and decrease inflammation). This newly out-of-balance immune system kicks off the inflammatory process within the body. This is what I call the "pre-autoimmune disease" state, where inflammation has become insidious and your body is "percolating" an autoimmune disease. This is where symptoms are moderate to severe and are affecting your quality of life. This stage is where you start hearing diagnoses such as Fibromyalgia, PTSD, IBS, Chronic Fatigue Syndrome, Thyroid issues/disorders, Leaky Gut, clinical depression, adrenal issues, moodiness, anger issues, asthma, migraines, CPRS, gluten sensitivity, myalgias, joint and muscle pain and more. Blood work may show no, to very little to moderate inflammation in blood markers such as CRP (C-reactive protein) and SED rate. The farther in this stage you are, the more inflammation the blood markers will reflect. You may even waffle back and forth between a "negative" and borderline "positive" on the ***ANA titer*** test, which detects and measures the amount of antinuclear antibodies in your blood (detects autoimmune disease). This is ***a very dangerous territory*** not only because of the level of inflammation in your body but also because these symptoms are starting to take a *physical, emotional, social,* and *financial* toll. This can easily increase depression and anxiety which both feed the developing disease and in turn inflammation drives the depression and anxiety. A ***VICIOUS CYCLE has begun,*** that can be difficult to get out of and it is usually during this stage that antibodies are able to start being detected and an autoimmune disease develops and takes over. *THIS IS THE POINT WHERE IT CAN ALL SPIRAL OUT OF CONTROL!!!*

Unfortunately, many doctors, including Rheumatologists, consider these "pre-autoimmune diseases" as a separate illness from full-blown autoimmune diseases and refuse to treat them as such. I went to a new Rheumatologist recently because my last one retired, and during my first visit, I was told that I needed to go to my primary care physician to have my Fibromyalgia treated. He immediately wanted to get me started on a heavy-duty TOXIC immunosuppressant medication for my SLE (Lupus). I told the doctor that since I *now know* what caused my illnesses (domestic abuse from a 30-year marriage), I am going to try healing therapies specific for such traumas, such as limbic system therapy, somatic movement therapy, and maybe some EMDR. (all standard healing protocols for trauma based illnesses) He looked at me like he didn't understand a word I was saying. I wasn't speaking "French"; I was just speaking *psychology, interpersonal neurobiology,* and a little *neuroscience,* for the most part. I could see the wheels turning in his head, but he just didn't get it. After a long pause, he clapped his hands together and wished me good luck. Needless to say, I never went back!

Sources:

Van Der Kolk, B. (2014). The Body Keeps the Score. Penguin Books.

Kendall, R. (2001). Studies on Hysteria. Science Direct. https://www.sciencedirect.com/topics/psychology/studies-on-hysteria

Jones, J. (2018). Quantumhurting.com (IAMTHESTORMWARRIOR.COM). https://iamthestormwarrior.com/science/

~~~~~~~
~~~~~~~

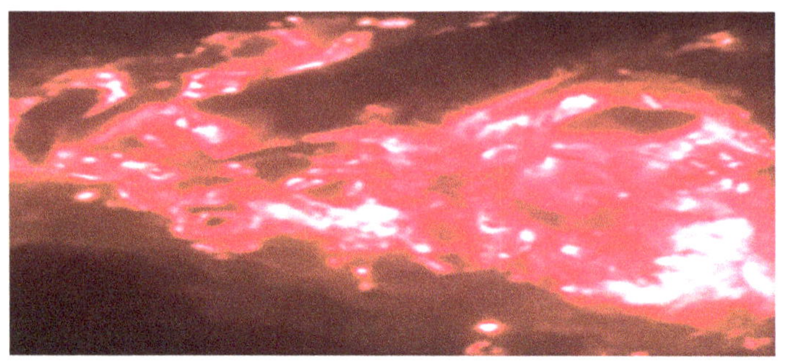

MY PERSONAL THEORY ON
THESE ILLNESSES AND DISEASES

The mystery of autoimmune diseases may not be that much of a mystery after all... Maybe we've just been looking in some of the wrong places... Although the number of people developing autoimmune diseases is on the rise, they are still a mystery to many people, including many doctors and scientists. According to the John Hopkins University website, there are over 100 autoimmune diseases, many with sub-categories. They are also at an all-time high here in the U.S. According to the "National Institute of Health," "up to 23.5 million Americans suffer from autoimmune diseases." There is a full spectrum of symptoms that range anywhere from *annoying* all the way to *death*, depending on which disease, the severity, and the system under attack.

The body's immune system beginsto attack healthy tissue by releasing pro-inflammatory cytokines, which cause inflammation at the site of the attack. Attacks are either organ-specific or systemic, where antibodies can be found in cells all around the body. These attacks on healthy tissue result in much pain and other complications, such as *severe inflammation* that can be destructive and cause arthritis and organ damage. And just to clarify, people do not die from autoimmune diseases, per se; they die from the *complications* they cause. For example, when Lupus causes the immune system to attack, let's say, a person's kidneys, as is the case in *lupus nephritis,* it can cause kidney failure, which, of course, can be fatal.

When my body developed Systemic Lupus Erythematosus years ago, my symptoms manifested mainly as total body joint and muscle pain, severe exhaustion, and cognitive difficulties. I did have a couple of bouts of pleurisy (where your immune system attacks the lining of your lungs and is extremely painful). I know others who have SLE as well, yet their symptoms (where their immune system has chosen to attack) are different from mine.

Until recently, there have only been a few "known" causes of autoimmune diseases. Mainly a few viruses, bacteria and environmental toxins, and even then, scientists are still not sure of the exact etiology or mechanisms of how it happens. Every single study or academic paper I have ever read regarding a "possible cause" for autoimmune diseases is unable to clearly explain the exact process from beginning to end, and they all state that much exploration and research still needs to be done to understand how and why this happens. In other words, scientists and researchers have uncovered bits and pieces of a process that can cause a malfunctioning immune response (which does not necessarily mean a full-blown autoimmune disease that is chronic over time). However, they still don't know many of the "hows" or the "why"s. For the most part, they've figured out so far that the Epstein Barr Virus (Herpes Virus #4), Herpes Virus # 6 and possibly #7 (Roseola), retrovirus and rotavirus, and the Coxsackie B Virus (CBV) can trigger autoimmunity. Links below. Please keep in mind these studies do not appear to have taken proper consideration that interpersonal trauma causes autoimmune diseases.

Recently, there's been a lot of talk regarding the gut microbiome as a possible "cause" of autoimmune diseases and even depression. I've seen massive marketing campaigns for the sales of micro, macro, pre, post, and everything else "biotics" and nutrients "especial'" that are claiming to cure autoimmune diseases, all based on some fairly recent studies and largely due to the newer field of Functional Medicine.

PLEASE DO SOME INVESTIGATING BEFORE YOU RUSH TO BUY THESE EXPENSIVE ITEMS! ESPECIALLY IF YOUR AUTOIMMUNE ILLNESS IS ABUSE OR TRAUMA-BASED. I'll sum it up here quickly by saying that I don't believe anything they could sell you to ingest is going to undo or repair all of the mental or deep-seated psychological damage/phenomena and trauma responses such as learned helplessness, cognitive dissonance, paranoia, or the other mal-adaptive coping mechanisms that you developed to survive in the situation or relationship, which occurs in abusive situations and relationships. Just like nutrients, supplements or "good bacteria" cannot re-attune your out-of-sync emotional and rational brains or keep our amygdala from mistaking too many things and situations as "dangerous." Please understand that nutrients and supplements, etc., can nourish and repair the physical tissue in our bodies and restore what our bodies are low on or missing, but they cannot repair invisible psychological damage. Also, NO WHERE IN ANY OF THESE STUDIES HAS IT SHOWN THAT they are curing these diseases, specifically, or that certain gut bacteria or anything in the gut microbiome begins, causes, or starts autoimmune diseases or depression. Most are a *result of* and part of a process already set in motion by another root cause, which needs to be addressed. These studies have only been able to show correlations, relationships or links, which hardly come close to a "cause." According to the article "Links Between Gut Microbes and Depression Strengthened" on the Nature.com website, "These findings do not PROVE cause and effect, and only show correlations between specific gut bacteria, their metabolites, and neurological symptoms." A recent study was done in Belgium with only a thousand cohorts (a longitudinal study over time) and again, even though this study was done on humans, it was NOT able to prove or even show that gut microbiome or any of its contents causes these terrible diseases or depression. What this study did show, however, was that there is a relationship between the microbiome and depression. According to Jeroen Raes, Senior Researcher in this new study, "None of that (their findings) proves that bacteria somehow contribute to-or protect from depression." At best, this study has shown us that the gut microbiome may feed depression. Still, it is definitely not causing it, much less autoimmune diseases. These studies include bacteria such as, Entreobacteriaceae family, Bordetella, Borrelia burgdorferi, Bacteroides fragilis and Enterococcus gallinarum (in the gut microbiome). Scientists have listed *molecular mimicry, epitope spreading, bystander activation, and immortalization of infected B cells* as some of the *possible* ways these viruses and bacteria may cause immune responses. I've also seen a few "nutritional and supplement" companies that are engaging in "scare campaigns" to frighten people into believing that just about everything you put in your mouth or come in contact with in the environment, can and will cause autoimmune disorders and diseases. If that were truly the case, *WE'D ALL HAVE AUTOIMMUNE DISEASES!*

Some environmental toxins have also been identified as possible causes of autoimmune diseases. Metals such as mercury and lead and toxic chemicals such as formaldehyde, ethylene oxide, and BPA have also been implicated as possible causes, but again, the exact mechanism is not fully understood. Some vaccines, food additives, and chemicals have also been implicated as possible culprits, but again, nothing definitive has been found.

So how is it that as many as 23.5 million Americans have autoimmune diseases but there are so few "real known causes"??? This doesn't make any sense when you consider the vast amount of people suffering from these diseases. These few viruses, bacteria, and environmental and chemical toxins *cannot be responsible for all these full blown diseases*. It just seems statistically impossible.

None of these numbers seem to jive, fit, or make sense when we look at these diseases from a purely medical and scientific framework (template/context, etc) like science has been doing with our current "Medical Model" here in the United States. If we look, however, at these diseases and the massive number of people being diagnosed with them in a *"Psychosocial"' or "Social" framework, THE HIGH AMOUNT OF AUTOIMMUNE DISEASES MAKES PERFECT SENSE! So do the "hows" and the "whys," and the process and mechanisms can be explained from beginning to end. THERE ARE NO MISSING PUZZLE PIECES...*

Recent research in the relatively newer fields of *neuroscience, interpersonal neurobiology, and developmental psychopathology* and the experts at the forefront of this research, such as Dr. Stephen Porges (The Polyvagal Theory), Dr. Bessel Van Der Kolk (author of the best-selling book- "The Body Keeps the Score), Dr. Dan Siegel (expert in the" field of interpersonal neurobiology), Dr. Peter Levine and others, have shown us that certain traumas, child abuse, domestic abuse, the intense negative emotions that go with those, and the body being stuck in physiological and chemical *"fight or flight"*, as a result of such abuse or trauma are not only ***CAUSING (the catalyst) the vast majority of these deadly autoimmune diseases but are also the culprit for many other*** "pre-autoimmune disease" illnesses as well. *This is what happened to me...*

Child and Domestic abuse are at EPIDEMIC PROPORTIONS here in America and the world and have been for a long time. There are an estimated 10 MILLION people who experience domestic violence/abuse each year (primarily women) in the United States (according to Wikipedia), and another 7. 5 MILLION reports of child abuse in 2017 (according to the U.S. Dept of Health and Human Services). These staggering numbers not only repeat themselves and increase year after year after year...**NO WONDER SO MANY PEOPLE HAVE AUTOIMMUNE DISEASES!!!** Please keep in mind that those numbers only represent those that were "reported," which means it's fair to estimate that these numbers are probably 3 to 5 times higher. And that's not even factoring in all the poor war veterans whose PTSD or subclinical PTSD symptoms from war trauma have caused their bodies to **develop a pre-autoimmune disease or worse.**

The treatment protocols for trauma and abuse-caused illnesses are very different from the routine traditional protocols that are now in place for these illnesses and autoimmune diseases. This can also explain why current treatments don't heal us, especially in the long term. People, myself included, have been receiving futile (and very toxic and dangerous) treatments and medication that cause severe side effects that rival the symptoms they're supposed to treat. Something very wrong with that picture. Real treatment for trauma/abuse-based illnesses is very different and does not involve going to a medical doctor for medication, shots, or other traditional treatments, so these people are not receiving proper treatment when they should be. If we ever expect to heal from these terrible *storms* in our bodies, there needs to be a tremendous pendulum shift in the way our medical industry views not only these illnesses but also the way they are treating them. We need less toxic medication and much more mind and body healing techniques and practices, many of which are *free of cost*. More Eastern Medicine principles, beliefs, and techniques need to be incorporated and employed to heal the hyperactive systems that drive the inflammation that causes these diseases. It is time for the Western Medicine "EGO" and its "GREED" to step aside for the more promising and healing Eastern medicine beliefs, mindsets, and practices. There has been enough research and studies showing how trauma and abuse cause our central nervous systems to become "revved up", like an engine running at too high rpm's, which, in turn, causes a cascade of systemic failures. These include the faulty rebalancing of the immune system to a more proinflammatory state, which creates and sends out pro-inflammatory cytokines to attack healthy tissue (inflammation). This research has also shown how mirror neurons, memory cells, and molecular mimicry are also involved in this process. SO WHY DOES OUR MEDICAL SYSTEM STILL TREAT AUTOIMMUNE DISEASES ALL THE SAME-ORGAN OR SYSTEM-SPECIFIC??? IT IS THE INFLAMMATION AND THE ROOT CAUSE OF THAT INFLAMMATION THAT NEEDS TO BE ADDRESSED AND TREATED INSTEAD OF JUST TREATING THE SYMPTOMS OVER AND OVER. Sorry...I didn't mean to yell, but as someone who lived the above scenario for a very long time, I am very passionate about this. Our Medical system here should no longer be able to turn a blind eye to this fact.

Great resources are, Stephen Porges' "Polyvagal Theory" and the works of Dr. Dan Siegal, Dr. Peter Levine and the book "The Body Keeps The Score", by Dr. Bessel Van Der Kolk. Also, please check out the **"ACE Studies",** which explains the causation and correlation between childhood abuse and neglect and the development of autoimmune diseases later in life. It is not only ***disturbing and pro-found***, but is also a scary eye opener to the fact that we all need to start being a lot nicer to each other.

Sources:

Orbai, A. Autoimmune Disease: Why Is My Immune System Attacking Itself? John Hopkins Medicine. https://www.hopkinsmedicine.org/health/wellness-and-prevention/autoimmune-disease-why-is-my-immune-system-attacking-itself

Autoimmune Diseases. National Institute of Health (NIH). https://www.niams.nih.gov/health-topics/autoimmune-diseases

HHV-6 as a trigger of autoimmune disease? HHV-6 Foundation. https://hhv-6foundation.org/autoimmune-disease/the-possible-role-of-hhv-6-as-a-trigger-of-autoimmune-disease

Ashton, M., *et al.* (2016). Incomplete Immune Response to Coxsackie B Viruses Associates With Early Autoimmunity Against Insulin. *Nature.com.* *https://www.nature.com/articles/srep32899#citeas*

Houen,G. & Trier,NH.(2021).Epstein-Barr Virus and Systemic Autoimmune Diseases. Front Immunology.PubMed Central. https://pmc.ncbi.nlm.nih.gov/articles/PMC7817975/

Links between gut microbes and depression strengthened. (2019). https://www.nature.com/articles/d41586-019-00483-5

Van Der Kolk, B. (2014). The Body Keeps the Score. Penguin Books.

~~~~~~~~
~~~~~~~~

MY THEORY-PART 2

My Doctor sent me to a different Rheumatologist this time as a second opinion because my symptoms were worsening. The initial blood work that prompted him to send me to the first Rheumatologist showed a low positive ANA TITER of 1:80. (Illustration # 1) The first "Rheumy" told me I was not testing positive for an autoimmune disease but that I had the hallmark symptoms of Fibromyalgia. This was in November of 2001. When my symptoms increased in the following months, I did not trust that diagnosis. I felt there was something more to it, so I went back to my primary care physician to have him retest my blood. It was in April of 2002, at this point and my ANA TITER test came back at 1:320! (Illustration #2). This is significant because the Antinuclear Antibody Titer test measures the presence and level of antinuclear antibodies in the blood. The higher the number on the right, the more you have. The new "Rheumy" did blood tests, and the results of those came back as testing positive for Systemic Lupus Erythematosus (SLE), which is a very serious and deadly auto-immune disease that affects women at about a ratio of 10:1 over men (I also have a theory on why women get struck down with these diseases so much more than men!) When he told me I tested positive for systemic lupus erythematosus, I WAS FLOORED...to say the least! I think my life may have even briefly flashed before my eyes, and I just remember thinking, "What does this mean for my future? The future of not just my physical body, but the future of my family, career, quality of life and, and, and... wow do these thoughts go on and on! It is VERY SCARY being diagnosed with such a debilitating disease for which there is no cure. It rocks you to your very core. It changes everything. It was one nasty CURVEBALL!

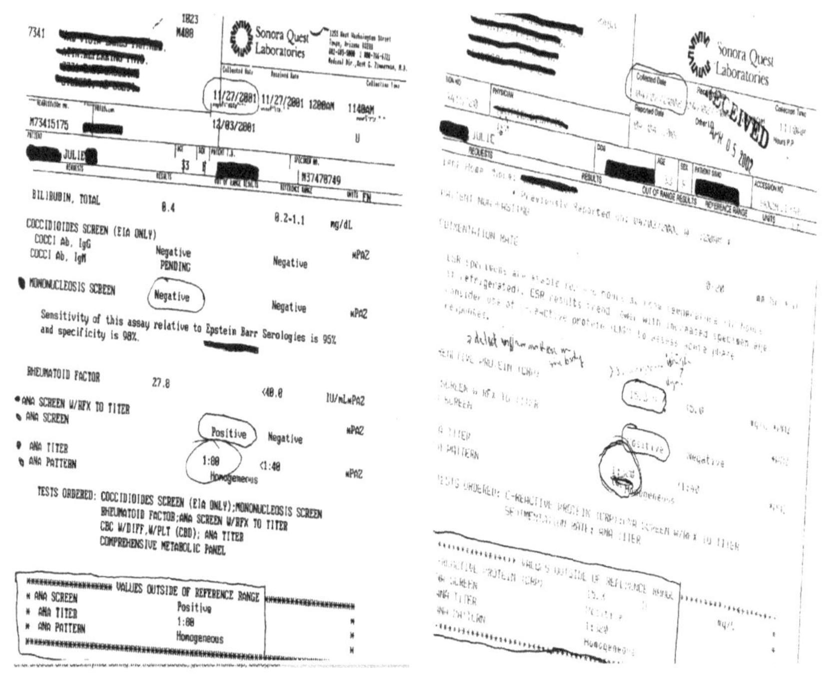

Illustration #1   Illustration #2

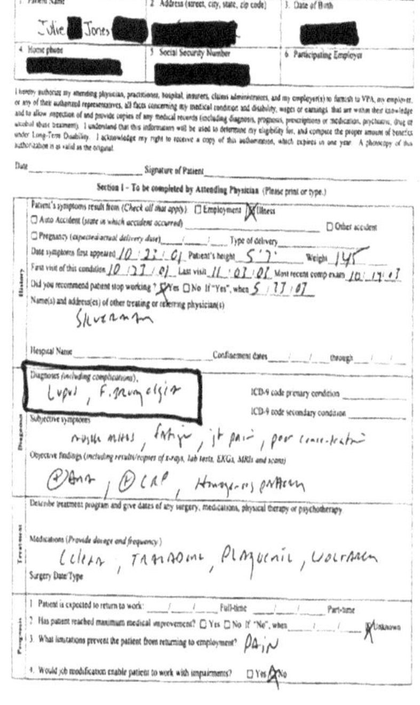

Illustration #3

LETTER TO SOCIAL SECURITY EXPLAINING WHY I COULD NO LONGER CONTINUE MY EMPLOYMENT BECAUSE OF THE ILLNESS.

ATTACHMENT FOR SECTION 2- LETTER "B" OF FORM SSA-3368 BK
"HOW DOES YOUR ILLNESS, INJURIES OR CONDITIONS LIMIT YOUR ABILITY TO WORK?

The daily pain and stiffness of arthritis in my hands, wrists, shoulders, knees, and feet made it a constant struggle to fulfill my duties as an active Phys. Ed teacher. My job requires that I demonstrate various skills several times per day, as well as, continually walk around to supervise students. Arthritis of my hands and wrists makes it difficult and painful to write and use the computer, as well as, write on the chalkboard, which is also part of my daily duties.
The constant physical and mental fatigue I experience from both the Systemic Lupus AND Fibromyalgia only add to the difficulties of doing my job effectively and efficiently. It is imperative that I stay alert and on top of things because I am responsible for approx. 30 students at any given time during the day.
The unpredictability of the muscle weakness, pain, and brain fogs, (confusion, forgetfulness, and inability to concentrate) make it nearly impossible for me to be at work, much less do my job. When I am having a bad day, (which is often, regardless of being on meds) I have to take pain meds and lie down because I have no strength to even sit up. I have had to call in sick, go in late, leave early and have someone cover my classes so I could go lie down in the nurse's office many times throughout the year. I lost wages because I exceeded my number of sick day allowances.
The constant infections that I get due to the Systemic Lupus, (U.T.I., bladder, strep throat, sinus, tonsillitis, flu, etc…) also caused me to miss many days of work as well. One factor which can aggravate a lupus flare and increase symptoms is sun and fluorescent light exposure. As a Physical Education teacher, I was outside in the Arizona sun quite often.
Having to deal with these problems on a daily basis has really taken a toll on my morale and mental health. I often feel despair because I know that I will have these problems for the rest of my life. I used to be a very physically active person. I played softball for the University of Arizona where I was a two-time Division I All-American and part of their 1991 National Championship team. Lupus and Fibromyalgia are destroying the very thing that made me such a successful and gifted athlete-my body. What once defined me and made me special is now failing me and robbing me of an active life with my family and career. How painfully ironic.
All the claims which I have made here can be verified by my Principal, Dr. Robert

Ok, now that you know a little bit about my diagnosis story, let's get back to my theory…Here it is…I BELIEVE THAT FIBRO-MYALGIA, CHRONIC FATIGUE SYNDROME, THYROID, STOMACH AND GUT ISSUES, IBS, etc… IS YOUR BODY BEING IN THE "PRE" AUTO-IMMUNE DISEASE (PRO-DROMAL) STATE, WHERE TRAUMA AND/OR TOXIC,

OVERWHELMING AND/OR CHRONIC STRESS/AN-GUISH, HAS BEGUN TO WREAK HAVOC IN THE BODY INCREASED INFLAMMATION BUT ISN'T FAR ENOUGH ALONG TO DEVELOP INTO A FULL BLOWN AUTO-IM-MUNE DISEASE AND THEREFORE DOES NOT SHOW UP IN BLOOD MARKERS...yet. Simply put, I think fibromyalgia and similar illnesses are the beginning stages of an auto-immune disease percolating... a toxic inflammatory storm brewing within. I believe that sometimes fibromyalgia and the like never progresses into a full-blown auto-immune disease depending on variables of the stressor (specific type/ duration, etc.) and the specific individual (psycholog-ical make-up, coping ability, level of arousal and alexithymia during the trauma/abuse, genetic make-up, biological system vulnerabilities, their current environment, etc.) I also believe that a major cause (of the vast majority) of Fibro, auto-immune diseases, Chronic Fatigue Syndrome, Crohn's Disease, gut and thyroid issues, and the like, is NOT viruses, bacteria, toxins, vaccines, food additives, etc., but psy-chological trauma and the chronic/toxic stress, torment and mental anguish (intense negative emotions) from adversity, abuse, abandon-ment, rejection, verbal, emotional, psychological, and neglect in child-hood and/or as an adult, or anywhere in between. The newer Sciences are starting to back this up, especially when you look at these illnesses through the framework of Dr. Stephen Porges' "Polyvagal Theory," as well as the exciting new abundance of findings in the fairly new-er sciences of neuroscience, interpersonal neurobiology and develop-mental psychopathology that has not been entirely or easily accessible to the general public yet. According to Dr. Bessel Van Der Kolk, at the forefront of this topic), in his book "The Body Keeps The Score: Brain, Mind, and Body in the Healing of Trauma"- "Research from these new disciplines has revealed that trauma produces actual physi-ological changes, including a recalibration of the brain's alarm system, an increase in stress hormone activity, and alterations in the system that filters relevant information from irrelevant." Dr. Van Der Kolk states that "being traumatized means continuing to organize your life as if the trauma were still going on-unchanged and immutable-as if every new encounter or event is contaminated by the past. After trauma, the world is experienced with a different nervous system. Traumatized people have a tendency to superimpose their trauma on everything around them and have trouble deciphering whatever is going on around them. Traumatized people look at the world in a fundamentally different way from other people. Trauma is not just an event that took place sometime in the past; it is also the imprint left by that experience on the brain, mind and body. Trauma results in a fundamental reorganization of the way the mind and brain manage perceptions. These attempts to maintain control over unbearable physiological reactions can result in a whole range of physical symptoms, including Fibromyalgia, Chronic Fatigue Syndrome, and other autoimmune diseases", Dr. Van Der Kolk, added.

I'm here to raise awareness and help educate because, during my learning/healing journey, I immediately noticed a big disconnect between what science knows and what the general public knows, especially newer information and findings regarding how trauma, abuse, and the like, are an immense cause of these terrible storms in our bodies. I remember vividly how I was once that person that was grasping for answers as to why I got sick, especially in the absence of the other risk factors or "possible causes." It is genuinely a terribly helpless feeling to be without these answers and up against such a formidable and invisible opponent that had taken over my body and turned my life upside down. My hope is that this information has enlightened you or maybe resonates with you the way it did for me. This knowledge has allowed me to make sense of my illness, its origin, risk factors, and I think, most importantly, this knowledge has given me the opportunity to play a very active role in my own healing journey. Instead of spending so much time in a medical doctor's office, being a GUINEA PIG for heavy-duty toxic drugs whose side effects rival the ailments they treat, and feeling that I had little to no control over the trajectory of my disease, I am now in control of my healing. All this new information truly reinforces what we've suspected all along- body and mind are intrinsically connected, and that adversity, trauma, abuse and the like cause such a profound emotional reaction in its victims, it literally makes them sick.

Enter "Siggy" and "Joey"…

The famed neurologist, Dr. Sigmund Freud and Dr. Josef Breuer, seemed to already "know" this way back in the late 18th Century, with their quote, "Psychical trauma-or more precisely-the memory of the trauma-acts like a foreign body long after its entry must continue to be regarded as an agent that is still at work." Now if they knew it way back then, my question is how or why did that message get lost somewhere along the way in our western medical system. Or did it get hidden??? Was it because BIG PHARMA began to control, dictate and reward systematically throughout the 'medical industry' and made sure that treatments mainly include medication, which funnels everything back to them??? Hmmm………

I am focusing on trauma/abuse/stress as the underlying cause of these illnesses since that is what happened to me. It's not only chemicals, toxins, and the possibility of vaccines and food additives that are supposedly causing these internal storms. It is also the intense gut-wrenching emotions and chronic or toxic stress from abuse and trauma that affect the different systems in our bodies negatively and can reset them to a chronic faulty setting which leads to chronic inflammation and disease…autoimmune diseases. Abuse and trauma (especially repeated) at the hands of a loved one or caretaker creates a special "toxic" kind of chronic stress and deep mental torment and anguish that is particularly damaging to its victims because of the epic inherent internal struggle and conflicting internal impulses, thoughts and deep feelings of wanting and needing to love this person (the abuser) but also wanting and needing for the abuse and pain to stop. This removes the natural protection against trauma for the victim, which is feeling safe with our loved ones. This destabilizes the victims' stability and footing, not only within themselves and their emotions as they internalize their abuse, but with the people around them and in their environments. We have an innate need to feel "safe," but as long as we are experiencing terror from the loved one, we cannot feel safe. Where terror exists, safety cannot. I can tell you firsthand that this is a total mindfuck of epic proportions. The love/hate dynamics leave you in total anguish. When someone you love is abusive to you, it feels like you have been turned inside out, literally.

Genetics do not "cause" these disorders and diseases outright. They are more of a factor in the process. In fact, abuse and trauma can actually change our genes during our lifetime through a process called "epigenetics." Trauma leaves a chemical mark on genes, and this means that the imprint of trauma can be passed down from generation to generation. How a person processes adversities, depending on their personal psychological make-up, coping ability, the extent of the abuse/trauma, when the abuse occurred, current environment, and vulnerability of biological systems, all factor into how stress and intense emotions manifest in their victims and how sick they will get.

Now that neuroscience and the related fields of interpersonal neurobiology and developmental psychopathology have shown us that intense emotions (which always involve the mind, heart and gut) and stress, especially chronic and toxic stress, are indeed catalysts, even causes, for all these ailments and diseases, there is much confusion to clear up. I feel there are too many "lenses" or "layers" that these symptoms and illnesses are being viewed through and that is over complicating the understanding of how and why they develop and they manifest in a person. Take fibromyalgia and chronic fatigue syndrome, for example, you have two completely different names and diagnosis but the symptoms are nearly identical, with so many overlapping. One is characterized by more pain and one is characterized by more exhaustion, so basically that means that they are only separated by the "degree" of a symptom versus different symptoms altogether. Why do we need an entirely different name for something so incredibly similar? The biggest problem, I think, is that most people do not realize just HOW sick stress can make you and that trauma and abuse has the ability to make you deathly ill with terrible diseases. I think another big reason is that the drug companies like to take a certain set of symptoms, create a name for it so they can sell a drug for this specific newly named "disorder" or "syndrome" that has been "created". Maybe not in that exact order but I feel they're guilty of that. It's about GREED and that almighty dollar! Don't even get me started on what the drug companies have done with opiates and how their marketing was ripe with deception and drew millions of people into the grips of not just psychological but physical addiction and dependency!

What if we stripped away all these layers and lenses that create confusion, make understanding difficult, and just re-examine these illnesses from a more social framework and "big picture" perspective? Now think about this for a moment… What if these symptoms causing "illnesses," such as Fibro, CFS, PTSD, etc., are all the same illness that start the same way- a result of an outer "assault" (trauma/stress/anguish/abuse/neglect) from external forces? The body consciously and subconsciously reacts and adjusts to these external assaults by going into a hyperarousal/ hypersensitive state, which is where the pain comes from, where the feedback loops of the HPA axis (which will leave you feeling 'wired but tired"), Dorsal Vagal Complex (DVC), Sympathetic Nervous System (SNS) and Ventral Vagal Complex (VVC) all kick into high gear which becomes their new default setting. The nerves tell your muscles to stiffen and harden to prepare for the assault or perceived assault. This is the point of this illness where the patient is symptomatic (pain, stiff, sore muscles, fatigue, gut issues, headache, anxiety, depression, cognitive/sleep difficulties, etc.). Still, this illness has not developed enough to be seen in bio markers, with the exception of a maybe abnormally high rate of inflammation and perhaps an increase in proinflammatory cytokine levels. Once it's been verified that abuse/trauma/stress is the culprit, these patients should ALL be treated with the same healing protocols (depending on the level of severity). This includes "bottom-up therapy," which focuses on the amygdala and other geographically lower and more primitive brain regions where past trauma actually lives and hides. This includes limbic system therapy and body-based therapy. These types of treatment activate self-awareness and interoception so the patient can access their "emotional brain," which is first needed to heal from trauma. The use of body-awareness techniques, rhythmical movements, sensory motor therapy, yoga, meditation, walking, exercise, and breathing all help to ground the victim and repair the misattunement between the mind and body that these victims experience. These therapies also quell and reverse the hyperarousal symptoms since trauma lives in our visceral sense and emotional brain. This is called "self-management" and is at the core of recovery. Unfortunately, "mainstream Western psychiatric and psychological healing traditions have not paid much attention to", according to Dr. Van Der Kolk, in his best-selling book, "The Body Keeps The Score: Brain, Mind, and Body in the Healing of Trauma:

It is Eastern medicine that understands and employs these treatment techniques and has been using them for what is probably thousands of years. "Top-down therapy" and talk therapy, which includes Cognitive Behavioral Therapy, are typically not as helpful with victims of trauma because they address the thinking and logical parts of the brain (mainly the frontal lobes), which actually go off-line and get deactivated long-term, during the "trauma response' in victims of trauma. Victims stay in this state because of the hyperactive amygdala, which keeps its host in a state of flight/flight or freeze." According to Dr. Bessel Van Der Kolk, "The fundamental issue in resolving traumatic stress is to restore the proper balance between the rational and emotional brains so that you can feel in charge of how you respond and how you conduct your life." (as opposed to feeling disconnected, fragmented thinking, angry, tightly wound, frazzled messes) He also stresses the fact that "we have a host of inbuilt skills to keep us on an even keel." This means we can directly train our arousal system by the way we breathe, chant, and move, a principle that has been utilized since time immemorial in places like China and India and in every religious practice that I know of, but that is suspiciously eyed as "alternative" in mainstream culture."

Source:

Van Der Kolk, B. (2014). The Body Keeps the Score-Brain, Mind, and Body in the Healing of Trauma. Penguin Books.

~~~~~~~
~~~~~~~

THE POLYVAGAL THEORY

A much better understanding of why we behave
the way we do-inside and out.

In 1994, Dr. Stephen Porges introduced us to *The Polyvagal Theory*, which has been instrumental in providing us with a framework and organized system of understanding the three neural circuits of social regulation and co-regulation with those around us, (1) Social Engagement (feeling safe and maintaining rest and digest mode), (2) Fight/Flight/Mobilization (adrenaline surges get you ready for fighting or fleeing) and (3) Immobilization (shutting off/dissociating from the stressor, danger, etc. and shutting down when we feel we cannot escape the danger/stressor). According to Dr. Porges, this framework "allows all those subconscious emotions and feelings deep within our underlying states to percolate information upward into our brainstem and transmit information to our higher brain structures, enabling access to different brain areas and cortical functions." This basically means that this information is taken from our lower most primitive areas, where we may not notice these feelings or why we have them, and transfers this information to our higher level thinking areas of the brain where we become conscious and aware of them so that we may take appropriate action for these emotions, sensations, etc. Until recently, Western science has largely ignored the importance of the ability of the pneumogastric nerve to bidirectionally communicate important information to other body systems that correspond with our immediate surroundings and the people in it. This is truly perplexing and frustrating since it has long been a "tried and true" central component in many traditional healing practices in various other parts of the world, including China and India. But in 1994, Dr. Stephen Porges' introduced us to *The Polyvagal Theory*, which brought undeniable attention to and helps us have a much better understanding of the critically important vagus nerve (formerly known as the pneumogastric nerve), its expression and management of emotions in humans as well as animals and how it plays a specific role in how someone responds to traumatic events. According to his official website, Dr. Porges, PhD. Is a "Distinguished University Scientist" at Indiana University, Director of the Traumatic Stress Research Consortium at Indiana University, Professor of Psychiatry at the University of North Carolina, and a professor Emeritus at both the University of Illinois at Chicago and the University of Maryland. In 1994, he proposed the Polyvagal Theory, which links the evolution of the mammalian autonomic nervous system to social behavior and emphasizes the importance of physiological state in the manifestation and expression of behavioral problems and psychiatric disorders. His work has helped broaden our understanding of not just our central nervous system in general but specifically how it responds to trauma. The vagus nerve allows communication bi-directionally (both ways) between the heart, gut, and brain when experiencing intense emotions, both positive and negative. It consists of 2 branches, the ventral-front facing and dorsal-rear. Each branch is linked to a different but specific behavioral and physiological coordinated response when faced with a traumatic event or situation. (ie; threat, fear, danger, stress.) We, as humans, are biologically driven to respond to distress using a predictable framework. (1) social engagement-our most natural state (should be everyone's default setting and state of being) of rest and safety, enables us to tend and befriend, rest and digest and make and maintain connections with those around us, to relax, play, love, and so forth. Basically, we have the inherent ability to nurture ourselves and others. When in danger or distress, it is natural for us to turn to this environment for reassurance, connection, and safety. However, if we are unsuccessful (our parent, caretaker, intimate partner, or friend is unresponsive or uninterested), our newer vagus shuts off, and (2) mobilization takes over. If our attempts to defend ourselves through mobilized fight, flight or active freeze responses are also unsuccessful (we are not quick enough, loud enough, or strong enough to protect ourselves or engage in protection), we *(3)* drop down the hierarchy again and our dorsal vagus initiates *immobilized* defense responses, such as dissociation, shutting us down and diverting energy to preservation of life on the inside, whilst potentially even feigning death on the outside.

Why the Polyvagal Theory is important;

- It shows us that we as humans are biologically driven to respond to stress using a predictable framework.
- Explains how we look to those around us to help decipher and put danger/stressors into the proper context.
- It helps us understand how and why our distress response might not be activated, for example, in the context of child sexual abuse, where systematic acts of grooming take place. The environment, actions, and behaviors of the abuser often condition their prospective victim in such a way that it prevents the activation of the nervous system, so those "alarm bells" never go off in the victim due to desensitization. Basically, predators are very good at *fooling* your "gut feeling," which is a very scary thought.
- It allows for compassion and empathy where otherwise there would be judgment, ostracizing, shunning and rejection, abandonment, etc. It gives us an understanding of another's

reactions and responses towards us or in relation to us. For example, suppose someone acts angry or fearful of us when we mean no harm instead of judging and shunning them. In that case, we can understand and act with empathy and compassion because we know that they have experienced some type of trauma/adversity that has put them into survival mode, which leaves a person feeling threatened, defensive, unable to focus well, selfish, and with volatile emotions, reactions and outbursts.

- It gives us a much better understanding of why, in some extremely dangerous and scary situations, our bodies may shut down, prevent us from responding with any kind of physical action, and cause us to go into a dissociative state. It is vitally important that we remember this is an innate survival response meant to protect us.

- It promotes self-awareness. It allows us to be consciously aware of our deepest emotions, feelings, and responses so that we may actively think about them in real-time and take appropriate and corresponding actions.

- Promotes social awareness. It allows us the ability to take the perspective of and empathize with those around us, as well as accurately interpret the meanings of cues in our environment including the ability to accurately interpret the emotions of others.

- It also helps us to understand the impact of trauma as a sustained response to an event which happened in the *past*. Over time, if the social engagement system is not used successfully one will decrease capacity to use this and develop a 'hardwired' autonomic nervous system response to trauma and its triggers. As more and more of the world is perceived as unsafe, these people may come to rely on their defensive states to negotiate their environments, making social engagement very difficult.

Finally, this theory highlights the value and importance of human relationship. When we are in a "fight or flight" response, or when we are immobilized (freeze state) it highlights that we are experiencing defensive reactions of the nervous system. This may be due to real threats, however if we have experienced a history of trauma this activation will also occur from perceived threats. The ultimate aim is to firstly be safe and secondly return our central nervous system to the state where we can rely on Social Engagement. We can do this by turning towards real connections with friends, partners, parents or pets.

Western medicine and science should no longer be able to intentionally ignore, deny, or hide the fact that this new knowledge has had a profound effect on and is literally transforming our understanding of trauma and how it affects our physiology long term (as when the memory of trauma/abuse is encoded into our viscera), and how to recover from it.

Sources:

Porges, S. https://www.stephenporges.com/

Porges SW. The polyvagal perspective. Biol Psychol. 2007 Feb;74(2):116-43. doi: 10.1016/j.biopsycho.2006.06.009. Epub 2006 Oct 16. PMID: 17049418; PMCID: PMC1868418. https://www.ncbi.nlm.nih.gov/pmc/articles/PMC1868418/#:~:text=Third%2C%20the%20Polyvagal%20Theory%20(Porges,flight%20or%20social%20engagement%20behaviors.

~~~~~~~~
~~~~~~~~

DEPRESSION IS NOW BEING SEEN AS THE BEGINNING STAGES OF THE 'FREEZE' RESPONSE (IMMOBILIZATION) IN THE FIGHT/FLIGHT OR FREEZE RESPONSE TO DANGER AND TRAUMA

Through new research conducted by biological anthropologists, neuroscience, and an overall better understanding of the critical vagus nerve (through the Polyvagal Theory), experts now believe that depression, PTSD, and anxiety are actually "adaptive responses to adversity" instead of mental illness/disease or chemical imbalance of the brain. They believe that depression is "the beginning stage of the FREEZE state (immobilization) in "fight/flight or freeze hierarchy. The freeze state is the body preparing for death, and it is your body's systems shutting down as a last resort response because it knows it can neither "fight" nor "flee" the situation. For example, a young child that is being victimized and abused by their own parent cannot fight, as the parent is much stronger than the child. The child also cannot flee (flight) because they cannot just get up and leave their home. They have nowhere to go and no way to take care of themselves. The result is that the child's survival instinct of "freeze" kicks in, and his system adapts to his volatile and abusive environment by shutting down, exhibiting a set of symptoms collectively known as *depression.* This is a very important finding because it tells us *it is actually the body that first detects danger and sends off the internal alarm bells, which then initiates an innate protective defense strategy that helps us survive dangerous situations.* Part of this defense strategy is sending messages to the brain, which adjusts accordingly (chemical changes, etc).

The traditional medical model tells us it is the brain that initiates depression (that depression develops in the brain as some illness), but current scientific findings are showing us otherwise. This would absolutely explain why antidepressants do not work well, especially in the long term. Yes, antidepressants are notorious for wearing off after a while... It makes sense why they would stop working after a while when you look at depression through a "biopsychosocial model". No matter how much chemical medication you put in your body, your current "depressing" environment will always override any small amount of medication you put in your system! If your depression is caused by past trauma and adversity, no medication is going to permanently override the chronically hyperactive and traumatized central nervous system that still acts like it's in danger, or the cascade of physiological effects and the dysfunctional thought processes and maladaptive coping mechanisms that follow. I have experienced this firsthand. According to the authors of this academic paper, "Despite widespread and increasing use of antidepressants, rates of anxiety and depression do not seem to be improving. From 1990-2010, the global prevalence of major depressive disorders and anxiety disorders held at 4.4% and 4%. At the same time, evidence has continued to show that antidepressants perform no better than placebos." The paper goes on to explain how "the worldwide rates of both anxiety and depression have held steady at 1 in 5 people but yet in war-torn and high conflict regions and countries, the rate jumps to 1 in 5 people having anxiety, depression, and PTSD." Those statistics help to solidify the fact that it is our immediate surroundings and environment (external forces) that are the culprits. The authors also noted that since the very beginning of record keeping on the effectiveness of antidepressants, has yet to show that they are an effective treatment for depression!

Source:

Escalante, A. (2020). Researchers Doubt That Certain Mental Disorders Are Disorders At All. <u>Researchers Doubt That Certain Mental Disorders Are Disorders At All</u>

~~~~~~~
~~~~~~~

IS IT ADHD/ADD OR REALLY DEVELOPMENTAL TRAUMA DISORDER/ COMPLEX TRAUMA (CHILDHOOD VERSION OF PTSD?)

This can be an unnerving question. Especially if you have a child who has been diagnosed with ADHD/ADD...like I have. I first came across this possibility when I was reading a book by the world-famous Dr. Bessel Van Der Kolk, "The Body Keeps The Score; Brain, Mind, and Body in the Healing of Trauma," which I will refer to often as it is a significant source for me, but not the only source.

What I learned in this book really rocked me to my core, to say the least! I had more of those "light bulbs going off in my head" moments as well! The kind where I say to myself "OMG this makes total sense" which is immediately followed by "OMG I have to spread the word so other people can know this too!" It made me think about my child and the poor children whom I had taught at a middle school who grew up in a chaotic, volatile, abusive, or neglectful home environment, where most students came from abusive, neglectful emotionally absent, and unsupportive homes, that had also been diagnosed with ADHD and for which stimulant medication did not help. After much research, I now believe the majority were misdiagnosed with this elusive disorder, which has no seemingly real point of origin and should have been diagnosed with a trauma-based disorder such as Developmental Trauma Disorder (also known as Complex Trauma (or Adverse Childhood Experiences), instead. This is a child's version of PTSD. as a result of chronically enduring abuse and trauma from their primary caregiver, (intentional or not). ADHD/ADD and Developmental Trauma Disorder/ Complex trauma/ACE's require very different treatment protocols-most ADHD/ADD treatments focus on organizational and time management skills. In contrast, the trauma-based disorders require treatments designed to dig deeper and treat the psychological and emotional turmoil and ongoing visceral sensations that accompany such traumatized individuals.

Let's first take a look at what these disorders are exactly ...According to the Center for Disease Control website, ADHD/ADD is a common neurodevelopmental disorder that favors boys by a ratio of 3:1 and includes symptoms such as poor impulse control, difficulty paying attention, being overly active (as if driven by a motor), talking out of turn (known as blurting), constantly losing and forgetting things, daydreaming, squirmy, fidgety, making careless mistakes, difficulty in resisting temptation and trouble getting along with others. According to the CDC website, there are several "possible" (meaning they don't know for sure) causes such as premature birth and low birth weight, brain injury, exposure to environmental metals or toxins such as lead, drug/alcohol/tobacco use by the mother during pregnancy, but no known cause has yet to be found. Earlier assertions that sugar and too much television/video games as a cause has NOT been supported by research.

The statistics for ADHD are staggering, according to the CDC website, the cases of ADHD/ADD have increased dramatically over the last 20 years. In 2019, 9.4% (I've also seen as much as 11% on other credible websites) of 2-17 year olds had this diagnosis in the U.S. That's 3.1 MILLION children and a 43% increase in diagnosis since 2003! This meteoric rise in cases of ADHD/ADD, can largely be attributed to not only the media blitz of advertisements about ADHD medications and doctors being quick to diagnose those who have even the slightest of symptoms for no other reason than to "have a diagnosis" or to enhance an average student's academic performance and the pressure put on teachers and schools to deliver high achievement scores. The typical traditional treatments for this disorder include stimulant medications and behavioral therapy, talk type therapies. Diagnosis is a multi-step process because there is no single test for diagnosis and consists of a physical exam (to rule out other causes) and an ADHD/ADD checklist which is filled out by teachers and parents regarding the history of the child. Comorbid disorders that appear to go along with this diagnosis might include, OCD, Oppositional-Defiant disorder/Conduct Disorder, Anxiety, Depression, Borderline Personality Disorder, Tourette's Syndrome, Bi-polar and learning disabilities, Impulse Control Disorder and more.

Now let's look at "Developmental Trauma Disorder" also known as "Adverse Childhood Experience" or "Complex Trauma", which share almost *identical symptoms* of ADHD/ADD but have very different origin/cause and treatment protocols and is very similar to PTSD in adults but according to Dr. Bessel Van Der Kolk, "PTSD does not fully capture the developmental impact of childhood trauma because a child's early experiences occur in the context of a developing brain, the social interaction and neural development are inextricably intertwined." This means that basically, a child's brain develops based on the internalization of both affective and cognitive characteristics of their primary caregiving relationships. Unfortunately, trauma at the hands of a loved one produces the most damaging and toxic type of stress and trauma. It causes deep tumultuous emotions that the victim may not be able to handle or process within their psyche or have words to express their pain. This is known as "ALEXITHYMIA" and can make the situation and therefore the psychological and physiological damage even worse, This very "special" type of trauma that abusers save *especially for their loved ones*, starts at home with the abusers being primary caregivers such as parents and causes what's known as "TOXIC STRESS." This type of stress and consequential physiological and psychological cascade of problems it causes is because the child who instinctively relies on and loves their caregiver, is fighting a tormenting internal battle and impulse of needing and wanting their caregiver but they also know that this caregiver is the source of their pain, suffering and neglect. (This is also true for victims of domestic violence.) They want and need love but they also want and need to escape and get away from the pain and suffering, after all... where there is terror, there is no safety. *TERROR AND SAFETY CANNOT EXIST TOGETHER*, as they are contradictory. This epic internal clash of conflicting and opposing forces causes a destabilization in the child's homeostasis which then sets the stage for further problems across all developmental domains including a nervous system that is chronically ramped- up and ready to fight or go numb and collapse even though the trauma is over. ***Common symptoms include the exact same symptoms as ADHD/ADD and all the other disorders I listed above in the ADHD paragraph.*** Why is this?

During an act of abuse, a child has the ability to blank out (dissociate and depersonalize themselves), even when merely being yelled at. This is a way they can make themselves "disappear", so that their mind is not in the present and therefore not having to "endure". These dissociation states can also be MISTAKEN for the "daydreaming" and "checked out" symptoms of ADHD/ADD. According to Dr. Van der Kolk, the thalamus (also known as a filter of incoming information and gatekeeper), of an abused child also breaks down and causes a "sensory overload" where the floodgates of incoming information (sensory and environmental) is wide open so the child's brain gets overwhelmed and over- stimulated and compensates by closing it all down and so they begin to "hyperfocus" as a coping mechanism. When this breakdown happens, the cost to the child includes the ability to feel alive, feel as "one" with their own bodies and filtering out various sources which would bring the child pleasure, excitement and happiness. The broken down thalamus also causes problems with attention, concentration and learning new things...JUST LIKE ADHD/ADD! The ramped up central nervous system of an abused child will cause them to act out without much control over their emotions or impulses because they've lost their innate ability to sooth and modulate themselves and their behavior and tend to see everyone as a potential threat. Their emotions become dysregulated and difficult to control. They will constantly misjudge social cues from those around them and act as if they have a "chip on their shoulder." Poor impulse control is a hallmark symptom of ADHD/ADD but it could also be seen as a *traumatized child acting out and/or re-enacting the trauma, or their failed attempts to escape.* This also fills the victim with shame, which unfortunately is a cornerstone of addiction. It's also important to point out that Dr. Van Der Kolk, in New York Times best-selling book, which also contain the latest works from Dr. Stephen Porges (the Polyvagal Theory), Dr Dan Siegel (Developmental Psychopathology) and others at the forefront of this newer research, explains that, other "pseudo-diagnoses" symptoms such as the ones listed above in the ADHD/ADD paragraph could also be caused by trauma and abuse, which has shown to be a lifelong ordeal and causes many problems such as developing auto-immune diseases (yes, the toxic stress from being abused can cause auto-immune diseases and many other PHYSICAL ailments), later on in life, unless there is intervention with a PROPER diagnosis and proper therapy based on that diagnosis. You can also find more information on this topic by taking a look at articles on the "ACE Studies", which confirms this as well.

We now know that ADHD is mainly perceived now as neurodiversity! It's not a disorder, it's not an illness, or sickness, it is in fact, a very highly adaptable trait that is a superpower in the right circumstances, situations, careers, etc. A trait that develops as a result of childhood adversity. It creates a massive well of inner energy. This allows them to have the energy, internal motivation to not just be inquisitive about the world around them, but the extra energy it takes to explore and research at a very deep level. It allows them to roam, discover and create.

Diagnosis cannot happen in a 15 minute doctor's appointment or 2 or 3. WE need to do our own due diligence as parents in research and fact finding the correct answers, which takes time, but it's a hell of a lot better than continuing to give a traumatized and abused child, who has an already hyper-aroused and over- stimulated Central Nervous System, stimulants and incorrect types of therapy because of a hastily made ADHD diagnosis. This can have disastrous results! Traumatized and abused children have very different treatment protocols than ADHD/ADD. I hope this information has helped to shed a little light on this new possibility!

Sources:

Van Der Kolk, B. (2014). The Body Keeps the Score.

Porges, S. The Polyvagal Theory. https://www.stephenporges.com/

Attention Deficit/Hyperactivity Disorder (ADHD). (2024). https://www.cdc.gov/adhd/data/index.html

~~~~~~~
~~~~~~~

PART 3

ABUSERS/ PSYCHOPATHS/SOCIOPATHS AND NARCISSISTS- INTRASPECIES PREDATORS

They can sell ice cream 🍦 to an Eskimo…but like an entire lifetime supply and at full price, with a few unnecessary add-ons…. maybe some sunscreen and flip flops, and make you feel really good about the transaction. You may also feel compelled to refer a friend."

Psychopaths are ***INTRASPECIES PREDATORS***.YIKES! This means they hunt and prey on their own species. Like a shark preying on other sharks, kind of... The first thing I would like to do here is help clear up some of the confusion, misconceptions and beliefs of what a true **"Psychopath"** really is. It appears there is an ongoing debate as to whether they are born or created. Some schools of thought say true psychopathy is born and sociopaths and narcissists are created. A classic "nature vs 'nurture" question. Well, it's actually BOTH! This is how it works-the majority of psychopaths are born that way yes, but nurture (or ironically a lack thereof) can create and /or re-enforce their development as well. For example, if an otherwise normal baby is born into an orphanage and lays in a crib for hours untouched, unloved and neglected, it's amygdala and areas that make up the emotional brain do not develop properly. Same is true for a child born into a situation where it is not wanted and that is reflected in the parents behavior, will most likely not have an amygdala and emotional brain components developed as much as a child born into a loving home who grew up in a stable environment. Now here's the thing…Let's say that a child is born into a family who happens to not want it. The lack of nurturing, care, affection, etc., will inhibit the growth of the emotional brain, and if severe enough, it could cause psychopathy. If the abuse is severe and prolonged, the effects would be even more severe. Meaning that this child will most likely grow up with minimal emotional affect, lack of empathy and apathy, most likely have a strong dislike and disregard for people and want to use them for their own gain and show selfish and self-serving behaviors and are quick to anger. The one emotion they do appear to feel with any real depth.

Actually, the term "Psychopath" is no longer a 'clinical diagnosis' in the DSM-5 and neither is "Sociopath". Ever since Alfred Hitchcock's thriller movie "Psycho" came out and scared the hell out of everyone by implying that they are all a bunch of crazed serial killers, the Psychology community decided to move away from the frightening term and instead calls it "Antisocial Personality Disorder" and is also sometimes referred to as "Malignant Narcissism." There's more, much more…Actually, Dr. Robert Hare, the doctor who created and developed the Psychopathy Checklist and the revised version (PCL & PCL-R), states in his article, "Psychopathy and Antisocial Personality Disorder: A Case of Diagnostic Confusion", on the Psychiatrictimes.com website, "Traditionally, affective and interpersonal traits such as egocentricity, deceit, shallow affect (lack of emotions), manipulativeness, selfishness, and lack of empathy, guilt or remorse, have played a central role in the conceptualization and diagnosis of psychopathy (Cleckley; Hare 1993; in press); Widiger and Corbitt). In 1980 this tradition was broken with the publication of *DSM-III*. Psychopathy-renamed antisocial personality disorder- was now defined by persistent violations of social norms, including lying, stealing, truancy, inconsistent work behavior and traffic arrests.

Among the reasons given for this dramatic shift away from the use of clinical inferences were that personality traits are difficult to measure reliably, and that it is easier to agree on the behaviors that typify a disorder than on the reasons why they occur. The result was a diagnostic category with good reliability but dubious validity, a category that lacked congruence with other, well-established conceptions of psychopathy. This "construct drift" was not intentional but rather the unforeseen result of reliance on a fixed set of behavioral indicators that simply did not provide adequate coverage of the construct they were designed to measure.

The problems with *DSM-III* and its 1987 revision *(DSM-III-R)* were widely discussed in the clinical and research literature (Widiger and Corbitt). Much of the debate concerned the absence of personality traits in the diagnosis of ASPD, an omission that allowed antisocial individuals with completely different personalities, attitudes and motivations to share the same diagnosis. At the same time, there was mounting evidence that the criteria for ASPD defined a disorder that was more artifactual than "real" (Livesley and Schroeder)."

The term, "Antisocial Personality Disorder" is also a little deceiving and a bit of a misnomer because it gives us the impression that these people shun other people, society and avoid social interactions altogether, but that could not be farther from the truth! These predators LOVE getting in the mix with other people because that is how they find and hunt their "prey" and sustain their "fuel". These people are SOCIAL PREDATORS! Mixing in with and befriending lots of other people is not only their livelihood but it's a means to an end for them.

Based on the one I lived with for my entire adult life (over half my life span and without even realizing what he truly was until our divorce) and my own personal research, I totally disagree with this new categorization in the DSM 5-R. True "functioning" or as I refer to them, "successful" Psychopaths are in a league all their own and therefore should have a very specific and definitive assessment, construct and category. Especially now that science has the ability to identify them through very specific biological markers, neuro-wiring, brain scans, as well as by physical and social markers and 'tells", which I discuss in detail in this section. The terms "Sociopath", "Psychopath", and "Antisocial Personality Disorder" don't really explain what exactly these people do or what exactly they are capable of, so amidst the confusion and lack of accurate and proper categorization on the part of the DSM-5, between these terms to properly differentiate between these individuals, I've chosen to created my own term for those more on the Psychopathy end of the spectrum who are very capable of destroying another person's life without ever needing to lay a hand on them, although many do as a means of control and intimidation. This term is not only self-explanatory but also captures the true essence of what they do and are capable of. That term is "SOULSPIRIT MURDERERS." It tells you exactly what they do without having to look it up but mostly *because that is also exactly what it feels like…*

These Soulspirit Murderers are very smart, cunning, capable and unsuspecting, as well as, being calm, cool and collected, as opposed to their more emotionally volatile and impulsive counterparts and not so divergently intelligent Sociopaths. Sociopaths (many but not all are narcissistic) tend to be the "fringers" of society (but not always), who are emotionally volatile and often find themselves in trouble with the law, whereas the true Soulspirit Murderers (Functioning Psychopaths, who are ALL narcissists) are more likely to be the ones able to live within the confines and parameters of the law, social policy and norms. They're more likely to live in big cities and highly populated suburbs where there are massive amounts of and different varieties of people to prey on. Living amongst a large population allows them to hide and blend in better so they are not easily identified or outed. Even so, when not busy using or manipulating someone, they would still probably prefer to spend much of their time in solitude, because after all, they loathe normal people and our full range of emotions. Emotions are a silly obstacle to them. They are many things but most of all, THEY ARE THE LAST PERSON YOU WOULD THINK IS A PSYCHOPATH! That's the scary part. They wear their "social masks" well! Think of it like this...sociopaths are more like "wrecking balls" in their actions and psychopaths are more "snipers" who are possibly part ninja and magician. They're intelligent, dynamic, well spoken, charismatic and you might or might not notice their lack of affect (emotions) but they can easily make up for and distract you from that deficit with humor, specifically "shock humor"- the kind of humor that shocks other people when they hear it. They bravely and boldly say and joke about things that are taboo or things most of us wouldn't dare bring up in public and it works very well for them! My ex-husband was a *master* at this...Their "no filter, no boundaries" topics and conversations are usually quite engaging and it's also a great way for them to get a "feel' for each of their audience members (potential prey) reactions, to see who's uptight and uncomfortable or accepting, entertained and therefore, casily sucked into their powerful vortex of manipulative negativity to be used.

They are great storytellers....""This one time at band camp…" No, actually they are "gifted" in this area. They have a list of several "patented" entertaining stories of their past that they will tell and retell over and over and over and, and, and…...you get the picture! I can't tell you how many times I 'd watch this freaky little "Pied Piper" scenario play out where people would just gather around my ex when he started telling his stories. He was too handsome, too hilarious, too charismatic, and too smart, and he knew how to "read and work a room." He was/ is also very aware of this as well. You will get sick of hearing these same stories time and time again and you will notice that various aspects or details are changed (usually with many embellishments) depending on the story teller's audience at the time. These *Soulspirit Murderers* tend to gravitate to such professions as politics (be sure to vote in Nov. 🙄), CEO's, sales, law, law enforcement, you know...anywhere that puts them in a position of power over other more vulnerable people they can prey on. They like to put themselves in positions where they appear to be doing ***humble helpful*** work for GOD and the church. They like to enlist as church leaders and clergy, or at least appear to be doing work for the improvement of mankind, the environment, or their community. They are ***masters*** at "hiding in plain sight!"

There are many things to look for, *if you know what to look for,* when trying to figure out if someone has this type of destructive behavior because they are *pathological.* Meaning they have "narrow" patterns of this antisocial behavior, so basically they cannot help but to keep repeating it throughout their lives, making modifications when and where necessary in order to stay out of trouble and within the expected boundaries. It's been internalized and ingrained into their personality. They may be able to control themselves for a short period of time, let's say, for example at the beginning stages of a relationship, when they know they must be on their best behavior, because their goal and "end game" depends on it, but it won't last for long. The destructive behavior will eventually rear its ugly head again and again!

Sources:

Hare. R. The Psychopathy Scales. https://www.hare.org/scales/

Hare, R. (1996). Psychopathy and Antisocial Personality Disorder: A Case of Diagnostic Confusion. https://www.psychiatrictimes.com/view/psychopathy-and-antiso-cial-personality-disorder-case-diagnostic-confusion

Hare, R. (1996). Psychopathy and Antisocial Personality Disorder: A Case of Diagnostic Confusion. https://www.psychiatrictimes.com/view/psychopathy-and-antiso-cial-personality-disorder-case-diagnostic-confusion

~~~~~~~
~~~~~~~

SOULSPIRIT MURDERERS

**What a BEAUTIFUL creature… its beauty is
engaging and draws you in, doesn't it? Well, it's also
extremely DANGEROUS and *DEADLY, so stay away.***

Part of the term, "Soulspirit Murderer", which I use to refer to these types , was taken from the term "soul murder", used by Dr. William Neiderland when describing what happens when a child (or an adult in this case) is abused to the point they begin to lose sight of who they are, what they feel, who they can trust and their perception of reality. Lack of awareness and denial are cultivated here. This is crushing to your spirit and soul...

True "Soulspirit Murderers" (the ones that walk among us), have "special capabilities", mainly because of their high level of intelligence, lack of real emotions, high level of apathy and ability to control their impulses. It is this intelligence and ability to control their impulses that in part allows these creatures to be able to function in society as opposed to being locked up in prison for anything from white collar crimes to very heinous crimes. There's some debate out there as to whether they have above average intelligence or not. I even read a small study that declared Psychopaths as less intelligent than the average person. I strongly disagree with this and here's why- That particular and most other studies on these creatures are done with those who are incarcerated. *The extremes.* Think about it...where else are they going to find these social deviants-these creatures don't typically run off to a psychologist's office to 'kick it" on the couch and discuss their evilness, or anything else for that matter. The only 'kicker' here is that they don't think they have a problem (all the other people do), which also leads me to believe there are *far more than what statistics represent.* Many of the incarcerated ones (the unsuccessful ones) are in for committing horrible crimes. Now the way I see it, if they are incarcerated, then they weren't smart enough to evade the law, *OR*, their deviant compulsions and obsessions were so strong, they were completely overriding their sense of reason, logic and control, so they end up committing the act impulsively, which means a sloppy crime scene so they get caught, *OR*, they are the extreme ones (the worst of the worst) that are literally "born that way" and are further created in childhood, with the corresponding underdeveloped or non-existent parts of the brain. This leaves them literally without the part of the brain where empathy, compassion and emotions live. Dr. Robert Hare (psychopathy expert and creator of the Hare Psychopathy Scale), likes to use the explanation of, "they can read the words to a song, they just can't hear the music. It's like being *color blind* but with regards to emotions." No wonder they have a big ax to grind with humanity! Most of these extreme versions had traumatic and even horrific childhoods. Some of the most evil of them all, Ted Bundy (the all-american creeper), John Wayne Gacy (the "pervaphile" clown who liked to show young boys his "tricks"), or Todd Kohlhepp (the creeper real estate agent turned part time serial killer) fit into this category. They commit such horrid crimes so often that the "law of averages" and "forensics" alone says they're going to get caught and thrown in prison eventually.

After much research...I've come to the conclusion that the smarter ones are definitely out here...*with us*... And I believe they're above average intelligence and ability to control their impulses (at least for a little while), is why...It makes these social predators extremely cunning, insidious, full of guile, able to maintain their patience and control enough to stay within social and legal parameters. They take the time to meticulously plan their crimes often with back-up or contingency plans in place, just in case. They have learned how to control their impulses and obsessions to a degree. Or should I say they've learned how to *HIDE and DISGUISE them!.* They appear to be very organized and obsessive-compulsive (OCD) because in order to stay 5 steps ahead of everyone (as they do), keep their lies and deviant plans secret, they must keep things in perfect place and in impeccable order so as not to accidentally expose themselves or cross-contaminate their ***dual realities.*** These qualities alone make them extremely good at reading people, manipulation and figuring out ways (using their divergent thinking style) to garner success, fame, riches, people or whatever the hell they please, at the expense of others.

The higher level Narc's (intelligent psychopaths), the ones out here free ranging it with us, are extremely good at this type of behavior and tactics. They don't have the dysregulated and hard to control emotions that get in the way and serve as obstacles, as is the case with the lower level narc's (sociopaths). Make no mistake, these are the *"cool cats"*, the ones that are emotionally deficient. They either don't have the emotions or what they do have is very shallow and have a "switch" they can turn it on and off as it suits them. That is the big difference, and their higher level divergent type of intelligence, of course. These creatures have learned how to "mimic" real emotions and the behaviors, facial expressions, postures and body language they need in order to move about freely and undetected in society. They have to in order to blend in. For example, a normal person will not steal because not only do they "know" it's wrong, but it "feels" wrong too. In stark contrast, the narcissistic psychopath also cognitively knows stealing is wrong but are much more likely to do it because not only do they make their own rules as they go along but because stealing doesn't "feel" wrong to them. It doesn't feel like anything except mild entertainment or a degree of satisfaction... there's a void of emotion where "guilt and shame" would be for the normal person. They tend to look at things from a pure "problem solving perspective", without taking the emotional variables, implications or consequences into consideration at all. Their behavior is predicated on these creature's pathological need to be in control of their situations and environments, which is driven by their insecurities and shortcomings. They live in the *moment*. Neither past nor future matters to them when they are in that *moment*. It is all that matters to them, not considering consequences because they're not thinking about them at all, when they are in their *moment*. Please remember though… no matter how far these people pump their chest and egos out… their insecurities are sticking out that much further!

If only the narcissist psychopath could understand this, right? Well they most likely will not be able to because they typically lack any kind of self-awareness or insight that would allow them to do so. These creatures are so self-centered and egocentric that they must live in a false reality that is skewed to their favor and only makes sense to them. Their reality is much different than ours and that's why so many of the things they did and do, do not make sense to you. In this reality, they are the master of the universe and cannot accept or bare to be anything less. They go through life with this false facade' and will try to annihilate anyone who attempts to tear it down. It's always best to steer clear of these real life vampires, they are human wrecking balls that bash and smash their way through *our lives*.

Sources:

Hare, R. (1996). Psychopathy and Antisocial Personality Disorder: A Case of Diagnostic Confusion. https://www.psychiatrictimes.com/view/psychopathy-and-antisocial-personality-disorder-case-diagnostic-confusio

<div align="center">~~~~~~~</div>

THE SIGNS-
Of the Psychopath, Sociopath, and Narcissist...

The signs. Now I understand, many years later...My ex actually in some ways *TOLD ME WHO HE REALLY WAS*...I just didn't know what I was hearing or what it meant. He also had no problem and was quick to instigate conflict or drama as well.

- He would never get rattled in high pressure situations and/or during confrontation type scenarios. I was not like this and noticed he was and when we discussed it, he would tell me he didn't get nervous or flustered in confrontations and actually got off on them and thrived on them. I didn't get that at all... now I do-because of his high intelligence he knew the odds were always in his favor so it was a dopamine rush for his low dopamine system and I'm sure, a great power surge, as well.

- He used to brag about being a bully in school. YUCK!!!! He would laugh and relive his bullying mis-deeds to me and others, obviously not understanding what he was really doing, the harm it causes or the gravity of it.

- I would have to bear witness to many of his lies that he told people-even when he didn't have to lie. That's the part that got me. He lied even when he didn't have to. He would tell big elaborate lies and relished in the creativity of what he came up with. One time when we visited his home state, he got in touch with an old high school friend and he and his wife ended up inviting us to a big homemade Italian dinner that wife would prepare for us the next day. When the next day came, he decided that he didn't want to go over there after all so proceeded to make up a big elaborate lie that involved "borrowing" a scenario from a John Grisham or a James Patterson Novel. Instead of feeling bad or guilty about what he had just done, he was very proud of coming up with such a great lie...

- He would freak out on the kids when they were really little (too little) and exclaim things like, "He doesn't care if he gets in trouble", "He doesn't fear punishment" and "You have to know it's the wrong thing to do even if it doesn't feel wrong, you have to know in your mind that it is". The kids were still so young and I thought those were odd things to say to a kid. Or anyone for that matter. I had never heard such explanations but apparently he had at some point in his earlier life. People don't come up with such odd *parenting gems* like that on their own.

~~~~~~~
~~~~~~~

<u>HOW TO SPOT THESE CREATURES</u>

"I have a switch I can turn off and on"~ a psychopath
I know… in reference to his itsy bitsy shallow emotions.

These *creatures* are very good at what they do, which makes them difficult to identify. They are masters at taking your defenses and walls down and making you feel comfortable, entertained, engaged and at ease around them. So much in fact, that they can even fool our 8th sense "gut feeling" (interoception) into thinking they mean us no harm. That's the truly scary part about it for me. When trying to spot a psychopath (aka Soulspirit Murderer), there are some specific red flags (tells) you can watch for as you try to steer clear of these ultimate social predators.

THEIR EYES...The eyes are said to be the windows to the soul and they can tell us much about the person behind them. They are also a direct indicator of the emotions we are feeling at that moment in time. Our pupils are directly related to something called "emotional arousal", which means that if we see, think about, recall, etc., something pleasing or shocking or anything that provokes an emotional response in a person, our pupils will dilate because of the emotional reaction it causes. Psychopaths are emotionally deficient, so their pupils will not dilate like a normal person would when looking at what would normally be arousing (either positive or negative) images, etc. Although they may have beautiful and aesthetically pleasing eyes, they won't be "bright and shiny" but more like there's a flatness or shallowness behind them or even deadened. This is actually a phenomenon known as "dead eyes", that is unique to the psychopath. You may also notice their eyes will not light up when talking about family, loved ones or anything they supposedly love. If something is sad or upsetting, their eyes will not reflect their emotion. When talking to one, you may notice that their eyes are not "connecting" with yours even though they are looking at you. It may look like they are looking right in front of your eyes (they are stopping their gaze just short of your eyes) or are looking right through you. They may even look past you when talking to you or everywhere but your eyes... (Now, this could also mean they are shy or on the spectrum if not in the presence of other related symptoms and signs). There's also something known as the 'psychopathic stare" and you'll *know when you're the subject of one because it's that stare that's way too intense and way too long. You'll be the one who has to break this creepy stare!*

THEIR WORDS... Because psychopaths wear a "*mask of sanity*" (their "act" of being a good well-meaning person as opposed to the scary predator behind the mask), in public and around most people, they have to carefully edit and filter their thoughts before they become words and that thought process takes time, so they are more likely to use a lot of "stall words", also known as "disfluencies", such as "uh' and "uhm", in order to interrupt their speech and give themselves enough time to figure out what to say, according to Jeffrey Hancock, the lead researcher and an associate professor in communications at Cornell University. Psychopaths are also very likely to ask you "probing" and invasive type questions (questions designed to make you divulge personal information) so they can figure out your assets and vulnerabilities. They will also divulge too much personal information but this is done strategically so you put your guard down and do the same. When they ask you what your favorite things are, they will say it's their favorite too. What a coincidence- you two must be made for each other...... NOT!!! They will brag, especially about things they've done that they *shouldn't* be bragging about. You know, the inappropriate and downright questionable things they enjoy talking about doing, (like being a bully as a child), that make you *feel uncomfortable* and you question it. When their actions or words make you feel awkward or uncomfortable, or you find yourself questioning them or being a little confused by them, please know, *THAT IS LITERALLY YOUR 8TH SENSE AND SUBCONSCIOUS TELLING YOU, "HEY... YOU NEED TO LOOK INTO THIS SITUATION BECAUSE IT IS NOT GOOD FOR YOU!!!!!!"*

THEIR LAUGH- Yes, there is such a thing as the "psychopathic laugh" or "psycho laugh", as I've accused my ex of exhibiting even before I realized he really was one. These laughs are usually done in a higher octave than normal, come right on the heels of one of their power plays or some kind of abusive behavior against you where they prevailed, and each "ha ha" is deeper than the last, reflecting their satisfaction with themselves. These creepy and self-proclaimed victorious verbal outbursts are usually accompanied by a "gleam in their eye", as I have found. (not to be mistaken for a light in their eyes, which requires real emotions.)

THEIR SWITCH- They have a "switch"- It's called an "empathy switch" and it's usually on the "off " setting just by virtue of their overall personality traits and disposition. Most functioning psychopaths (the ones who can maintain *themselves* enough not to be incarcerated or who got in trouble early on, and learned to "hone" their deviant skills and figured out better ways to stay out of the slammer , eh ehmmm), have some level of empathy and emotions, but they are severely stunted (aka. shallow effect.) This means that they can easily "wall off" anything that feels like empathy or emotions to them as it suits them by "switching their switch to the "off" setting if it isn't already there by default. They are naturally very good at "compartmentalizing" and separating their actions from any kind of emotion, which makes it very easy for them to commit a multitude of different types of crimes against people, physical and otherwise. To them, they are just merely solving a problem that gets them what they want or need, but to the rest of us, we usually take into consideration if our and how our actions might affect others and adjust our actions accordingly.

THEY ARE PUNISHMENT RESISTANT AND REWARD DRIVEN- so basically this means that they choose their behavior not based on the potential consequence but by the potential *reward*. They don't "fear" punishment or negative consequences like the rest of us so it's not a good deterrent. They respond better to rewards for good behavior, than punishment for bad behavior, if that makes sense! I really think the only thing they genuinely fear besides their own demise, is monogamous long-term intimacy/relationships!

THEY HAVE AN UNCANNY TENDENCY OF PAYING UNUSUALLY CLOSE ATTENTION TO THINGS AND ELEMENTS THAT ARE RELEVANT TO THEIR CHOSEN GOAL,

but have a deficit when it comes to acknowledging peripheral (secondary) information and integrating that to make fair, well informed logical choices. This means they are great at hyperfocusing and bad at multitasking! This is because they lack something called "automatic perspective taking", which means they can't or choose not to look at things from someone else's perspective. In other words, they don't put themselves in someone else's shoes in order to help make a better decision. This is where their lack of empathy comes from. How can you "feel" for someone if you don't know how they "feel", ya know?

THEY DON'T SEE THE 'BIG PICTURE"- They have difficulty forecasting their future (usually financial) or learn from their mistakes- according to research co-author, Arielle Baskin-Sommer, of Yale University, in her research published in the "Proceedings of the national Academy of Sciences." "These individuals have difficulty integrating information across contexts. One way to examine that problem is through cost-benefit decision making. (decision making based on weighing the cost vs. the benefit of the result of the decision about to be made) "It may be that several of their behaviors like sensation seeking, engaging in criminal behavior, etc. is a result of the failure to notice cues in their environment, integrate that information, and use it to make future choices. It is almost like every situation a psychopath encounters is brand-new to them," she added. "They are not informed by history or use that new information to direct their future. It then becomes clear why they continually have encounters with the law; if you are unable to weigh the costs and benefits and integrate or remember contexts in which the similar situation has gotten you into trouble you are less likely to inhibit that behavior."

The unique neural wiring and structural and functional differences in these individuals leads to, decision making that excludes factoring in emotional variables or elements and maladaptive decision making processes that do not allow them to accurately forecast the trajectory and outlook of their future or correctly judge appropriate levels of danger of a potential situation. Many of these types of "red flag" patterns of behavior take time to reveal themselves and when they do, the damage has usually already been done. Please, if any of this sounds familiar, do some investigating!

Source:

Steele, B. (2011). The Words of Psychopaths Reveal Their Predatory Nature. https://news.cornell.edu/stories/2011/10/words-psychopaths-reveal-their-predatory-nature

Baskin-Sommer, (2018). Psychopaths Fail to Automatically Take the Perspective of Others. https://pubmed.ncbi.nlm.nih.gov/29531085/

~~~~~~~
~~~~~~~

<u>Narcissism</u>
Public enemy #1

The Narcissistic Spectrum

(Empathy) * ------((-------------------------------))--------* (Apathy)

((most people have the ability to slide back and forth within this range, depending on the situation))

NOTE: The above scale is not a formal scientific scale (obviously); it is just a visual aid to help readers understand the concept.

The farther someone is toward the Narcissistic end of the spectrum, the more they are plagued by narrow-minded, mal-adaptive and immature coping skills that hyper focus on their "self" and their needs regardless of who they have to hurt, abuse or manipulate to achieve it. When they lash out, it is literally the equivalent of an "adult temper tantrum", which is the result of their stunted emotional maturity, as a result of, usually some form of abuse, maltreatment or neglect in their own early childhood, whether it was intentional or unintentional. Narcissism is likely a result of not being loved enough, wanted enough, being payed attention to enough, a mis-attunement between caregiver and the child early on, genetic factors or some neurobiological factors (the connection between the brain and behavior and thinking), according to the Mayo Clinic Website. They can also be created by loving a child too much, telling them and making them believe they are better than or more special compared to others and should receive special treatment and much adoration and attention. So basically, a Narcissist can be created by either too much or not enough love and attention or early childhood *attachment issues.*

On the exterior, the Narcissist is arrogant, has an exaggerated sense of self-importance, monopolizes conversations (for control, attention and adoration), is rigid, controlling and belittles others. They expect special favors and think they deserve the best of everything even though many have never had any kind of real achievements or displayed the capabilities or talents to justify any of it, and as a result, will often manufacture or exaggerate achievements and accomplishments. They have an all-around unwillingness to acknowledge, be concerned with, or feel compassion for others and their needs, unless there is something it is for them. All these traits make them great bullies and very abusive! They have a "high conflict personality", which means they don't play well with others... unless of course, they're wearing their "Mask of Sanity"!

The sad thing about Narcs is that although they have a tough and obnoxious exterior, sadly, they are plagued by feelings of inferiority, low self-esteem and shame. Their tough exterior is just a well-designed "suit of armor" they use to protect their fragile inner selves from that "savage and painful" outside world that was not nice to many of them early on in their lives. They act as if they have a "chip on their shoulder," or as if they've been slighted by others. The sad truth is that most were more than likely victims of some degree of abuse as a very young child, which included, shaming and humiliating the child, or neglecting their needs in some way, resulting in feelings of inferiority, possible abandonment, low self-esteem and deep vulnerability. These are all things that destroy a child's spirit and soul, not to mention their sense of self- worth. This also most likely happened or started prior to or during their emotional development stage, which leaves them emotionally dysregulated (unable to control their emotions and therefore behavior, so they "act out"), with shallow emotions or with no emotions at all because the neurons and neural pathways in and between those parts of the brain never fully developed due to the lack of stimulation in those areas. They shut their painful emotions down during childhood maltreatment, shaming, neglect, etc. as a coping mechanism and therefore the proper range, depth and control of their emotions never properly developed so they perpetually operate in "survival mode"-the short-term (that becomes chronic) fear- based mode someone goes into, when faced with danger, an attack or severe stress and the like. Normally, we should be in the relaxed state of "homeostasis", which is the calm, emotionally regulated physical and psychological balance maintained within a person. Narcissism can be seen as a "safe" way for these people to live because it keeps them from having to feel the unbearable pain they had to feel when they were that vulnerable, shamed, "not good enough", child.

In the case of the overly loved and doted on child who grows up to be a Narc, their parents instilled into them that they are perfection (or should be), very special, better than anyone and so any time the child makes a mistake or falls short of their parent's high standards of expectation of them, they are filled with unbearable feelings of shame, embarrassment, inferiority and feeling they have let the idealizing parent down. This leads to strong gut-wrenching emotions that the child learns to "wall off" or numb out in order to avoid them at all costs. In any case, they learn to project their vulnerabilities, short-comings and problems onto other people, which ironically, usually results in the very thing they are trying to avoid the most- namely rejection and abandonment. This can also result in a "failure to launch" situation where the child knows it will never be able to live up to the parental expectations out in the real world so they never really attempt to go out there and live on their own.

There is some hope for people who suffer from this high conflict personality disorder. It's not curable but it can be treatable. The problem here is that most Narcs don't believe they have a problem or are the one with the problem. Oh, the irony!

According to Craig Malkin Ph.D., in his article, "Can Narcissists Change", on the PsychologyToday website, "as a therapist, I've seen first-hand that when we change relational patterns, it often transforms even the most inflexible "trait" into something softer, gentler-not a fixed feature, but a protection that eventually yields to touch and intimacy in all the ways one would hope. Narcissism is a way of relating. Not everyone can shift into a more flexible form of intimacy, but some can." I also feel like the way society is today, with everything we want or need at our fingertips and at lightning fast speed, more and more of these self-entitled, greedy and apathetic creatures are being created every day.

I hope this sheds some light on not just what a narcissist *really* is but also on their inner workings and why they are the way they are. Best wishes and thank you for reading!!!

The Mayo Clinic Staff. (2023). Narcissistic Personality Disorder. https://www.mayoclinic.org/diseases-conditions/narcissistic-personality-disorder/symptoms-causes/syc-20366662

Malkin, C. (2013). Can Narcissists Change? https://www.psychologytoday.com/us/blog/romance-redux/201309/can-narcissists-change

~~~~~~~
~~~~~~~

THE "ANTISOCIAL CLUB"

"All that glitters is not gold… sometimes it's really
just thinly gold plated tin held on by duct tape"

People who are considered to be abusers, such as, **sociopaths, psychopaths** and **narcissists** are all members of a very special "social club", which Psychologists like to refer to as "those with **"Antisocial Personality Disorder"**, and they have a lifetime membership. In order to be a member of this "very special club", you need to exhibit and excel at special skills in areas such as- screwing people over and not really caring much about it, then throwing them away, and seeking out excessive attention and adoration, especially for things not really achieved. Speaking of "achieve", you can even "achieve" *higher* club status if you are also able to brag about your misdeeds in a cold and uncaring manner. Yes, if they happen to possess copious amounts of apathy --well then that will get them a higher status and ranking for sure! Oh, to be so adored! These people like to live outside of the social contracts that the rest of us are "bound" by and make their own rules. They tend to regard real laws and rules more as, "rough guidelines" or "mere suggestions", or meh, not at all. The problem with these types of people and the destruction they cause, is that the crimes they commit are usually the non-violent, interpersonal, moral and ethical ones that are *invisible* and therefore hard to identify, quantify or collect as tangible physical evidence or proof.

They rate fairly high on the psychopathy scale and are mainly characterized by 4 specific domains according to the PCL-R (Psychopathy checklist- revised) scale, which is used to rate the level of psychopathy in an individual. These domains are; interpersonal, affective, lifestyle and antisocial. According to the article, 'Diagnosing Psychopaths", on the Psychology Today website, Scott Bonn, Ph.D. states that, *"The interpersonal traits include glibness (in conversation-insincerity, lack of forethought, superficial charm- think used car salesman), grandiosity, pathological lying and manipulation of others. The affective traits include a lack of remorse and/*

or guilt, shallow affect, lack of empathy and failure to accept responsibility. The lifestyle behaviors include stimulation-seeking behavior (because they have "chronic" boredom due to low levels of dopamine and approx. 4 times the dopamine released for "rewards"), impulsivity, irresponsibility, parasitic orientation and a lack of realistic life goals. Antisocial behaviors include poor behavioral controls, early childhood behavior problems, juvenile delinquency, revocation of conditional release and committing a variety of crimes."

Dr. Scott Bonn goes on to say that, *"An individual who possesses all of the interpersonal, affective, lifestyle and antisocial personality traits measured by PCL-R is considered a Psychopath. A clinical designation of psychopathy in the PCL-R test is based on a lifetime pattern of psychopathic behavior."*

"The results to date suggest that psychopathy is a continuum ranging from those who possess all of the traits and score highly on them to those who also have the traits but score lower on them. This PCL-R allows for a maximum overall score of 40. A minimum score of 30 is required in order to designate someone as a psychopath."

"The scores for those who are Psychopaths vary greatly, revealing that very high to low levels of the condition exist among those who have it. Non-criminal psychopaths generally score in the lower range (close to thirty) while criminal psychopaths, especially rapists and murderers, tend to score in the highest range (close to forty.)"

"No two psychopaths score exactly the same on the test. The average non-psychopath will score around five or six on the PCL list."

And lastly, Dr. Scott Bonn concludes, *"Dr. Hare and other experts, including <u>forensic</u> psychologists and FBI profilers, consider psychopathy to be the most important forensic concept of the early twenty-first century. Because of its relevance to law enforcement, corrections, the courts and related fields, the need to understand psychopathy cannot be overstated."*

Regardless of what people and doctors decide to call or categorize these creatures as, the most important thing to remember is that they have the potential to inflict unimaginable pain, physically, psychologically and otherwise. It is very easy for them to manipulate and abuse people because they can separate their almost non-existent emotions from their actions. They are pathological which means they have a narrow pattern of behavior that will eventually give them away. They can behave themselves for short periods of time but that narrow patterned behavior (deviant of course) will always surface, usually after a commitment has been made... like moving in with each other, engagement or marriage!

Bonn, S. (2023). Psychopathy: A Clinical Diagnosis. https://www.psychologytoday.com/us/blog/wicked-deeds/201610/psychopathy-clinical-diagnosis

~~~~~~~
~~~~~~~

Characteristics of an Abuser

"Handsome is as handsome does"~ my father
(in reference to my ex-husband)

It's important for me that I include the fact that men or women can be abusive and both can be victims, although the vast majority of victims are women. Abuse and violence happen in all types of relationships, whether it is a traditional heterosexual relationship or a same sex or other type. "Abusers" have some behaviors in common that can be seen as "red flags." This was taken directly from the www.ilrctbay.com website; (no known author)

Characteristics of Abusers

If the person you love or live with does these things, it's time to get help:

- Keeps track of what you are doing all the time and criticizes you for little things. *(This gives you a suffocating feeling and like someone is watching you at all times.)*
- Constantly accuses you of being unfaithful. (*This could be him 'projecting" his cheating on you-he's really the one cheating but accuses you of it instead)*
- Prevents or discourages you from seeing friends or family or going to work or school. (This encourages isolation, which is an extremely valuable tool for the abuser)
- Gets angry when drinking alcohol or using drugs.
- Controls all the money you spend.
- Humiliates you in front of others. (likes to use you as the butt of his jokes in public)
- Destroys your property or things that you care about. (may abuse your pets or lets them out free on "accident")
- Threatens to hurt you or the children or pets, or does cause hurt (by hitting, punching, slapping, kicking, or biting).
- Uses or threatens to use a weapon against you.

- Forces you to have sex against your will. (or what's known as "sex on demand')
- Blames you for his/her violent outbursts. (Look what you made me do.)

Characteristics of Abusers...Warning signs of potential violence:

- Abuser pacing the floor or circling you.
- Clenching/unclenching fists
- Facial expression (glaring)
- Shouting/yelling

Always be conscious of your own safety needs in all interactions involving an abusive person. Do not meet privately with a violence-prone individual. If you *must do so,* be sure someone is available close by in case you need help.

Abusers frequently have the following characteristics:

- Often blow up in anger at small incidents. He or she is often easily insulted, claiming hurt feelings when he or she is really very angry.
- Are excessively jealous: At the beginning of a relationship, an abuser may claim that jealousy is a sign of his or her love. Jealousy has nothing to do with love.
- Like to isolate the victim: He or she may try to cut you off from social support, accusing the people who act as your support network of "causing trouble."
- Have a poor self-image; are insecure.
- Blame others for their own problems.
- Blame others for their own feelings and are very manipulative. An abusive person will often say, "You make me mad," "You're hurting me by not doing what I ask," or "I can't help being angry".
- Often are alcohol or drug abusers.
- May have a family history of violence.

- May be cruel to animals and/or children.
- May have a fascination with weapons.
- May think it is okay to solve conflicts with violence.
- Often make threats of violence, breaking or striking objects.
- Often, they use physical force during arguments.
- Often use verbal threats such as, "I'll slap your mouth off", "I'll kill you", or "I'll break your neck". Abusers may try to excuse this behavior by saying, "everybody talks like that".
- May hold rigid stereotypical views of the roles of men and women. The abuser may see women as inferior to men, stupid, and unable to be a whole person without a relationship.
- Are very controlling of others. Controlling behaviors often grow to the point where victims are not allowed to make personal decisions.
- May act out instead of expressing themselves verbally.
- May be quick to become involved in relationships. Many battered women dated or knew their abuser for less than six months before they were engaged or living together.
- May have unrealistic expectations. The abuser may expect his or her partner to fulfill all his or her needs. The abusive person may say, "If you love me, I'm all you need- you're all I need".
- May use "playful" force during sex, and/or may want to act out sexual fantasies in which the victim is helpless.
- May say things that are intentionally cruel and hurtful in order to degrade, humiliate, or run down the victim's accomplishments.
- Tend to be moody and unpredictable. They may be nice one minute and the next minute explosive. Explosiveness and mood swings are typical of men who beat their partners.
- May have a history of battering: the abuser may admit to hitting others in the past, but will claim the victim "asked for" it. An abuser will beat any woman he is with; situational circumstances do not make a person abusive.

How dangerous is the abuser? Assessing lethality in an abuse situation:

Some domestic violence is life threatening. All domestic violence is dangerous, but some abusers are more likely to kill than others and some are more likely to kill at specific times. The likelihood of homicide is greater when the following factors are present:

1. **Threats of homicide or suicide:** The abuser may threaten to kill himself, the victim, the children, relatives, friends, or someone else;
2. **Plans for homicide or suicide:** The more detailed the abuser's plan and the more available the method, the greater the risk he will use deadly force;
3. **Weapons:** The abuser possesses weapons, and has threatened to use them in the past against the victim, the children, or himself. If the abuser has a history of arson, fire should be considered a weapon;
4. **"Ownership" of the victim:** The abuser says things like "If I can't have you no one can" or "I would rather see you dead than have you divorce me". The abuser believes he is absolutely entitled to the obedience and loyalty of the victim;
5. **Centrality of the victim to the abuser:** The abuser idolizes the victim, depending heavily on him or her to organize and sustain the abuser's life, or the abuser isolates the victim from outside supports;
6. **Separation violence:** The abuser believes he is about to lose the victim;
7. **Repeated calls to law enforcement:** A history of violence is indicated by repeated police involvement;
8. **Escalation of risk-taking:** The abuser has begun to act without regard to legal or social consequences that previously constrained his violence; and
9. **Hostage taking:** He is desperate enough to risk the life of innocent persons by taking hostages. There is a very serious likelihood of the situation turning deadly.

Here are more characteristics that many "abusers" share. I got these from the website 'www.psychology.com', author unknown;

- They tend to be insecure. Low self-esteem is a common trait in abusers.
- Needy with an unrealistic expectations of the relationship
- Distrustful
- Lies often
- Jealous
- Needs to be "right" and in control
- Possessive
- History of aggression
- Can be cold and apathetic towards people, children and animals
- Blames their bad behavior on others
- Suffer from untreated mental health issues
- Have a "Jekyll" and "Hyde" personality
- Can be psychopathic, sociopathic or narcissistic
- Don't respect boundaries- social or personal
- Don't respect laws
- Sadistic personality (derives enjoyment from hurting others)
- Substance/alcohol abusers
- Selfish and self-centered

Sources:

Lancer, D. (2017). The Truth About Abusers, Abuse, and What to Do. https://www.psychologytoday.com/us/blog/toxic-relationships/201706/the-truth-about-abusers-abuse-and-what-to-do

Kim, J. (2014). Why He Hits: The Psychology of an Abuser. Why He Hits: The Psychology of an Abuser

~~~~~~~
~~~~~~~

THE 90% RULE AND "WEB METHOD"

~How to use these rules to identify and deal with, Narcissists, Sociopaths, Psychopath (Antisocial Personality Disorder) and people with "high conflict personalities.

People with *"high conflict personalities"* such as those in the "Cluster B" group of personality disorders, which includes **Sociopaths, Narcissists (Narcs), Psychopaths** and **Antisocial Personality Disorders,** belong to. These people are considered to have a *pathological pattern* of narrow behavior which repeats itself over time. This makes it helpful in identifying them but that can also take some time. I feel like it makes good sense not to rush into any new relationship and form a commitment too soon-there are some things you just won't know about a person unless you've spent some extensive time with them in all facets of their life or even live with them for a period of time. Even then, there is no guarantee that you will notice or learn important aspects of their personality , or patterns of antisocial behavior. *Remember...they are "hiding" them from you and it is the most dangerous part of their personality.* It took me years to catch on to and realize some of my ex-husband's deviant behavior and ploys. There are *signs* though..

The **"90% Rule"** is one way of determining if someone's behavior is problematic and could lead to abuse or damage. This is how it works- According to author **Bill Eddy, LCSW, Esq.** in his book, *"5 Types of People Who Can Ruin Your Life"*, these people will do things and say things that 90% of the population *would not do.* If someone is displaying very negative behavior, ask yourself, "would 90% of the population do or say that?" If your answer is anywhere from "probably not" to "hell no-he's crazy!", then you are most likely dealing with one of these people. These people do not play well with others. They pretend to though, on the surface, but rest assured they are scheming ways to manipulate, use, and deceive you. These people will demand that you feel the same way they do about things and when you don't, they can get nasty. They may try to guilt trip you or even bully you into aligning with their beliefs and opinions. Don't let them use excuses like being tired, hungry, (hangry) or overstressed for behaving badly. When applying this rule, remove such excuses when trying to determine if a person's behavior is problematic.

Author and licenced clinical social worker Bill Eddy has another system for identifying these dangerous types of personalities in people, which he calls, "The WEB Method'. This is done by 'observing the person's words, your own emotions about them, and the person's behavior. Words (W) plus emotions (E) plus behavior (B) ='s WEB." states the author. He continues describing it as;

1. WORDS; Do the person's words fit the high conflict pattern of behavior?
    1. Are they preoccupied with blaming others?
    2. Do they often use all-or-nothing thinking? For example, "My way or the highway!" Or, "I hate everyone in that group. Don't you?" (*with a full-on expectation that you will agree with them*).
    3. Do they have a hard time communicating or controlling their emotions? *(For example, and from my own personal vault- Something terrible has happened to a close family member, you look to your partner for support but they are apathetic and unsupportive, or, they send you angry texts filled with F-bombs and threats because of some minor transgression or offense they 'perceived" you to have committed.)*
    4. Do they often make strong threats?
2. *EMOTIONS-* What do you feel around this person? When you're around them, or think about being around them, do you:
    1. Feel afraid or anxious?
    2. Feel inadequate or humiliated?
    3. Feel helpless or hopeless?
    4. Feel alone, isolated or ashamed?
    5. Blame yourself a lot for their behavior or statements?
    6. Try to talk yourself out of it or reduce *how you feel?*

7. Feeling incredibly positive-like the person is too good to be true?
8. Feel swept off your feet-too much?
9. Feel like the absolute center of this person's life-like an obsession?
10. Feel incredibly sorry for them-a helpless victim their entire life?

(This one is HUGE...Tune into your "gut feeling" more-it will tell you....)

3. BEHAVIOR- Has the person behaved in an extreme way?
    1. Would 90% of people do what the person did?
    2. Does this person treat you in an extremely negative way?
    3. Have you observed them treating others in an extremely negative way?

(A good example here would be if, let's say, your "new boo" treats you very nice so far but you notice he is unnecessarily rude, mean or disrespectful to the waitress serving you at a restaurant or his mother. If he is being rude to these people you can count on the fact that you are next.)

Source:

Eddy, B. (2018). *5 Types of People Who Can Ruin Your Life. Tarcherperigree-Penguin Books.*

~~~~~~~
~~~~~~~

PART 4

DOMESTIC ABUSE/INTIMATE PARTNER VIOLENCE

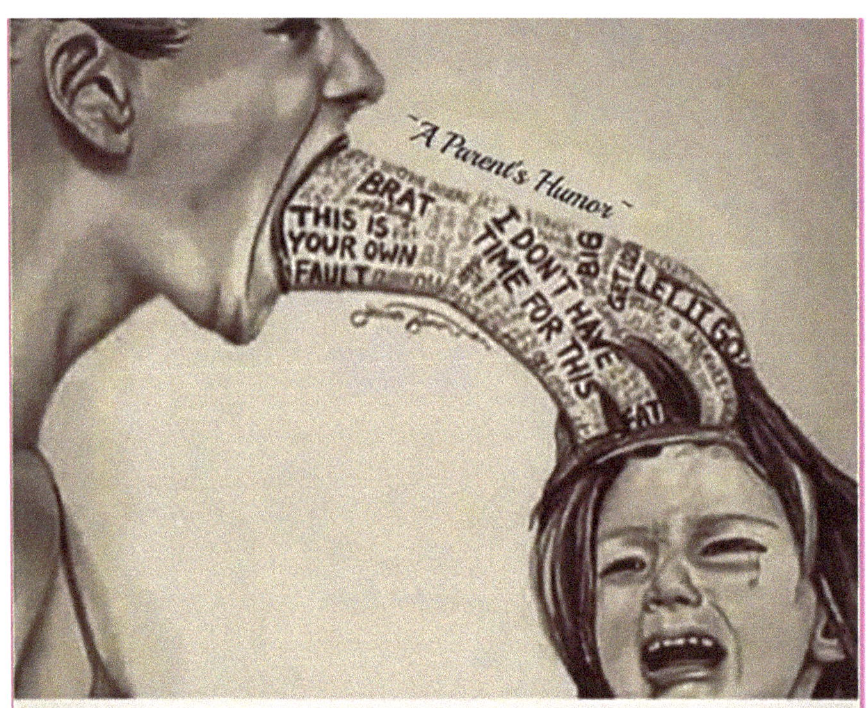

This is one of the most powerful image I've ever seen. study it & clean up your act for the sake of your children. Their minds are fragile, their emotions run deep. Don't destroy them mentally because words. You can never take back.

INTRO- DISTURBIA IN SUBURBIA

"Broken bones will heal, but the hurtful words, memories, and awful visceral sensations can last a lifetime."

It sets in slowly... like fog creeping up in the grass, just out of our field of vision and stealthily slithers, winding its way into the entire space that surrounds you, until it permeates all that you are and occupy.. Psychological abuse is incredibly damaging and it changes who you are. It changes your brain, your perceptions, your central nervous system, right down to our genes that are passed on to our children (epigenetics.) *IT. IS. EVERYWHERE…*

Wait...you mean stress can cause a person to develop an auto-immune disease??? Well, as it turns out...YES IT CAN!!! This very question, and subsequent answer is one of the main reasons I have been inspired to start my website and book, as it was the answer to a question that had eluded me for almost 2 decades! I was diagnosed with Fibromyalgia and then Systemic Lupus Erythematosus in the early 2000's after I started feeling sick, mind numbingly exhausted and was having weird little infections, seemingly out of nowhere, (just a few years prior I was an exceptionally healthy Division I athlete playing softball in the PAC 12). I had been physically well conditioned, mentally tough and had a very positive and happy disposition and was a well adjusted person but within just a few years' time I found myself very ill. Well long story short- I didn't learn/realize/was able to make the connection, that it was actually the chronic stress, intense gut wrenching emotions and trauma from being in an abusive relationship that took me on a wild and crazy ride for almost 30 years, that was the CATALYST and CAUSE of my illnesses! I didn't have any of the risk factors or contributors that typically or "have been known to" cause auto-immune diseases (not that there are very many supposed "KNOWN" causes anyway.) During my marriage, I knew that my husband could be exceptionally and unnecessarily wicked and cruel (especially verbally and emotionally) and could be violent and scary at times but I truly did not REALIZE that his behaviors, how he was treating me, the conditions at home that it was creating, and what I was enduring was considered ABUSE, in the eyes of the LAW. I think everyone is familiar with the domain of physical abuse by now but not many are familiar with the highly destructive, very insidious and long term damaging verbal, emotional, and psychological abuse, as well as, isolation, oppression and rejection. These are often more psychologically harmful than physical abuse because physical abuse tends to be cyclical with periods of calm in between, but verbal and emotional/psychological abuse can happen EVERYDAY and it feels very personal. Verbal, emotional and psychological abuse tears at your character, soul and spirit…

Trauma and abuse at the hands of a loved one is generally the worst kind because of the intense conflicting emotions, torment and instability involved. Chronic exposure to any type of abuse, including rejection, by a loved one, intimate partner or parent/caretaker (as is the case with child abuse), creates not only enormous amounts of extreme emotions and stress but it also creates a special kind of stress known as "Toxic Stress" that is especially damaging and has a long term physiological grip on its victims. Having to "walk around on eggshells" in a love/hate relationship is profoundly insidious and harmful. This type of stress happens primarily because there is an internal struggle of impulses within the victim; one that comes from that innate need to be loved, valued and taken care of by that loved one, (the abuser) and to look to them for safety. The other conflicting internal impulse tells them that their loved one is also the source of their pain and suffering and they need and want that to stop. This scenario creates a tormenting epic struggle within the victim and sets the stage for a full blown physiological chain of events that "resets" many of our internal biological systems including our immune system to a hyperactive and hypersensitive state, so that it keeps trying to fight off the enemy long after the enemy or traumatic event/s are over. These "memories" or "imprints" of the trauma also live on within our senses by manifesting viscerally as uncomfortable and sometimes unbearable inner sensations and feelings. Many times, the victim has no words or cannot verbalize the intense emotions they are feeling or even identify what it is their feeling. This is known as- ALEXITHYMIA. This alone, can directly cause the immune system to become a more 'proinflammatory' environment.

According to Dr. Bessel Van Der Kolk, who is at the forefront of this subject, in his best-selling book "The Body Keeps the Score; Brain, Mind, and Body in the Healing of Trauma" states that, "In our society the most common traumas in women and children occurs at the hands of their parents or intimate partners. Child abuse, molestation, and domestic violence are all inflicted by people who are supposed to love you. That knocks out the most important protection against being traumatized; being sheltered by the people you love. If the people whom you naturally turn to for care and protection terrify or reject you, you learn to shut down and to ignore what you feel." This creates an environment where in place of safety, there is terror and WHERE TERROR EXISTS, SAFETY CANNOT.

This profound internal dilemma along with the acts of abuse themselves, set off a coordinated series of behavioral and physiological responses known as "The Stress Response", which is aimed at protecting and attempting to return its host to homeostasis but with victims of abuse, this system becomes faulty. The Stress Response gets stuck in a repeating loop so the hypothalamus keeps telling the adrenal glands, via the HPA axis (the interaction between the hypothalamus, pituitary and adrenal glands) and part of the Central Nervous System, to keep secreting the stress hormones adrenaline (also known as epinephrine) and cortisol, (which is part of the "fight or flight" response to prepare the body for danger- real or perceived) while also communicating bi-directionally with the immune system. This communication takes place by way of small proteins and chemical messengers. Messengers in the CNS are hormones and neurotransmitters (which deliver information between neurons.) The immune system messengers are known as cytokines. These cytokines are small proteins which are released by cells. Although there are many different types of cytokines, the ones typically stimulated by the stress response are known as "pro-inflammatory" (causing inflammation) and are normally released from the immune system, in response to injuries to protect and heal tissue and in response to infections, to help fight off bacteria, germs and viruses, etc. This is one of the main causes of inflammation in the body, in the absence of injury or infection. Inflammation is at the heart of auto-immune diseases and many other illnesses and disorders. Sometimes these "pro-inflammatory' WARRIORS will attack systemically- all over the body (as is the case with my own Systemic Lupus Erythematosus) or they can attack in a concentrated area such as a single organ or only the myelin sheaths (the protective coating) of nerves, as is the case with Multiple Sclerosis..

While this process is happening, many other simultaneous changes to the body's other systems are going on as well and can become the default setting that our systems stay in, when faced with chronic abuse and trauma related toxic stress. For example, According to Dr. Bessel Van Der Kolk, in his best-selling book, explains how the insula (the part of the brain that collects input from internal organs such as, joints, muscles and our balancing system), interprets and integrates this information and when in this faulty state, will keep sending signals to your amygdala (the brain's smoke detector) which keeps setting off "fight or flight" and releasing surges of hormones. Dr. Van Der Kolk states that, "the insidious effects of constantly elevated stress hormones includes memory and attention problems, irritability and sleep disorders. They also contribute to many long term health issues, depending on which body system is most vulnerable in a particular individual."

The long term effects can be disastrous, far reaching, life-threatening and the cycle can last for generations. DOMESTIC ABUSE/ VIOLENCE, also known as "Intimate Partner Violence" or IPV, as defined by the National Coalition Against Domestic Violence is: "The willful intimidation, physical assault, battery, sexual assault and or other abusive behavior (emotional, verbal, psychological, financial, religious, racial, gender, reproductive, oppression, neglect and rejection), as part of a systematic pattern of power and control perpetrated by one intimate partner against another. The one constant component of domestic abuse/violence is one partner's consistent efforts to maintain POWER and CONTROL over the other." According to the National Center for Biotechnology Information (NCBI) website, it is also considered a Human Rights Violation and a public health issue across the world.

Our brain and bodies react the same way during verbal and emotional assaults as it does during a physical assault, which means that victims go into "fight/ flight or freeze" mode and starts releasing hormones such as adrenaline and norepinephrine to prepare the body for "fighting, fleeing or freezing" the assault but in the cases of chronic abuse, the response to threat continues in the body even when the actual threat has past. According to Dr. Bessel Van Der Kolk, in his best-selling book, "The Body Keeps the Score; Brain, Mind, and Body in the Healing of Trauma", states that, "Being traumatized (by physical, emotional, verbal or any other type of abuse), means continuing to organize your life as if the trauma were still going on- unchanged and immutable-as every new encounter or event is contaminated by the past. After trauma the world is experienced with a different nervous system. The survivor's energy now becomes focused on suppressing inner chaos, at the expense of spontaneous involvement in their life. These attempts to maintain control over unbearable physiological reactions can result in a whole range of physical symptoms, including fibromyalgia, chronic fatigue syndrome, and similar illnesses as well as autoimmune diseases."

Stress, specifically "toxic stress", which is born from, abuse and trauma at the hands of a loved one, other types of traumas (war), adversities and the intense negative emotions, torment and mental anguish that go with these events, are like literal wooden "splinters' or glass "slivers" we sometimes get stuck in our skin. If not removed or treated properly, they can fester, become infected, inflamed and cause further problems. Our bodies identify "toxic stress" and other threats as "foreign bodies invading the organism", just like a virus, bacteria, or environmental toxin. Our bodies react the same way…

The most destructive and pervasive form of domestic abuse is not physical, like many people would think and what appears to be the most common, but is psychological, which includes verbal and emotional abuse.

Physical abuse can heal over time in most cases although it can leave visible scars and much worse, but it is the intimate assault of your feelings, thoughts, belief systems, values, morals and perceptions that really de-stabilize and tear at a person's mental health and overall well-being. A real assault on your soul and spirit, it is very damaging to a person's psyche as well as physical body. Psychological abuse is designed to keep you off balance and control and maintain power over you. Over time it is detrimental to the victim's personal growth and autonomy. They are being stifled and not allowed to grow. The effects of verbal and emotional abuse are like splinters or shards of glass we get stuck in our fingers, if not treated, they will continue to fester, become inflamed and infected and cause further problems. Think of it this way~ Abuse and traumatic events are seen as "foreign bodies" and "dangerous", to our system, just like a bacteria or virus, and respond accordingly.

Domestic abuse comes in several different forms. The obvious one that everyone knows about is physical abuse but there are many less obvious forms that can be far more pervasive and damaging in the long term. Those forms include; verbal, emotional, psychological, sexual, financial, religious, reproductive, oppression, neglect, rejection and isolation. It all usually begins slowly with verbal abuse and escalates over time into other forms.

Tactics of verbal and emotional abuse can include, lying, bullying, coercion, intimidating, humiliating, demeaning, criticizing, ignoring, neglecting, a pattern of scaring or starting the victim, angry and violent outbursts, aggressive and intimidating postures, verbal threats, gaslighting (a form of psychological manipulation), and attempts to undermine the victim's sanity, status, footing, power and equality in the relationship.

Here are some examples of *psychological abuse* from my relationship with my ex-husband;

- If I didn't feel well (because of my illnesses) and didn't want to have sex when my ex-husband did, which was just about every single night and during the day literally, (sex on demand) many times he would try to bully me into it by threatening to cheat on me and a few times he threatened that he was going to call a former mistress of his, and a few times, he actually did. I can remember one time when his 6' 2" frame was standing over me as I laid in my bed in pretty severe pain. He was literally texting and trying to call her as I was looking up at him. If this isn't emotional and psychological abuse, I. DON'T. KNOW. WHAT. IS...

- He would often come home from work or elsewhere and would immediately attempt to start a fight by being jabby, or provoking in some other conversational way. This would allow him an "out" and a reason to leave the house again. It all became very obvious and habitual on his part, over time.

- When I would go grocery shopping, I would go to Walmart most of the time. It was the closest, the cheapest, and I was trying to be price conscious. Being the closest store was a huge deal because I spent most of my time bedridden with severe body pain from my illness. After I would return from shopping or just going to pick the groceries up, I would often get yelled at and reprimanded like I was a child because "I spent too much money" or for not telling him I was going shopping for groceries. I would also get criticized about what I bought. This happened all the time. I always bought healthy and nutritious food. I would spend between about $100 and maybe $150 for almost 2 weeks worth of food for a family of 4, the last several years of our marriage. We lived in a nice home and had above average income. Now here's the kicker... He would go shopping and buy almost all *JUNK FOOD*...I'm talking Ding Dongs, Twinkies, Ho-Ho's, donuts, cakes, pies, chocolate covered wafers, candy, chocolate bars, and a lot of those little round blobs of pink marshmallows covered in pink shredded coconut, and just about the entire Hostess end cap, with very little healthy food sprinkled in between. He'd make *HOSTESS* proud. I never heard him yell at or reprimand himself for his choices! Ha! What a hippo. (as in hypocrite, not as in weight gained from all the snacks.) Apparently the same standards did not apply to him. We both contributed to our monthly income. The moral of this story is that it didn't matter what I did or did not do, he was going to find fault with it and nail me for this perceived transgression. I was damned if I did and damned if I didn't. TO THIS VERY DAY…When I have to spend money, at the grocery store or otherwise, my heart races and I feel that awful surge of adrenaline, and that old familiar feeling of dread and apprehension. It's like my brain and body forget that I won't have to go home to that drama anymore. So annoying…

- One time when we were trying to move back to Phoenix from California, after we sold our business, and the kids were real little, we chose a house and were negotiating it. Well, my husband was anyway because he took control of all things. He assured me that all was going well and that it wouldn't be long before the house was ours. Well after days and days of not hearing anything from him, the realtor called me and said we have not heard from your husband in several days and that the stress was causing the owner's wife's illness to get worse. Well apparently, he assured them all was well also and then just dropped off the face of the earth. Come to find out, he had taken our down payment money and used it to rent a space in a strip mall to open a skateboarding shop. Now, this was back in the 90's when skate parks were popping up everywhere. I had no clue he was up to this until after he had signed the lease, etc. He hired his, just out of prison younger brother, to manage it, which was a big mistake. His brother, who sadly had spent much of his life being incarcerated, was nowhere near equipped to manage such a place. He quickly proved this by hiring his "old prison buddy", who went by the name of "Shaggy", to help ensure the business would spiral within months.

Now the above examples may not seem so bad but if you combine a couple or several of them at a time and are exposed to any combination on an almost daily or consistent basis, they're not so small. If they are capable of those types of behaviors, they are surely exhibiting similar behaviors in different contexts. I hope this helps in the understanding of how emotional/psychological abuse affects its victims and why it is so destructive.

Sources:

Van Der Kolk, B. (2014). The Body Keeps the Score- Brain, Mind, and Body in the Healing of Trauma. Penguin Books.

Learn More About Abuse. https://www.thehotline.org/resources/learn-more-about-abuse/

Huecker, M. et al. (2023). Domestic Violence. National Library of Medicine. https://www.ncbi.nlm.nih.gov/books/NBK499891/

What is Domestic Violence? National Coalition on Domestic Violence. https://www.thehotline.org/resources/learn-more-about-abuse/

~~~~~~~
~~~~~~~

WHAT TYPES COMMONLY ABUSE?

You can love them and hate them all at the same time…so is the conundrum and paradox of the abusive relationship.

Men, women, and children can all be victims, although the vast majority of victims are women. Why is this??? Well, there are many reasons. From a historical and cultural perspective, it can be argued that men have traditionally been indoctrinated both religiously and secularly for centuries into the belief system that they need to be "The man of the house," the strongest, most capable, productive, powerful, and dominant. Otherwise, there is a sense of threat to their masculinity and, for some, their very existence and sense of purpose. Most religions specifically encourage and cultivate male domination over females and also promote and facilitate inequality. It is because of this that physical and emotional abuse is predominantly a man's domain.

If you mix the above mindset with someone who has a personality disorder such as narcissism, sociopathy, or psychopathy (antisocial personality disorder/Cluster B), the damage can be profound, even deadly. People with these "Cluster B" personality disorders tend to be big abusers and also make up the biggest "sub-set" of abusers. It is their empty or almost empty emotional gas tanks, inability to form strong attachments with people (which leads to apathy), and their own inadequacies and hyper-fragile self-esteem that prime them to be abusers. Simply put- they tear us down to build themselves up to feed their hyper-fragile egos. And unfortunately, fragile and hyper-fragile egos must be fed, and the beasts are always hungry….Abusers aren't all "abusivey" right out of the gate, though. If they were, it would make most people run for the hills because their potential victim hasn't established deep enough positive feelings yet (or any at all) or a connection that would keep them with their abuser. Not worth it. They start off slow and stealth, a snide comment or a nudge here, a "no filter" rude joke and a shove there (all little tests, by the way), and before you know it WHAM…you are waist deep in it, and don't realize half of it!!! Abuse almost always occurs in relationships that have a power imbalance. This kind of abuse can happen every day, whereas physical abuse tends to be cyclical, with periods of relative calm and "great times" in between (another reason victims don't leave.) Most of the time, the abuser is "projecting" his problems or bad behavior onto his victim. Here are some examples from my own private collection: #1- he accuses you of cheating and stealing money from a joint savings account when he's really the one doing all of that. #2- he would constantly lecture me about not spending money when I would go shopping, even for groceries. For anything, really. It was a sport for him. When, in all actuality, he was the compulsive and impulsive spender who couldn't seem to stop. I have always been a small-town simpleton, not to mention I spent most of my marriage in various degrees of sickness and just didn't get out much at all. It was he who ran our money and finances into the ground while painting the town red. With what felt like *my* blood… He controlled the money, and he spent the money. Even my children are fully aware of this. Abusers are very good at accusing you of the things they are actually doing…

Physical abuse is obviously traumatic to the victim, but bones and skin eventually heal if the damage is not too severe. It is the long-lasting personal and intimate negative effects of chronic verbal, emotional, and psychological abuse that really do the immediate and long-term damage to a person. This is because it targets the thoughts, feelings, and perception of the victim and their reality.

Other issues, such as drugs or alcohol abuse and anger problems, can also lead to domestic abuse as well, but I'm focusing on those with moderate to severe personality disorders. These people can be very selfish, narcissistic, manipulative, exploitative and dangerous. They have the capability to greatly injure and even "murder" a person's soul and spirit. It's all about them, their selfish needs, and their deviant ways. Hence, they make sure it stays that way by using certain strategies (aside from physical threats and violence) to CONTROL not only their victim, those around them, and certain situations but also your perception of reality. Notice I said "perception" of reality...that's because what they attempt to do is distract you from the TRUE reality, which is them sneaking around behind your back, cheating, abusing finances, etc., using and manipulating people, making passes at your friends, even family members for personal and financial gain, and worse. Generally, just "severely running amok without dignity" is what I call it. Now, in order to maintain and CONTROL all the chaos they're creating behind the scenes, they need to have a certain level of POWER, and they do this by employing the systematic pattern of verbal, emotional and psychological ploys and strategies that play with our minds, keep us unsure, in a state of stress, anxiety and confusion and dependent upon them for truthful information and support. I remember feeling like, something was going on, or something wasn't quite right but I couldn't put my finger on it, so many times in my marriage and only if I would have listened to my gut because after our divorce, more information came to the surface and I have found out that those times when I felt like something wasn't quite right, were indeed the times when he was cheating on me or being deceitful and manipulative. It started when I was pregnant with my first child and shortly thereafter. Big lesson learned here-WE MUST LEARN TO LISTEN TO AND TRUST OUR GUT FEELINGS about people and situations!

If anything here looks familiar or strikes a nerve with you, you need to pay attention! If you're not quite sure what you are enduring qualifies as abuse, listen to your body and mind; they'll tell you, for you! If you truly are in an abusive relationship, your mind will be filled with confusion, cognitive dissonance, conflict, uneasiness, frustration, and maybe a feeling that you are going crazy. You may even feel like a mere shell of your former self. It may be difficult to even recognize yourself when looking at your reflection; you kind of recognize the person looking back at you, but she's changed... Physically, you may find yourself with stomach or digestive problems, headaches, anxiety, depression, mood swings, or periods of confusion because your reality might not make sense to you because the abusers' words and behaviors contradict each other. If any of this resonates with you, I urge you to please reconsider that relationship because I can tell you from personal experience that it will be very costly. It can cost you your self-esteem, sanity, career, and mental and physical health, and there will surely be chaotic and painful times ahead. Please arm yourself with this knowledge and be proactive! There are many resources out there that can help.

***WE DID NOT AND WILL NOT GO QUIETLY
INTO THE NIGHT, AND WE ARE FOREVER STRONGER
AND WISER FOR IT; OUR SCARS TELL US SO***

~~~~~~~
~~~~~~~

<u>WHY DO VICTIMS STAY?</u>

**"Just when you think you can take no more, here
they come dangling carrots and kindness in front of you."**

One of the most commonly asked questions (and most frustrating) is, "Why do victims stay when they are being abused?" I totally get it; if you take things at face value, it seems like a perfectly reasonable question because the solution seems simple, right? You're being abused by a person, so you remove yourself from them and their "vortex of negativity."...Problem solved.....right? IF ONLY!!! It's usually never that cut and dry, especially in longer relationships where everything is so deeply intertwined, like emotions, belief systems, children, mindsets, social circles, finances, property, etc., and where Cognitive Dissonance, Learned Helplessness and Stockholm Syndrome (Trauma Bond) have manifested and set it.

One of the obvious reasons we don't leave is that we don't want to leave the children alone with the abuser, so we stay to act as the "buffer." And I did, indeed, get "in-between" him and the kids many, many times. My ex was physically, verbally, and emotionally abusive to our children, unleashing yelling, screaming, and verbal assaults like no other. This included F-Bombs, literally every 3rd or 4th word, calling them terrible names that I won't mention here. This would basically tear at not only their self-esteem and worth but their SPIRIT and SOUL as well - and that, my friend, is very dangerous and destructive territory. YOU NEVER EVER WANT TO SHAME AND BREAK A CHILD'S SPIRIT. VERY VERY BAD THINGS CAN HAPPEN WHEN YOU DO. Children will internalize that stuff. The abuse began when the kids were about 4 or 5 years old. As they got older, it got worse. The ex has very serious anger issues, so when the children would commit an "offense" of maybe a "3" on the Richter Scale, his reaction would be way out of proportion, at about a "7," and his punishment for them was rarely age-appropriate either. I found myself constantly having to intervene (verbally and sometimes physically) to de-escalate the situation. It was terrible.

Another reason victims don't leave their abusers is a lack of knowledge regarding what constitutes "abuse" under the law, especially when it's not just physical. They may not even realize they are "victims of abuse" at all, as is the case with many victims. They might know that they are being treated very badly at times while not REALIZING that what they are enduring qualifies as abuse in the context of Laws and Rights. Criminal, Civil and Human Rights. This was my case. I knew my ex-husband was an a**hole (which he'll proudly tell you - ya, he's weird like that) and that I was being treated terribly, often, especially over the last decade, but I never *realized* that it qualified as verbal, emotional, psychological, sexual, and financial abuse as well as severe neglect and oppression. When I finally made this realization, I had already been divorced for several months.

He had me so far gone into the abyss of despair that I had no more to give and became sick and bedridden. Then, he "discarded" me without ever making any real attempt to seek help for me from any kind of doctor, clinic, facility, etc. Even though, as a spouse, he had a legal "duty to act" (per the marriage contract) to try to get me help but, he never did. I've since learned that he was out having SEVERAL affairs, as he later admitted to me after the divorce. As it turns out, the abuse I endured was so bad that it caused me to have severe depression, anxiety, and mental anguish to the point that it manifested physically. I developed Fibromyalgia and, shortly after, a serious life-threatening auto-immune disease named Systemic Lupus Erythematosus and, eventually, PTSD. I also had a suicide attempt. YES, ABUSE CAN AND DOES MAKE YOUR BODY SICK, DEATHLY SICK. Oh, you didn't know this? Well, neither did I...until I educated myself. KNOWLEDGE IS POWER! Welcome to the club!

A lack of financial independence, resources, and support outside the home (or perceived lack of) are other big reasons victims don't leave their abusers. I was in this position. I had become sick so early on in my marriage that I was no longer able to work and had little to no financial resources. Many times, the abuser is successful at isolating the victims not only from family and friends but from the outside world as well. Victims then feel trapped in general with nowhere to go, and if they work, their paychecks may be hijacked by their abuser, like mine were.

Many times, the abuser oppresses the victim by monitoring phone calls and emails and by making finances off-limits and un-reachable. The abuser may control all outgoing and incoming mail as well. My ex controlled all of this. Our mail was literally off-limits to me. We had one mail key, and the ex kept it on his keychain and took it everywhere he went...even out of town! If I asked for the mail key, I was always met with resistance. Eventually, I would just give up and follow "the path of least resistance" in order to avoid conflict and keep the peace, which is a common survival tactic victims will use to avoid conflict and the resulting abusive behavior. Abusers may allow a victim to only leave the house when absolutely necessary. This is yet another suffocating tactic that makes the victim feel as though their abuser is "everywhere."

Fear...can be paralyzing and is one of the biggest reasons victims don't leave their abusers. They are afraid that if they try to, there will be retribution and the threat of harm or death against them, their children, or their extended family.

Now, to truly understand some of the more deep-seated psycho-logical reasons victims don't leave their abusers, we must first look at the skewed dynamics of an abusive relationship and the intricate dance of interpersonal and psychological interactions between abuser and victim. I'll use my relationship as an example. My ex and I entered our rela-tionship when I was barely a couple of years out of college. I had little to no money or work experience. He, in contrast, was seven years older, employed as a manager of a retail chain store, and had his own money. He also had a lot of experience with life in general, something that I did not. Right off the bat, there was a big power imbalance going into the relationship. He had a lot more power than me from the get-go, and he saw to it that it remained that way.

Of course, I was madly in love with the guy. He was like no one and nothing I had ever experienced. He was handsome, had a boyish charm and charisma, and was funnier than anyone I'd ever known. He said all the right things at exactly the right time, and he professed that he had love for me, which made me believe it. It turns out I was being played by a smart and slithery psychopath who had already spent time in a maximum security jail for kidnapping an ex-girlfriend (ya, that's a FEDERAL OFFENSE) - all unbeknownst to me, until I was already too invested in the relationship and not to mention, he totally downplayed it. He had also been constantly in trouble with the law as a juvenile. I had no clue of the severity or gravity of what any of that really meant.

These abusive relationships often start out with various levels of love or adoration, but this all erodes over time due to the assertion and exploitation of the abuser's power over their victim. Abusers have an insatiable need to suck all that is good out of their victims. Power and control are how they feed and fuel their own empty souls. They murder ours to feed theirs. They are modern-day VAMPIRES.

Learned Helplessness is another big reason abuse victims don't attempt to leave their partners. This phenomenon happens when an animal or person is subjected to a negative and harmful stimulus that it cannot escape from or where they see no way out; they give up and just keep taking the negativity. This basically means that when we are in abusive situations that we feel we cannot control or leave, we resign ourselves to the fact that there's nothing we can do about it, so we give up and just keep taking it.

The survival tactic of Stockholm Syndrome is another big reason victims don't leave their abusive relationships. This is a manifestation of the "trauma bond," which is an attachment-type bond that is created and cultivated by the process of repeated abusive behaviors and experiences, in which the victim also receives love, attention, kudos, and positive reinforcement after the abusive act and during the cyclical times of peace in the relationship. This confuses the victim into believing that love and abuse go together and that they still have feelings for the abuser. This becomes a relationship pattern, and the bond becomes stronger over time. This pervasive pattern can be internalized as a belief system and sets the stage for victims to repeat this in future relationships... unless there is some intervention. This bond is a type of psychological alliance with their abuser where the victim feels a level of empathy for the abuser. Stockholm Syndrome can also be seen as an act of "surrendering to win" by the victim. Because we humans have that innate instinct and will to survive, we are pretty darn good at adapting to and bargaining for our immediate environments. Both our conscious and subconscious will find ways to avoid conflicts by using de-escalation, avoidance, or by resolving the conflict, as well as developing coping mechanisms that are almost always detrimental to their personal growth and relationships. These coping mechanisms are mainly *cognitive dissonance, following the path of least resistance, and the victim giving up entirely and resigning themselves to align with the abuser.* By aligning with their abuser, the victim can not only feel some emotional relief from their inequitable relationship but also deescalate otherwise intense and vicious attacks and situations. This can also be seen as a valuable tool of "empowerment" for the victim because it allows them to have some kind of a foothold in their abusive relationship where they may otherwise be completely annihilated by their power and control-hungry soulspirit murderers.

What I've learned is that the cycle of domestic abuse is very difficult to break. There are some very serious psychological phenomena and mechanisms that take place within these relationships that literally change and or create a false belief system the victim internalizes about themselves and the world around them. In order to be successful at breaking the cycle, there needs to be a pendulum shift in the collective belief systems that allow these abusive behaviors to happen in the first place!

Sources:

Morales, A.(2023).Stockholm Syndrome/Definition, Treatment and Examples.Study.com. Url; https://study.com/learn/lesson/stockholm-syndrome-symptoms-treatment-example.html?srsltid=AfmBOorXfUE712cD0w5njkOLy5aI5gYbAK-nCSw72YUDnvYzes0JZepOf

Wirta-Leiker, C.(2013).Why Aubse Can Cause Learned Helplessness.Growbeyondwords.com. Url: https://growbeyondwords.com/2013/05/why-abuse-can-create-learned-helplessness/

~~~~~~~
~~~~~~~

EMOTIONAL, VERBAL, AND PSYCHOLOGICAL ABUSE- HOW IT AFFECTS THE PSYCHE, SPECIFICALLY.

THE DIRTY DYNAMICS OF AN ABUSIVE RELATIONSHIP

So what makes a relationship abusive, anyway? Well, according to the "National Coalition Against Domestic Violence" website, "Every relationship differs, but what is most common within all abusive relationships is the varying tactics used by abusers to gain and maintain power and control over the victim." If you strip all the murky layers away and peel it down to its most basic component, abusive relationships are driven by *insecurities.* Although it may not seem like it because most of them have a tough facade, most abusers have some big insecurities (some deeply rooted from childhood), and the biggest sub-set of abusers come from the *Antisocial Personality Disorder*, "social club"…

After being married to one of this "social club's" most *dedicated and loyal members* for nearly 30 years (not realizing he was a "member" of this club at all until much later) and much research, I believe there are those that don't always abuse because of insecurities (fear based behavior to avoid a perceived or real consequence), but abuse to seek and achieve rewards/goals, (goal-driven behavior). Both are ego-related problems. In other words, their abusive behavior has less to do with insecurities (which involve actual emotions) and more to do with apathy (lack of emotion, Including empathy) and different neural wiring altogether, like producing about four times more dopamine when "rewarded," than the normal person does (and this would be why they are so "goal driven" and tend to hyperfocus on their "reward" they are seeking whether it be money, sex, social status, etc., you know...all the superficial and shallow things in life.) I also believe there are those that abuse for *both* reasons. Abusers, men or women, can be insecure about such things as their worth or place in society, job or family, or their value to others and/or to themselves. Sadly, for people like this, their entire self-worth can be dictated by how their intimate partner views them. For those with an unstable sense of identity and self-worth, this is often the case. Well, whatever the case, their victims never deserve the abuse.

A deeper look into the abuser's mentality tells us where these insecurities are really coming from...*fear.* These fears that drive the insecurities are mainly grounded in "fear of being seen as weak" and/or "fear of not being good/competent enough or loveable enough in some way." The abuser is weak or deficient in some way, and they know it, so they resort to abuse to make up and maintain authority, power and control. This gnarly little issue with the abuser's personality creates a *pathological need* for control and power, which compels the abuser to continue with abusive patterns of behavior that always involve not only not respecting your personal boundaries but flat-out plowing right through them (physical and otherwise). This creates a relationship of emotional extremes-loving/hating, withholding/giving, very high "highs" and very low "lows," and drama, lots of drama. These extremes give their victims psychological whiplash, and they start questioning their own reality, judgments, and sanity. I'm all for compromise and working towards shared goals in the relationship, where you feel you are a co-pilot, but when one is trying to steer, control, read the map, and make all the decisions, all by themselves and bully you into submitting to their choices, something is very wrong! Victims start feeling like they are losing control of their own lives and what's going on around them. You feel like your world is closing in on you, and you are powerless to stop it. It feels overwhelming, which further leads to a sense of powerlessness and hopelessness. *And so the downward spiral begins…*

Abusers also like to "supplement" their big power plays against you with smaller, more stabby jabby mind*uck tactics, like making unprovoked snide comments about what you wear, eat, watch on TV, your hobbies, your hair, make-up, child-rearing, cooking, and just your overall mere existence thoroughly disgusts them. For example, he would complain if I was going somewhere with him, including our kid's sporting events, and went for the casual look, saying things like, "It's a shame you can't look nicer or wear better clothes," or "that looks like shit on you," if he wasn't in such a generous mood. The problem is that when I would dress nicer, etc., to appease him, he would make remarks about, "Who was I trying to impress." Damned if I did, damned if I didn't, ya know? That is how they wear you down and is part of the devaluation stage these creatures put their victims through before they discard you. In the beginning, during the "idealization" stage, we are "the best thing that ever happened to them." This 180-degree turn is done, so you start questioning just about everything. This results in lower self-confidence in your decision-making skills and processes, so you start going to your abuser for the "OK" and confirmation on things before you act. This puts the control back in their hands when you feel the need to "run everything by them" to double-check your decisions on matters big and small. **Now, this can be very tricky if your abuser is intelligent in some ways, like mine, because you come to learn and respect their opinions and above-average intelligence on other fronts early on and during the relationship in various ways.** I know from personal experience that they're just using that intelligence to undermine yours!

It's often very difficult for the victim to detect any of these more subtle tactics or identify the abuse at all as they are going through it. Oftentimes, it takes loved ones, friends, or a counselor/therapist to point out the abuse when it is not purely physical in nature. A big one for me was that it was being pointed out to me that I was apologizing for things I did not need to be apologizing for. Sadly, I had been conditioned over time to look immediately to myself as the reason or problem when that was not the case many times. Most of the time, though, the victim never talks about it or allows others to even know anything is amiss at all. For others, it takes time away to get a good perspective and the ability to put their partner's behavior into the right context before they make the realization that abuse has occurred. For example, instead of putting my ex-husband's bad behavior into the "Daaaang, I guess he's just a really mean a**hole" (unofficial) framework, I should have been framing his behavior in the context of "the law" and "civil/human rights." If I had done this, I believe I would have been able to identify some of his tactics, but his others took much longer to reveal themselves. Also, these creatures are bound by their narrow patterned behavior, and it flat-out takes time for a pattern to emerge, especially when it is intentionally hidden in the beginning. In severe cases, the victim even has to confront the fact that their health has suffered as a result of that abuse. I was facing some pretty severe and serious abuse, as it is pretty easy to get "desensitized" or "conditioned" into "receiving" it. Especially when they are mixed with good and positive times (which distract and help the victim "get over" or "overlook" the abusive behavior), as abusive relationships always are. The "good times" are a crucial aspect of the actual abuse dynamic. This includes conditioning the victim that love and abuse go together when they DO NOT! I feel this is particularly true when there is not a lot of physical abuse involved because no one sees the physical marks or bruises, so no one knows to ask if they are ok.

Let's also not forget that some people don't even realize they're exhibiting behavior that is considered abuse and would prefer to change their bad behavior if they could. Well.......... this article isn't about them! Rest assured, these creatures know exactly what they're doing and spend much time and energy concocting and planning out their misdeeds. If any of the above descriptions made your "Spidey Senses" tingle, please... look into the matter (or person) because it seriously could mean the difference between a happy, healthy relationship or one where there is violence, volatility, and where there's a dark cloud over your head, where a toxic and enduring storm brews...

Sources:

Domestic Violence Statistics. https://www.thehotline.org/stakeholders/domestic-violence-statistics/

Identify Abuse- Recognizing Abuse is the First Step. https://www.thehotline.org/identify-abuse/

Dynamics of Abuse. https://www.thehotline.org/resources/dynamics-of-abuse/

~~~~~~~
~~~~~~~

DIFFERENT TYPES OF DOMESTIC ABUSE

Broken bones will heal, but the hurtful words, memories,
and awful visceral sensations can last a lifetime."

Below is a list I put together of the different forms of abuse and some examples, with help provided by the Womenagainstabuse.org website;

<u>PHYSICAL- These are obviously meant to control your person, injure, scare, intimidate, and take ultimate control over you.</u>

- Hitting, slapping, punching, and kicking you in any part of your body. (Any unwelcome physical contact.)
- Using fire or a hot surface to burn or attempt to burn you or pretend they're going to.
- Putting hands around your neck actual strangulation.
- Damage or threat of damage to personal property (pets, house, vehicle, important items)
- Refusing access to medical care and/or unnecessarily controlling medications/treatments.
- Coercing a partner into alcohol/substance abuse makes the victim more pliable and easier to control. Especially when the victim becomes addicted, they are really at the mercy of the abuser.
- Use of weapons to intimidate, coerce, or scare. Even using household objects as "'make-due" weapons.
- Excessive tickling and not stopping when asked to. (YES. This is a form of physical abuse, too!)

<u>EMOTIONAL-</u>

- Intimidation (verbal threats, threatening looks, and aggressive posturing): They may not hurt you directly but will throw or kick things to show you "what they are capable" of as a threat.

- Guilting, shaming, and humiliating. Abusers are very skilled at projecting their guilt, shame, and humiliation onto you in order to rid themselves of the terrible thoughts and feelings that accompany those things. (These are especially damaging as these are cornerstones of addiction)
- Insulting, name-calling, degrading (even pet names such as "chubbylicious" or "chubby pumpkin" are harmful.) Disguising your acknowledgment that they are overweight doesn't make it ok to point it out every time you want to call them by their endearing pet name!)
- Stalking. Abusers may continually make contact with you in person, by phone, or by using other technology to make you feel uncomfortable and fearful.
- Blaming the partner for every little thing that goes wrong. (projecting)
- Showing signs of extreme jealousy
- Isolating the victim- this serves to disconnect the victim from family and friends to strengthen and maintain the maximum amount of control.

<u>NEGATING, HUMILIATING AND CRITICIZING</u>

These abusive tactics are mostly meant to destabilize and undermine your self-esteem, trust, and confidence within yourself and your perception of how the world sees and feels about you. Unlike physical abuse, this abuse is constant (daily), harsh, and unrelenting in all matters.

Here are some examples:

- Character assassination. This usually involves the word "always." You're always late, wrong, screwing up, disagreeable, and so on. Basically, they say you're not a good person without even having any facts to the contrary. By adding *always* to their gripe, it creates the illusion (mostly just to them) that you are a bad person because if you're always doing something bad, it must be inherent or ingrained into us and part of our person, versus just bad behavior or action that happens from time to time. When they imply that we are incompetent or deficient in some way across the board and at all times instead of just occasionally like most of us, it's easier for them to justify their demeaning behaviors towards us. It's very self-gratifying for them to structure their complaints in such a way that you are *this or that* while in their delusional mind, they never are what they are accusing you of being. Oh, the irony!

- Shouting, yelling, and screaming/throwing adult temper tantrums. Screaming, shouting, and swearing are meant to intimidate and make you feel scared, weak, powerless, and humiliated. It may be accompanied by threatening physical movements and actions such as making a fist, fist-pounding, aggressive posturing, kicking, or throwing things.

- Name-calling. They'll blatantly call you "stupid," "a loser," and words too awful to repeat here. My ex's "go-to" put-downs for me were to tell me "I was a waste of skin" and that "I didn't know anything about anything, so shut the fuck up." (Even though I was the one with a Bachelor's degree from a DI University and accrued many certificates for higher learning, hours beyond that of formal education and career development, as well as a teaching certificate and in contrast he never went to his classes and eventually dropped out. But it wasn't because he wasn't smart, though…

- Put-downs of your interests. They might tell you that your interest or hobby is a boring waste of time and money or you're in over your head, meaning you're not good or skilled enough. The reality is that they'd rather you not participate in activities without them or where you could possibly be more skilled than they are. (there's a jealousy factor here)

- Patronizing comments and tone. "Aw, sweet cheeks, I know you want to learn, but this is just beyond your little skill set or level of understanding. Now, go to the kitchen where you belong and fix me something to eat."

- The use of sarcasm. Often just a put-down or dis in disguise as a joke or humorous phrase or comment. When you protest, they claim to have been teasing you and tell you to stop taking everything so seriously or that you are too sensitive. They exclaim, "It's just a joke' even though it really wasn't, and you know it.

- Embarrassment/creating drama in public. They argue, pick fights, divulge your secrets, or make fun of your fears, concerns, or shortcomings in front of your friends or in public.

- Minimize and dismiss your concern. You tell them about something that's important to you, and they completely minimize and disrespect the importance by saying that it's not a big deal or it's unimportant. They may cut you off mid-sentence by saying, "Ya, ya ya….can you hurry up and get to your point or end of the story?". Their facial expressions and body language, such as smirking, headshaking, eye-crossing/rolling, looking around, acting indifferent, and sighing(as if bored), help convey and reinforce the same dismissive message.

- "Joking around"The jokes might have a little truth to them or be a complete fabrication. Either way, you are the butt of these jokes. Remember the old adage, "There's much truth in jest".

- Insulting your physical appearance. They'll tell you, right before you leave the house, that your make-up looks clownish, your hair is ugly in some way, or that your outfit is too this or that (nothing of which is good). All of these factors instill a lack of confidence in our choices and ourselves.

- Pushing your buttons. Once your abuser learns your pet peeves or about something that irritates or frightens you, they make sure to pick at them every chance they get. They want and need that emotional reaction from you! *IT. IS. THEIR. FUEL.*

- Downplaying or belittling your accomplishments and achievements. Your abuser might tell you that your achievements mean little or nothing or that it happened so long ago that it doesn't matter now. They may even claim to be responsible for your achievements. They will even try to "one up" your accomplishments by stretching the truth or flat-out lying about something they "accomplished."

CONTROL, GUILT AND SHAME

Abusers like to use control and shame to make you feel bad, insecure, and even humiliated about your shortcomings, problems, thoughts, and behaviors. They do this as a means to establish, maintain, and increase their power.

Examples include:

- Verbal Threats. Declaring that they will take the kids and go into hiding or threatening to do something crazy, like harm the children in some way.
- Monitoring your every move. They want to know where you are at all times and demand that you respond to texts and calls ASAP. They like to mysteriously appear where you are, with the intent of verifying you are where you said you would be, even though you've given them absolutely no reason to think otherwise. Mine did this quite often.
- Electronic spying. They will spy on your internet history, emails, bank accounts, texts, voicemails, and call history. They might even demand your passwords while not giving up their own.
- One-sided/Unilateral decision-making. They take it upon themselves to open/close a joint bank account, purchase an automobile, decide to move, or cancel your doctor's appointment without consulting you at all. (By doing these things, they are telling you that your opinion and input doesn't matter and are not valuable to them or the decision-making process.)
- Establishing and maintaining financial control. They will secretly open a bank account in their name only at another bank and then quietly transfer funds from your joint account over to HIS new account at another bank, all unbeknownst to you. They might keep bank accounts in their name only and make you ask for money. You might be expected to account for every penny you spend while they're out spending freely and

overspending to the point it's detrimental to your finances. True story.

- Talking "'at you" instead of with you or to you/Lecturing. Making statements and responses that reflect the belief that you are beneath them. Talking "at you" as if you are a child.
- Giving direct orders, as if speaking to an employee or subordinate. Anything from "Put my food on the table now" to "Go get me some beer right now" orders are expected to be followed regardless of how out of line, irrational, or mean the demand is.
- Angry Outbursts. You were told to cancel that dinner with your friend or bring the dog in the house before it starts raining, but you didn't, so now you get to deal with an angry and volatile tirade about how impossible, incompetent, and uncooperative you **always** are.
- They treat you like a child. They try to dictate what you eat, wear, what to buy, how much to eat, or which friends you should hang out with (my ex demanded I get friends who were "hot.") Hmm, I wonder why... They'll even try to tell you how to feel and what to believe.
- Faked or phony helplessness. They may claim not to know how to do something when they actually do. Abusers are very well aware that sometimes it's just easier to do it yourself and enjoy taking full advantage of it.
- Dr. Jekyll and Mr. Hyde's level of unpredictability. They'll be fine one minute, then explode in an angry, profanity-filled rage out of nowhere, suddenly shower you with affection, or become highly irritated, dark, and moody at the drop of a hat to keep you guessing, off balance and ultimately walking on eggshells. It is psychological whiplash.
- They leave/walk away. In social situations, they may dramatically huff out of the room, which leaves you holding embarrassment, concern, and an overall lack of understanding as to what has just occurred. At home, leaving is used as a tool to keep the problem unresolved and power in their control. Leaving is also a strategy to avoid drama and de-escalate the

situation, but you will know when it's been weaponized. Feels totally different!

- Using "others" to solidify their claims. Abusers may tell you that "*everybody* thinks you're crazy" or "*everyone* says I'm right about this." They attempt to give the illusion that they have just "tons and tons" of people, possibly "everyone," on their side and supporting them and their claims, so you feel overwhelmed, insecure, and ultimately defeated about your opposing belief, claim, or viewpoint.

BLAMING, ACCUSING AND DENYING

These behaviors manifest as a result of an abuser's insecurities and real or perceived shortcomings. They want to create a ruling system in which they rule at the top, and you're at the bottom to be used as they see fit.

Here are some examples:

- Displays of jealousy. This could be due to a person, job, hobby, or accomplishment.
- Using inversion/180* turning the tables/flipping the script. Abusers lie to deflect/escape responsibility and divert blame, among other reasons. Lies for them have many applications. They can whip out an elaborate lie at a moment's notice, with almost ninja-like quickness and contextual accuracy. In order to make themselves appear as innocent as possible or to do the most destruction possible, they won't just tell a little fib or spin the story a little bit; oh no, they will completely invert the truth 180 degrees as far from the real truth as possible. For example, a staunch supporter, activist, and advocate against child sex abuse is suddenly arrested for, surprise--child sex abuse. That is a perfect example- they claim to be against the very thing they are guilty of- a 180-degree inversion of the truth. In their delusional minds, if they enjoy and are guilty of assaulting children and need to avoid detection, what better cover and way to hide than to appear to be the polar opposite

of what they really are and publicly condemn the very acts they commit, so they hold positions as advocates/activists/supporters. Do you see how that all works? Abusers may say you cause their rage and control issues by being such a pain or so difficult when it's really their issues and volatile personality that cause much of the turmoil, and they *know this*. They say things like, "Look what you made me do," or "This is all your fault." They refuse to take responsibility for their own actions.

- Denying factual information/claiming fact as false. An abuser will deny that a conversation between the two of you, an agreement, decision, or event ever took place when you know full well that it did. This is called **gaslighting**. It's designed to make you question your own memory, reality, and sanity. They'll say things like, "I never said that" or "You're just making that up." They will deny ever writing something even though you have the actual note/document as proof.

- Using guilt to control and manipulate. They might say something like, "You owe me after all I've done for you," in an attempt to get their way, on their terms, when and how they want, on demand. You may feel that you "owe" them in some way, but there are two people in this equation, so both perspectives need to be taken into account in terms of when, where, and how you repay, especially if their terms are overly demanding, unrealistic, coercive, abusive, harmful or detrimental to your health and well-being.

- Provoking/antagonizing, then blaming. Abusers are skilled at pushing your buttons to upset you. Once you've taken the bait and given them their desired reaction, the escalating argument is all your fault for creating it, even though you were just *reacting* to their initial unprovoked nasty actions. They may yell, "Wow-you're in a bad mood today," even though you were in a great mood up until that interaction with him...

- Denying they are abusive. When you call them out on their abusive behavior, abusers may claim that it wasn't that bad or it wasn't that big of a deal. They might say you misunderstood what they were trying to say or deny it completely. They then act as if it isn't even within the realm of possibility that they could be abusive, even though there were various official court documents and records from his past that prove otherwise.

- Accusing you of the abuse. They will say you are the one who has anger and control issues, and they're the helpless victim. My ex was very emotionally abusive and neglectful towards me at home, but while he was out in public, he got much sympathy, pity, and attention for having a sick wife at home. Aww, poor guy! He didn't bother telling them all that it was his abuse that was making me so sick and keeping me in bed...

- Minimizing/Trivializing your needs, concerns, or situations. They might keep trying to change the subject or distract you from your thoughts/conversation. They may insist you are overreacting and use phrases like "you're just blowing it out of proportion" to convey their apathy and indifference towards your concern and, let's face it, also your mere *existence* most of the time...

- Claim you have no sense of humor. Abusers enjoy making humorous yet embarrassing or humiliating snide remarks or "jokes" that are funny only to them, and when you don't laugh, they claim you have no sense of humor or tell you to lighten up. They will also purposely NOT laugh when you say something funny because this reinforces to you that they are only allowed to be the funny one. Their egos will not allow you to be funnier than them. Period.

- Blaming you for all the problems. It's all your fault. You aren't doing enough, not being supportive or nurturing enough, etc. They will claim you're not "strong enough" to handle them, yet fail to acknowledge or attempt to correct their own deviant, abusive, volatile, and indulgently self-serving behavior as any reason or possible cause of the problems. Maybe they should start to bring their ridiculous, irrational, and destructive behavior more in line with what is considered acceptable, positive, and constructive societal and personal boundaries and behaviors so *we* **ARE ABLE TO/HAVE THE SKILLSET TO HANDLE YOU!** Hey, there's a thought that literally never occurs to them...

- Destroying and denying. They might "accidentally" misplace or break your cell phone or other valuable items that are important to you. They might also "accidentally" let your dog out of the backyard to get back at you or cause you much distress. They may secretly remove your credit card from your wallet and then deny it or "lose" your car keys and then deny it. True story. I looked for my poor dog for hours in the dark in coyote country...

NEGLECT AND ISOLATION

Abusers will put their own emotional needs ahead of yours.

Examples include:

- Give you the Silent Treatment. They refuse to respond to your attempts at conversation in person, by phone, or by text.
- They dehumanize you. They'll look away or stare at something someone/else when having a conversation with them. They will act unengaged and indifferent to your words and physical presence to make you feel as if you are not worthy of their time or attention.
- They prevent you from socializing. If you have plans to go somewhere, they come up with reasons or pleas not to go, or they'll throw some immature drama-filled monkey wrench into your plans at the last moment or in the middle of.
- Trying to come between you and your family. They'll tell family members that you don't want to see them or make excuses why you can't attend family functions.
- Withholding love and affection. They refuse to physically touch you and refrain from holding your hand or even hugging you. They may also withhold sex.

- They overly demand respect. No disrespectful act or slight, real or perceived, will go unpunished, and you're expected to apologetically acquiesce.
- Ignoring/Tuning you out. They'll wave you off, change the subject, or just plain ignore you when you want to talk about your relationship.
- Divide and conquer. Abusers will attempt to turn others against you. They will tell friends, family, and co-workers that you're unstable and prone to hysterics, but crazy is their favorite word of choice.
- Claiming you are clingy/needy. They will shut you down by being unsupportive and scarce when you really need them to be supportive, present, and "plugged in." They may say things like, "What's the big deal?" and "You just need to get over it." These comments are really telling you that they don't care and don't want to be bothered with your stuff. Sometimes, they'll just straight up demand that you "stop talking about it."
- Attention entitlement. Abusers may rudely interrupt you in person, phone, or text conversations in order to demand your immediate and undivided attention, regardless of how significant your convo is and how insignificant their information is.
- Neglecting your most basic needs. If you happen to be ill or handicapped and require assistance with some things, they may purposely deny you help as a means of controlling you. When I was very sick and bedridden, my ex wouldn't help me with even my basic needs of taking a shower or helping me get dressed. One time, I was not able to wash my hair for approximately two weeks because I was in too much pain/ discomfort, and he was either gone for days or uninterested in helping me when he was home. Instead, he would yell at me for not moving fast enough. That was when he happened to be back home from cheating with his "niece-in-law," over 30 years his junior.
- Downplaying/Displaying of indifference. They see you physically injured, in pain, in emotional distress, or crying and do

little to nothing to help or tell you it's not that big of a deal as they roll their eyes.

- Telling you how to feel/disputing your feelings. Abusers will attempt to make you have the same beliefs and mind-sets as they do. They will demand that you feel a certain way even though it may completely contradict what you really feel or think about a situation. They want to strip you of your own freethinking and dictate what goes on in your head to better align with theirs. They'll exclaim that you're incorrect and actually try to convince you that you don't *really* feel that way; you just *think* you do. They demand you feel a certain way (that usually aligns with how they think and feel). Most of the time, because of the nature of the beast, these beliefs do not align with your own core beliefs or values. The state this puts a person in internally causes much inflammation and dysregulation in our body's chemistry.

<u>SEXUAL ABUSE</u>

Sexual abuse isn't as much about the sex as we might think it is. It is mostly about **power** (an angry power) and includes any sexual behavior performed without a partner's consent. Examples include:

- Blackmailing, coercing, or forcing a partner to have sex with other people when against the partner's wishes/will for the abuser's personal enjoyment or some type of payment. (human trafficking)
- Engaging in any type of sexual activity when the victim is not fully aware, coherent, or conscious or is afraid to say no
- Inflicting intentional physical injury, pain, or discomfort during sex. They may prolong sex even though it is painful to partner and have been made aware of it.
- Tricking or coercing a partner to have sex without protection/ sabotaging birth control methods. Forced pregnancies.

FINANCIAL ABUSE

Any behavior that maintains power and control over finances constitutes financial abuse. Examples include;

- Prevents victim from working. Due to inflicting injury or damage to the victim's body, hiding/damaging work clothes or vehicle, etc. Not allowing the victim to leave the house.
- Workplace harassment. They will show up in person or persistently call or email to engage with you at your work location.
- Financial control. They control all or most of the finances and leave you with a small allowance or nothing at all and no access.
- Damaging a partner's ability to obtain good credit/credit score. They may have you sign your name on a credit card, rental agreement, or any other application for credit, etc. (because they've already destroyed their own credit), then decide to stop paying the payment at some point unbeknownst to you and by the time you figure it out, your credit has been damaged. Abusers like to put you out "in front" and hide behind you and your good name when the damage they did rises to the surface, and someone needs to be held accountable. They are very skilled at this...

TECHNOLOGICAL ABUSE

Technology abuse includes the use of technology to monitor, control, and stalk a partner/victim. Technological abuse can happen to people of all ages, but it is more common among teenagers who use technology and social media to interact in a manner often unmonitored by adults. Examples include:

- Hacking into social media, email, bank, and personal accounts. Creating fake accounts to attempt to engage with you online or cause you damage. Abusers are very insidious in regards to their victim's technology accounts, etc.

- They use tracking devices/apps. Abusers use these to keep tabs on you, your location, and all forms of communication, incoming and outgoing.
- Trolling/spying on your social media sites.
- Password stealing. Attempting to steal your password or demanding to know their partner's passwords while not offering up their own to you.

Source:

Type of Abuse. https://www.womenagainstabuse.org/education-resources/learn-about-abuse/types-of-domestic-violence

~~~~~~~
~~~~~~~

WARNING SIGNS OF A TOXIC RELATIONSHIP

"When a man truly loves a woman, she becomes his weakness. When a woman truly loves a man, he becomes her strength." ~unknown

💥 Here are some warning signs you are in a toxic relationship. These are taken from my own private collection...

💥 Sign of a toxic relationship;

- Your partner makes you feel like you're not good enough. You feel your self-esteem dropping. Constantly picking at you and getting a rise out of your reactions. It's a SPORT to them, a way to entertain themselves as well because they live in a constant state of boredom.
- You are constantly being compared to other people. Appearance and otherwise.
- You feel like you're walking on eggshells because you don't know what kind of mood your partner is in or how they're going to react to you.
- You find that your "fight or flight" goes off when you hear them drive up or walk in the door. Mine would always go off when I would hear him pull into the driveway or walk in the door.
- You find yourself constantly trying to seek their affection, attention, and validation. You feel the need to make sure they still hold you in a positive light because you're just not really sure. They like it when you are in this state.
- They put you down and minimize or invalidate your words, ideas, feelings, thoughts, and beliefs. ("It's not that big of a deal," "Why are you so upset, you shouldn't feel that way, it's stupid")

- You find that your partner does not take responsibility for their bad behavior or intentional infliction of pain towards you. Instead, they blame you or project their problems onto you.
- You find yourself becoming withdrawn from family and friends.
- You show signs of depression and/or anxiety.
- You find that you are constantly asking yourself, "What did I do wrong?" after confronting them about their bad behavior.
- You start questioning your sanity. Really, you do.

✴ Now, in *stark contrast*, here are some signs of a healthy relationship;

- Both partners treat each other with mutual respect and compassion.
- "Trust" is not an issue in the relationship.
- Both partners are "nurturing" each other and the relationship itself.
- Both partners are able and willing to compromise when needed.
- Both partners are able to receive constructive feedback without it leading to verbal, emotional, or physical abuse.
- Both partners are able to care for their personal needs as well as their partners and the needs of the relationship.
- Both partners feel they can establish and uphold healthy boundaries with each other.
- Both people feel supported by their partners in their endeavors outside of the relationship.

~~~~~~~
~~~~~~~

GASLIGHTING

*"And she was called crazy and delusional by the
very man who systematically tried to drive her there."*

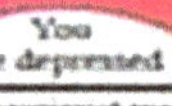

According to Wikipedia, "**Gaslighting** is a form of psychological manipulation in which a person seeks to sow seeds of doubt in a targeted individual or in members of a targeted group, making them question their own memory, perception, and sanity. The tactics of denial, misdirection, contradiction, and lying gaslighting involve attempts to destabilize the victim and delegitimize the victim's beliefs.[1][2] Instances may range from the denial by an abuser that previous abusive incidents ever occurred to the staging of bizarre events by the abuser with the intention of disorienting the victim. The term originated from the 1938 Patrick Hamilton play *Gas Light* and its 1940 and 1944 film adaptations (both titled *Gaslight*), in which a character tries to make his wife believe that she has gone insane to cover his criminal activities. When he turns up the gas-fueled lights in the upstairs apartment in order to search for a murdered woman's jewels, the gaslights in his own apartment grow dimmer, but he convinces his wife that she is imagining the change. The term has been used in clinical and research literature, as well as in political commentary."

GASLIGHTING is a form of *psychological and emotional abuse* that abusers use to maintain power and control over their victims. *It is like psychological violence and warfare, a form of mind control that is emotional bullying*. This tactic can also set the stage for *Stockholm Syndrome*, a manifestation of the very real *Trauma Bond* phenomenon.

The process of gaslighting-- the lying, denying, using people, the duality, creating confusion, projections, character assassinations, and manipulations starts off very slow so the victim doesn't realize they're being brainwashed, and it becomes incredibly insidious, in terms of family, friendships, social circles, jobs and more. I like to use the "frog in a pot of boiling water" metaphor to help explain this: If you drop a frog in a pot of boiling water, it realizes it immediately and tries to escape due to the extreme temperature change, but if you put a frog into water that is room temperature and turn the heat up very slowly, (like how some people hard boil eggs), it won't even notice until it's too late (especially if the man keeps distracting the frog) until it's too late! The metaphor goes something like that. The point is that the victims are similar to the frogs in room temperature water, and the abuser turns up the heat in slow increments by the process of GASLIGHTING, so the victim doesn't realize it until so much damage has been done, and sadly some victims don't ever make that realization at all. I was a frog 🐸 for a long time, but as I grew older and wised up, I began noticing inconsistencies in my ex's stories, behaviors, and things that just flat-out didn't make sense. Be ready for anger and the run around when you confront them or ask for clarification, though! My ex was quite the GASLIGHTER and is nearly famous for "talking out of both sides of his mouth" here in these parts. It's been especially noted by a couple of his former bosses, his ex-wife, his kids, and myself. I remember he would literally contradict himself in almost the same sentence sometimes when he was" off of his game." Once I started noticing this, it became easier to pick up on, and I started confronting him about the duality and contradictions in his words and behaviors. When my ex felt I was backing him into a corner about his lies, etc., his preferred weapon of choice from his deviant bag o' tricks was the 'ol "distract and redirect" play. If this technique sounds familiar to you, it's because parents are taught to do this with their children when they are misbehaving. It's actually a great technique when it's properly used with children, but the anti-socials of the world have gone and weaponized it. SUPER! This play reminds me of those cons off the Vegas strip who used to have people play the shell game where they switch up three coconut shells real fast and tricky like, with a ping-pong ball hiding under one of them. Have you ever won that game? Ya, me neither. These cons make sure we don't, just like relationships with them. Relationships are a game to them, with a winner and a loser. They win, and we lose ...unless. Unless we arm ourselves with the knowledge of how to deal with these abusers and "Soulspirit Murderers" or to avoid them entirely. Anyone can be susceptible to the GASLIGHTING process. This tactic is also very popular with cult leaders, dictators, and politicians... Surprise! Ya, I know... you're not really surprised by that last set of facts.

If any of this seems familiar to you or resonates with you on some level, please do yourself a big favor and investigate. And as always, listen to what your body and mind are telling you; they pick up on things "we" don't notice! They, after all, have the ULTIMATE vested interest in your sanity, happiness, and survival!

Source:

Gaslighting. https://en.wikipedia.org/wiki/Gaslighting

<div align="center">~~~~~~~</div>

11 WARNING SIGNS OF GASLIGHTING

Here is a list of 11 Warning signs of GASLIGHTING, according to author Stephanie Sarkis, PhD, in her book "Gaslighting: Recognize Manipulative and Emotionally Abusive People- and Break Free";

1. "THEY TELL BLATANT LIES. You know it's an outright lie, yet they are telling you this lie with a straight face. Why are they so blatant? Because they are setting up a precedent. Once they tell you a huge, outrageous lie, you're not sure if anything they say is true. Keeping you unsteady and off balance is the goal." *Back when I was a softball pitcher and wanted to keep hitters off-balance, I'd throw change-ups and offspeed curveballs... Well, my ex kept using this strategy in our relationship. I felt off-balance almost the entire marriage.*

2. "THEY DENY THEY EVER SAID SOMETHING, EVEN THOUGH YOU HAVE PROOF. You know they said they would do something; you know you heard it. They out and out deny it. It makes you start to question your reality and the more they do this, the more you question your reality and start accepting theirs."

3. "THEY USE WHAT IS NEAR AND DEAR TO YOU AS AMMUNITION. They know how important your kids are to you, and they know how important your identity is to you. So those may be one of the first things they attack. If you have kids, they tell you that you should not have had those children. They will tell you you'd be a worthy person if only you didn't have a long list of negative traits. They attack the foundation of your being."

4. "THEY WEAR YOU DOWN OVER TIME. This is one of the insidious things about gaslighting--it is done gradually, over time. A lie here, a lie there, a snide comment every so often...and then it starts ramping up. Even the

brightest, most self-aware people can be sucked into gas-lighting-it is that effective." *Insert the frog in the pot of water metaphor here!*

5. "THEIR ACTIONS DO NOT MATCH THEIR WORDS. When dealing with a person or entity that gas-lights, look at what they are doing rather than what they are saying. What they are saying means nothing; it is just talk. What they are doing is the issue." *This is where you're going to find the big 'disconnects'!*

6. "THEY THROW IN POSITIVE REINFORCEMENT TO CONFUSE YOU. This person or entity that is cutting you down, telling you that you don't have value, is now prais-ing you for something you did. This adds an additional sense of uneasiness. You think, "Well, maybe they aren't so bad." Yes, they are. This is a calculated attempt to keep you off-kilter and, again, to question your reality. Also, look at what you were praised for; it is probably something that served the gas-lighter." *Sounds like that darn shell game again-they let you win just enough to keep you playing.*

7. "THEY KNOW CONFUSION WEAKENS PEOPLE. Gaslighters know that people like having a sense of stability and normalcy. Their goal is to uproot this and make you con-stantly question everything. And humans' natural tendency is to look to the person or entity that will help you feel more stable-and that happens to be the gaslighter." *Grrreeeaaattt... Superrrr...*

8. "THEY PROJECT. They are a drug user or a cheater, yet they are constantly accusing you of that. This is done so often that you start trying to defend yourself and are distracted from the gaslighter's own behavior." *So when your "Boo" starts accusing you of cheating...rest assured that it is your "Goo" most likely is!*

9. "THEY TRY TO ALIGN PEOPLE AGAINST YOU. Gaslighters are masters at manipulating and finding the peo-ple they know will stand by them no matter what- and they

use these people against you. They will make comments such as, "This person knows that you're not right," or "This person knows you're useless too." Keep in mind it does not mean that these people actually said these things. A gaslighter is a constant LIAR. When the gaslighter uses this tactic, it makes you feel like you don't know who to trust or turn to, and that leads you right back to the gaslighter. And that's exactly what they want: Isolation gives them more control." *They like to "divide and conquer"!*

10. "THEY TELL YOU OR OTHERS THAT YOU ARE CRAZY. This is one of the most effective tools of the gaslighter because it's dismissive. The gaslighter knows if they question your sanity, people will not believe you when you tell them the gaslighter is abusive or out of control. It's a master technique." *My ex used this pre-emptive ploy with me, telling me, my children, family, and friends that I was CRAZY and DELUSIONAL so he could justify his leaving me when I was very sick with an auto-immune disease and mostly bedridden. I've seen a few psychiatrists and have never been diagnosed with any type of personality disorder whatsoever, but my ex sure was when he had a psych evaluation when he went AWOL in the Air Force and when he spent time in maximum security jail here in Az. for kidnapping an ex-girlfriend and now that I think about it, he probably also had at least one back when he was breaking into people's homes when he was a juvenile. No, I did not know any of this until after I was too invested in the relationship and thought I could change him. Big Mistake! Turns out he left me because he was actually cheating on me with multiple women and finally settled on his relative, by marriage, who is about 35 years younger than him. I had to remind him that people with his kind of profound personality disorders of the cluster B variety are, in fact, the ones that are delusional. He strongly disagreed with me.*

11. "*THEY TELL YOU EVERYONE ELSE IS A LIAR. By telling you that everyone else (your family, the media) is a liar, it again makes you question your reality. You've never known someone with*

the audacity to do this, so they must be telling the truth, right? No, It's a manipulation technique. It makes people turn to the gaslighter for the "correct" information–which isn't correct information at all."

Sources:

Sarkis, S. (2018). Gaslighting: Recognize Manipulation and Emotionally Abusive People. *https://www.google.com/search?q=Gaslighting%3A+Recognize+Manipulative+and+Emotionally+Abusive+People-+and+Break+Free&oq=Gaslighting%3A+Recognize+Manipulative+and+Emotionally+Abusive+People-+and+Break+Free&gs_lcrp=EgZjaHJvbWUyBggAEEUYOTIGCAEQRRg60gEIMzQ5NmowajSoAgiwAgE&sourceid=chrome&ie=UTF-8*

~~~~~~~
~~~~~~~

MEN AS VICTIMS OF DOMESTIC VIOLENCE

According to statistics on the "National Coalition Against Domestic Violence" website, "1 in 4 MEN have experienced some form of physical violence by an intimate partner." That statistic is just for "physical abuse and doesn't even consider other forms of pervasive abuse such as verbal, emotional, psychological, financial, etc., which many times can be more damaging in the long term than physical abuse. Physical abuse is usually "'cyclical," but verbal and emotional abuse is a more intimate form of abuse and happens every single day. I found some interesting information on this topic, which serves to shed some light on this quiet dilemma;

The below information was taken from the psychcentral.com website.

Battered and Abused Men:

Most of us recognize that men experience verbal and emotional abuse at the hands of women; less well accepted or admitted is the fact of physical abuse. In our society, we think of women as the victims and men as the aggressors in physical abuse. The fact that women are more likely to be severely injured in domestic violence adds to the problem of recognizing male abuse. Nevertheless, it happens - frequently. In fact, men are just as likely to be seriously injured when a woman becomes violent because women are more likely to use weapons in the course of an assault. If a male client indicates that his girlfriend or partner assaulted him, believe him. A man will find it harder to discuss his pain with you than will a woman, and even harder to admit to being a victim. It is easier to attribute an injury to a sports mishap or workplace accident than to admit to a doctor or police officer it resulted from domestic violence.

Facts:

1. Fewer men report abuse. They are ashamed to report being abused by women.
2. Healthcare and law enforcement professionals are more likely to accept alternative explanations of abuse from a man. They will believe other reasons for the presence of bruises and other signs of injury.
3. Our justice system often takes the word of the woman above the word of the man in abuse cases. It is just more believable that the aggressor was the man, not the woman.
4. Men are more likely to tolerate the pain of abuse than women. They "grin and bear it" more. And again, many are ashamed to seek medical help for abuse.
5. Unless a woman uses a weapon, she usually does not have the strength to inflict injury.

Abused men are as likely as their female counterparts to have low self-esteem. People can come to believe that they are somehow responsible for what happened. People cling to the hope that things will get better: that the woman he "loves" will quit when their relationship is better adjusted or the children get older and show more responsibility. These are all pretty much the same excuses women make for remaining with men who batter them.

Are you abused? Does the person you love…

- "Track" all of your time?
- Constantly accuse you of being unfaithful?

- Discourage your relationships with family and friends.
- Prevent you from working or attending school?
- Criticize you for little things?
- Become angry easily when drinking or abusing drugs?
- Control all finances and force you to account for what you spend.
- Humiliate you in front of others?
- Destroy your personal property or items with sentimental value?
- Hit, punch, slap, kick, or bite you or the children?
- Use or threaten to use a weapon against you?
- Threaten to hurt you or hurt the children?
- Force you to have sex against your will?

Below is a list of things you can do to help yourself:

- Tell friends he trusts.
- Make safety arrangements such as:
  - Leaving the relationship;
  - Finding a safe place to go, and
  - Changing his phone number and/or locks.
- Telephone a domestic violence hotline or shelter and:
  - Talk to a worker;
  - Find out about his legal rights; or
  - See a counselor - separately or with Lisa.
- Gain the support of witnesses when possible.
- Take notes detailing dates, times, and what occurred.
- Phone 911 when Lisa becomes physically abusive.

Abuse Checklists:

Below is a self-assessment quiz to help you determine if you are being abused. You may be suffering abuse even if you answer "Yes" to only a few questions.

You may be becoming or already are a victim of abuse if you:

- Feel like you have to "walk on eggshells" to keep him/her from getting angry and frightened by his/her temper.
- Feel you can't live without him/her.
- Stop seeing other friends or family, or give up activities you enjoy because he/she doesn't like them.
- Are afraid to tell him/her your worries and feelings about the relationship.
- Are often compliant because you are afraid to hurt his/her feelings and have the urge to "rescue" him/her when he/she is troubled.
- Feel that you are the only one who can help him/her and that you should try to "reform" him/her.
- Find yourself apologizing to yourself or others for your partner's behavior when you are treated badly.
- Stop expressing opinions if he/she doesn't agree with them.
- Stay because you feel he/she will kill him/herself if you leave.
- Believe that his/her jealousy is a sign of love.
- Have been kicked, hit, shoved, or had things thrown at you by him/her when he/she was jealous or angry.
- Believe the critical things he/she says to make you feel bad about yourself.
- Believe that there is something wrong with you if you don't enjoy the sexual things he/she makes you do.
- Believe in the traditional ideas of what a man and a woman should be and do -- that the man makes the decisions and the woman pleases him.

*** IF YOU OR SOMEONE YOU KNOW IS A VICTIM OF ABUSE, PLEASE CONSIDER TAKING ACTIONS TO REMOVE YOURSELF FROM THAT PERSON AND SITUATION."

***SOME RESOURCES;

* National Domestic Violence Hotline- 1-800-799-7233 (SAFE)

Website; www.ndvh.org

- Men Stopping Violence- 1-866-717-9317

Website; www.menstoppingviolence.org

- A Call To Men- 1-917-922-6738

Website; www.acalltomen.org

- National Gay and Lesbian Task Force- 1-202-3935177

Website; ngltf.org

- National Center for Victims of Crime- 1-202-467-8700

Website; www.victimsofcrime.org

Source:

Smith, K. (2021). Invisible Victims: When Men Are Abused. Psych Central. https://psychcentral.com/blog/invisible-victims-when-men-are-abused

~~~~~~~
~~~~~~~

DOMESTIC VIOLENCE/INTIMATE PARTNER VIOLENCE IN THE GAY COMMUNITY

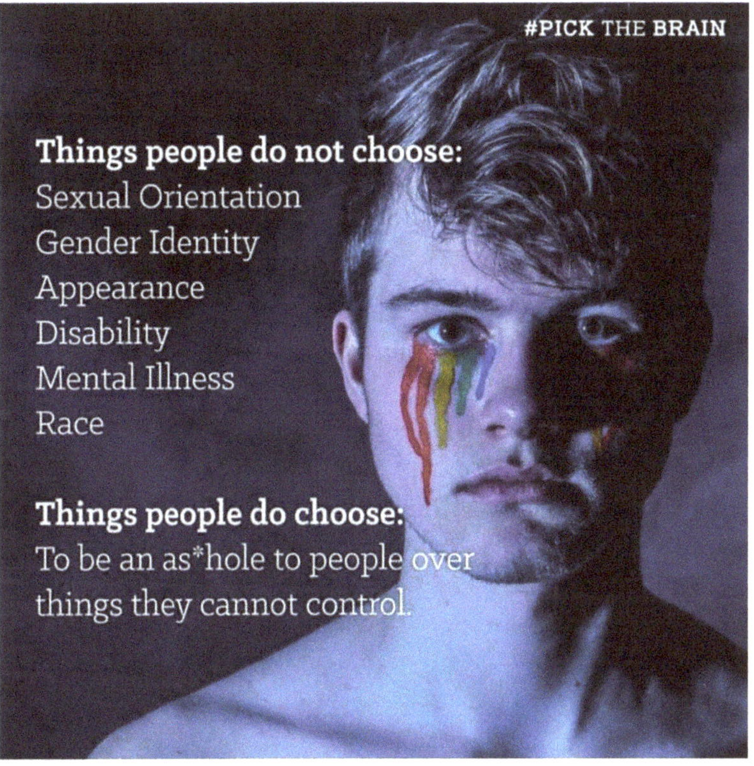

 **Suicide Awareness / Prevention**

I wanted to make sure I included the LGBTQ community in my website not only because they often get overlooked in the "stop domestic violence" movement but because some of the most amazing people I know are members of this community, so it is very close to my heart. After some research, I realized that this community suffers greatly from abuse and trauma. In fact, the rates of abuse and violence are higher than in the heterosexual community! I'd like to share some sobering statistics with you…

According to the "ncadv.org' website in the article, "Domestic Violence and the LGBTQ Community," (which is no longer available online) Sadly, "LGBTQ members fall victim to domestic violence at *equal* or even *higher rates* compared to their heterosexual counterparts."

**** HERE ARE SOME STATISTICS FROM THE WEBSITE;

* 43.8% of lesbian women and 61.1% of bisexual women experienced rape, physical violence, and /or stalking by an intimate partner at some point in their lifetime, as opposed to only 35% of heterosexual women.

* 26% of gay men and 37.3% of bisexual men have experienced rape, physical violence, and/or stalking by an intimate partner in their lifetime, in comparison to 29% of heterosexual men.

* In a study of male same-sex relationships, only 26% of men called the police for assistance after experiencing near-lethal violence.

* In 2012, fewer than 5% of LGBTQ survivors of intimate partner violence sought orders of protection.

* Transgender victims are more likely to experience intimate partner violence in public compared to those who do not identify as transgender.

* Bisexual victims are more likely to experience sexual violence compared to people who do not identify as bisexual.

* LBGTQ Black/African victims are more likely to experience physical intimate partner violence compared to those who do not identify as Black/African American.

* LGBTQ white victims are more likely to experience sexual violence compared to those who do not identify as white.

* LGBTQ victims on *public assistance* are more likely to experience intimate partner violence compared to those who are not on public assistance.

The LGBTQ community has unique problems when it comes to domestic and intimate partner violence. One of the biggest ones is using "outing" the person as a tool to control and abuse. Many people in this community have not "come out of the closet" yet, so to speak, so the threat of someone they love divulging their "secret" to the world is beyond mortifying, and many will do anything to not let that happen, including reporting the abuse Young people in this community are also generally not ready to fully discuss their sexuality much less being abused because of it. There is also a problem with reporting intimate partner abuse or violence within this group; some reasons include not trusting the police or other authorities as taking them seriously, the fear of harassment, or having to deal with "homophobic" mindsets of police and court officials. There is a certain level of shame or guilt that many of these people deal with, and that can also prevent them from seeking help or even talking about it with anyone. Many are victims of religious persecution or harassment because of the false and rigid mental construct that hamstrings and hinders those with black-and-white religious beliefs and those "white knucklers'." Transgender individuals also have unique problems when it comes to domestic and intimate partner violence, some of which include being called names that assault their "identity." What some people don't understand is that they automatically fear or try to find a reason to discredit or condemn it, even when it involves committing "religious hypocrisy" many times without ever trying to otherwise educate themselves about it (Remember…PSYCHOLOGY SAYS~ when people engage in acts of hatred or condemnation, it says a whole lot more about them (and not in a good light) than it does about you or their "perceived" problem with you!!! People also like to 'project' their problems onto other people by getting angry and abusive with others (you). Again, they are the ones with the problem, not you!!! It's a 'they' problem, not a "you" problem!

This community, in general, feels as though they have definite barriers, biases, and obstacles when it comes to equality. And rightfully so on many levels. They are still trying to find their footing when it comes to being treated as equals on many important fronts, so I think it's very important to include them on my website. Even more so once I realized their rates of abuse and violence are higher than in the heterosexual community which itself is much too high. Tis saddenedme greatly. Also please remember, these statistics *only* represent what has been *reported*. I hope this article helps to raise awareness of this epidemic. *(Updated in 2024-As a result of the additional letters added to this ever growing acronym and increasing problems with biological males "identifying" as a female to take advantage of some gainful situations. It is clear that the only males trying to crossover into women's sports are the ones who failed in their men's categories, not some random Joe off the street who'd just like to "give it a try." There is a direct and specific agenda and goal in this case. also, if you are a male "identifying" as a female-you need to stay the hell out of our women's bathrooms and dressinhg rooms, too! This absolutely screams "pervert," regardless of what you think. (Just because you want to "identify as something" does not mean that the rest of us have to go along with the delusion as well.)*

Sources:

Kane, C. Working With Survivors. https://www.thehotline.org/resources/working-with-survivors-equipping-survivors-with-their-voice

Understanding Intimate Partner Violence in the LGBTQ+ Community. (2022). https://www.hrc.org/resources/understanding-intimate-partner-violence-in-the-lgbtq-community

~~~~~~~
~~~~~~~

PART 5

A LITTLE ABOUT ME
("I AM THE STORM" SECTION)

*"THE DEVIL USED TO WHISPER IN MY EAR, "YOU'RE NOT STRONG ENOUGH TO HANDLE MY STORM"…….
TODAY, I TOLD THE DEVIL, "I AM THE STORM…AND I'M COMING FOR YOU AND YOUR KIND…"*

<u>INTRODUCTION</u>

I came across the above saying a few years back, right when I was making the big realizations of what had really happened to me in my marriage. It resonated so deeply with me when I read it that it gave me full-body chills for like a full minute. They just kept coming.

Oh, the storms I weathered from him…and not just the day-to-day battles that you have with someone who has a personality disorder. They don't just have it "sometimes"; they have it all the time. This is not a tell-all book or a tattle session for me, and I don't feel the need to spill every single little thing he did as far as behaviors, but just to give you an idea of the range of his behaviors during our relationship in terms of severity, I feel one of the worst behaviors was when I was about 32 years old and teaching at the time, he had come to pick me up from work and instead of turning right on the freeway, to go home, he turned left heading to the Superstition Mountains and desert. He was clearly mad (we had just had our other vehicle repossessed), and he started speeding up and saying that he was going to take me out to the desert and leave me there. Now, mind you, this was daytime in May, so it was hot. After hearing this out of his mouth, I panicked and knew I had to do something, so I grabbed the wheel and started pulling on it. Not exactly sure why- I think I just knew that if he drove me out to the middle of nowhere, I did not stand a chance, so I had to act in that moment. It caused enough disruption that he finally relinquished and ended up driving us home. We were having a lot of issues with him not coming home when he was supposed to, and he would just show up hours later with no good excuse and excessively spend money out of our account. I did not know where it was going. Years later (about five years ago), I learned that during one of his kidnapping attempts on an ex-girlfriend years before I met him, he held her at gunpoint and, put her in his car, and was attempting to drive her "somewhere." (Sounds familiar?!?) Apparently, this was an M.O. of his. He also spent a fair amount of time in "adult timeout" for the act as well. And others. You think he would have learned his lesson. I think back now to that day in the car, and now I know there was a very good chance that he had a gun with him as well. He had the past "patterned behavior" that one of these creatures would have, of being constantly in trouble with the law as a juvenile, spending time in juvenile court and detention for things like breaking into neighbors' homes because it was fun. I'm sure he got a big dopamine hit off of it, which is hard to accomplish in the daily lives of a dopamine-deficient psychopath. Other things that hinted at his psychopathy during our marriage but that I did not realize was that, one time, when we had just moved to a different town, we were unpacking boxes in the garage, and he came across some old paperwork from when he got a dishonorable discharge from the U.S. Air Force for going AWOL. I was already in the house by then and did not see the paperwork, but he told me the psychiatrist who conducted his exit assessment said he was narcissistic. (This was interesting because before that, at various times, he also told me that his current boss (at the time) and ex-wife had also told him he was narcissistic as well.) After he said this, he paused for a moment and said, "You should see what else he said," in a way that told me whatever that "else" was was even worse than a narcissist. I asked him what else it said, and he would not tell me. He tried to and succeeded in changing the subject. He said he'd already put the paperwork away and stuck the box in the attic. I didn't give it too much thought because we were very busy that day, and I forgot about the conversation at the time. Back then, we did not have the internet to consult for answers, and I did not make the connection. Back then, I did not know that the only thing worse than narcissism is psychopathy. The combo can be lethal.

The last couple of years of the marriage were the worst......The final unraveling was when I found out he was messing around with a woman that was affectionately known as "The Village Idiot" (for a few reasons), among other things, so as I spiraled down from this information, he began seeing his niece-in-law, which is about 30 years his junior and was leaving me at home in a urine-soaked bedroom, in severe pain and not able to take care of my basic needs such as showering. My bedroom carpet was so urine-soaked from my two dogs because they weren't being taken outside enough or properly, and one had developed a urinary tract infection. I did not have access to money to pay for a carpet cleaning, and my ex would not pay for it. Made the entire house smell bad. He would not deal with it, but he would not let me do anything about it, either. The smell permeated my room and my lungs. Very unnecessarily cruel and sadistic behavior, in my opinion. There were a few times that I had to go without washing my hair for a couple of weeks because I couldn't lift my arms up to wash my hair due to the severe total body arthritis and pain. When he did show up after being gone days at a time, he would be very mean and say terrible things to not just me but the kids. I had teenage kids at home at the time.

About a year later, after moving out of that home after the divorce and realizing what had really happened to me, I happened to be looking at one of my son's college books for "Criminology" and came across some life-changing information. Information that was a catalyst for this truth finding journey. I was flipping through the pages of this book, and I got to the section on HUMAN RIGHTS. As I'm scanning the page, something catches my eye…… "I have the right to…" I immediately start reading this section of the actual human rights, and as I'm reading, my head starts spinning a little. Turns out this man had been systematically obliterating many of my basic human rights for YEARS! That was a hard pill to swallow, but there were two more bigger pills in the next couple of chapters waiting to choke the shit out of me. After taking that information in, I continued on to the CIVIL RIGHTS/LAWS section. I also made some sad realizations after reading this section as well. You mean I can sue him in court on a tort??? WOW! I never realized! As I choked this information down, I moved on to the CRIMINAL LAW section. Oh my GOD, did I about fall over in my chair when I got to that part …

Then, I made the realization that I am considered fully handicapped by both the federal and state governments and started looking up those special rights and domestic violence penalties. It turns out they are **three times** more harsh than if the victim were not considered a vulnerable adult! I remember, well, the night this all happened. I remember feeling like my reality had turned on its side (again) by about

180 degrees. I ended up in my walk-in closet, sitting on the floor, on the phone with my mom, telling her all this, and I remember I was rocking. Crying and rocking. I think I stayed in that closet for close to an hour. My poor mom!

Now, all of a sudden, I had a tremendous decision to make. Was I going to file criminal charges against this man, the father of my children, and put him in prison for possibly years and years??? Talk about a big girl's decision to have to make. This weighed heavily on me. This would not just affect both of us but several children and others as well.

After much thought, research, and consulting attorneys, I decided not to pursue any charges against him because it would be a massive and expensive undertaking, but mostly because I knew he would lie under oath. How do I know this? Well, for starters, he has psychopathy, and they will cheat and also because I watched him with my own eyes, lying in court before when I had filed a restraining order against him very early in the marriage when he rushed and tackled me, just like a damn lineman in football. One of the reasons I think the other invisible abuses were so bad was that he knew he should no longer try to put his hands on me early in the marriage.

I thought, I will handle this my own way on my own terms. I decided to write the book! I will use my "right" to make things right!

~~~~~~~
~~~~~~~

THE TRANSITION FROM VICTIM TO SURVIVOR

"If you had to go through it, you might as well learn to grow through it!"

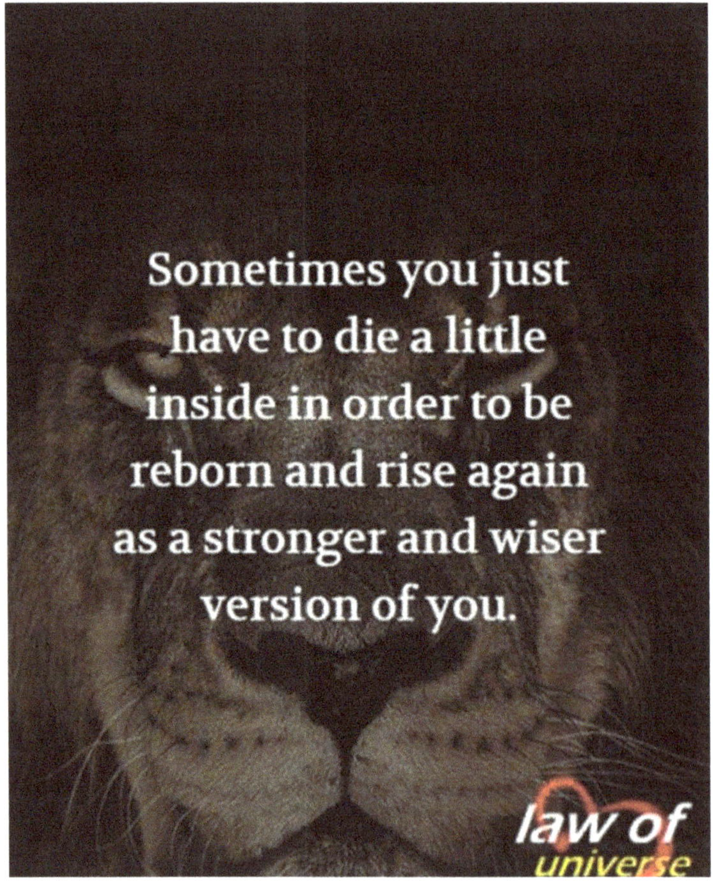

The term VICTIM doesn't have to be a "static" term or even a "state of being," and it certainly doesn't have to be your final destination! WE HAVE THE ABILITY TO MORPH OUR REALITY FROM THE REALM OF "VICTIM" INTO THE REALM OF "SURVIVOR"!!! With some help, I personally believe that we actually have that power within us... I KNOW WE DO!!!

Being a survivor of domestic abuse means finding our footing again with ourselves, those around us, and our communities. It means finding our own way in this world again, one that encourages self-love and growth instead of a controlling and stifling existence. It also means learning to believe and trust in our own realities again. This is not an easy one for us because we've lived for a long time in someone else's version of what they wanted our reality to be. After all, we were brutally deceived and treated very badly by the ones we loved the most, which unfortunately produces a very toxic type of damaging stress and mental anguish. Being a survivor also means clawing your way back towards the light with whatever strength is left of your badly broken and battered soul and spirit because you feel total annihilation closing in. Sometimes, it gets so close you can feel it breathing down the back of your neck, waiting for another moment of weakness to close in on you. It is much too close for comfort much too often. The Devil is constantly whispering in your ear that you are not strong enough to handle his storm…

Being a survivor also means remembering being at annihilation's doorstep, where it could have gone either way, and being very thankful I'm still here. Being a survivor also means learning to believe in the power of the human spirit and our ability and capacity to heal ourselves and each other. Especially when there is nothing expected in return, it means forging our own paths again, some of us with not much time left, instead of following the path of least resistance. It requires us to get out of our "comfort zone" and grow as a person. Doesn't feel like a good thing, but it is! It means no more walking on eggshells or having your "fight or flight" go off every time you hear them drive up, open the door to come into the house or hear their footsteps coming your way. It also means that the "critical" voice in your head is no longer "theirs" but is your own once again, and eventually, we learn to speak kinder to and go easier on ourselves because there's no way we could have known what we were in for or up against. We didn't stand a chance and they made sure of it. It does not take "two to tango" in these cases. It is a dance belonging only to the abuser, our feet stuck on theirs, flinging you in whichever direction they please and still managing to be five steps ahead of us all the while. They try to convince you it's country music you're listening to while you could swear you're hearing 70's Rock.

Being a survivor means learning to be our own advocate. It means finding courage, being brave, and speaking out to help and educate others with this newfound wisdom, even when we'd rather someone else be the example and do the educating. It means being a voice for those that don't have a voice or for those that have a voice but aren't "allowed" to use it. It means finding happiness in the little things and trusting people again. It is a time of personal growth where we learn to find ourselves all over again; this new person we've become, a version of our former selves, takes a while to get acquainted with. Finding the parameters of this new "me" isn't easy. We've been worn down and broken down, turned inside out, and lost a part of ourselves along the way. Parts of us may have even died during this journey, but remember, with death comes transformation and rebirth! Like a **PHOENIX**!!! As domestic abuse survivors, we have gone through a metamorphosis and have been transformed, and OH MY... what we've gained in wisdom, strength, and compassion!!!

WE ARE STRONG RESILIENT, AND WE DID NOT AND WILL NOT GO QUIETLY INTO THE NIGHT.

SHE

~~~~~~~
~~~~~~~

DEPRESSION AND THE DARK TIME

A Peek Into The Mind of a Severely Depressed Person.
"THE DARK TIME'

"Please come now, I think I'm falling.
I'm holding on to all I think is safe,
It seems I found the road to nowhere,
And I'm trying to escape,
I yelled back when I heard thunder,
But I'm down to one last breath,
And with it, let me say...
Hold me now,
I'm 6 feet from the edge, and I'm thinking,
Maybe 6 feet
Ain't so far down."
~CREED, "One Last Breath."

This was the last piece written before I launched my website. It's a tough one to write, much less think about. Sometimes, it seems like so long ago, and sometimes it seems like it was just yesterday. I'm at a place now where I can go back and "re-visit" for a little while. Just a very little while, though, then my mind bounces me right back out of it. I remember in fragments. They come ripping through my mind's eye like shards of mirrored glass with jagged edges. They explosively enter as quickly as they exit. It always comes from the top left of my mind's eye and quickly exits to the middle right. Always the same way. Much like a lightning bolt, and they have the same impact. The specific memories imprinted on them are shiny and reflective...just like the mirrors they superimpose themselves upon. Those memories... It's hard, though; old emotions and sensations stir as I write about this time in my life. The time when I was in my deepest, darkest despair, mind, body, spirit, and soul. A time when the autoimmune disease my body developed was at its worst, and I had spiraled into a very dangerous place known as severe depression. I was in constant full-body pain much of the time. Many times, it was often severe- the kind of pain that makes you shiver and your teeth chatter because your body is on the verge of shock from the overwhelming intensity and amount. This pain is everywhere, head to toe. I think even my hair may have hurt back then... I call this period in my life "THE DARK TIME." The days, months, and years where I was too sick to even get out of bed most of the time. I realized that in order to be able to help other people, I would have to share and "divulge" events that are deeply personal and painful. So, (insert deeeeeep breath here) here goes…...

I will never forget all those times, laying there, seemingly "gorilla glued" to this place called "bed." I spent a lot of time there listening to life pass me by. Resigning myself to the fact that this is my life now, and this is just how it's going to be from here on out. A battle just to make it through every single day. One that starts when I wake up every morning. It's a repeating cycle, a little like "Groundhog Day," over and over, like a hamster on a wheel. Sometimes, you can psych yourself up enough to make it slowly out of bed, and sometimes you can't. It's miserable to feel so defeated before your day has even had a chance to begin. All the promises of a new day are snuffed out before they've even been given an opportunity to come to fruition. I will never forget the sounds I would hear as I laid there in deep despair. The sounds of kids playing, cars driving by, neighbors doing yard work, birds chirping, people going to and from work, kids swimming, and all the other sounds that make life in suburbia go around. All the sounds that confirmed that life was indeed passing me by. Tucked away in my little corner of the world, I remember trying to imagine what everyone might be doing on such beautiful days. We have so many beautiful days here in the "The Valley of The Sun." I remember always thinking that I wish I could be the people I was hearing, even just for a little while, where I could be outside playing, running, dancing, like my old self, my body free of pain, my mind free of anguish and my future full of hope and promise. Free from this invisible monster that had invaded my body, mind, and spirit. The "dark aether" that had taken me over.…

To me, each one of those days I had to be in bed represents a day that I could have been living my life to the fullest. I could have been more involved in my children's lives, activities, and school. You see, when someone has a chronic illness, it's not just the patient that suffers. Their family, friends, and everything they are involved in are affected. The ripple effect is much bigger than anyone realizes. You go from owning, directing, and being in charge of not only your daily life, activities, and the general trajectory of your life all the way to spending days in bed, body on fire with pain, ratted and matted hair, and smelling like death. You've been in bed for days and not being able to walk because the swollen joints in your feet make each step feel as though you are walking on sharp rocks. It's hard to get very far, let me tell ya! I couldn't believe how painful my feet were, so one day, I looked up how many joints the human foot has. Well, to my shock, it has 33 joints! That's a lot! It also contains over 100 pieces of tendons, ligaments, and muscles, which also become inflamed and very painful in connective tissue autoimmune diseases like mine. No wonder my feet hurt so bad!

Depression, and especially severe depression, alter the way you think and perceive everything. When you have depression, it's as if you feel or sense a "heaviness" within you. You can't quite put your finger on it, but it might feel like there's a dark, heavy cloud over your head that is bearing down on you. Sometimes, you can feel the pressure of it. The lens through which you look/perceive things and situations, and just life in general becomes very muddled and dulled out as if smeared with mud. Your thinking and thought processes become distorted and affect your decision-making, and you have difficulty concentrating on anything for any length of time. It becomes incredibly difficult to think about anything more in-depth than just the 1st or 2nd layers. Except for your problems, of course. Those you'll obsess about…Many times, you can't even concentrate, and your thoughts are fragmented and disrupted. There is much time spent in "dissociative states," where your mind goes "somewhere else" and your brain "checks out" because it cannot deal with what is happening in the present. You spend a lot of time feeling like you are physically **FROZEN** or can't move. It's like your arms and legs weigh 100 pounds each, and they are literally too heavy to move.

You try to move them, but you can't; they won't budge, so you give up and tell yourself you'll try again later. When you do finally feel like you can move, it's as if you're trying to wade your way through a room full of molasses. Everything feels like it's going in slow motion, including your thoughts. When and if you do make it to your "destination," which can often just mean the bathroom or another nearby room, your heart, lungs, and muscles act as if you just had to run up five flights of stairs. Those times are few and far between because you mostly just stay in bed. It literally feels like you have become paralyzed. You want to move, but you can't. You are trapped in your own body. I remember convincing myself many times that I would make a damn good mannequin. Every little chore or errand you need to take care of seems like a MONUMENTAL TASK. A task that you don't have nearly enough energy for, and besides, it's going to hurt way too much. Even if the place you need to go to is just down the street, in your head, it seems like it's a million miles away, so you automatically become extremely overwhelmed and withdraw and dissociate once again, not only because that is your safe place but because the shame of not being "capable anymore" is too much to bear also. I cried a lot. I cried all the time, actually. I would walk into the kitchen, see the dishes piled up in the sink, get completely overwhelmed (another MONUMENTAL TASK), and hobble in pain back to my "safe" place and cry. Then I would think about all the things that I needed to do, such as house cleaning, laundry, and showering, and the list in my mind went on and on until I would cry myself to sleep.

Depression also lies to you. It whispers in your ear things like, "Everyone would be better off without you," "You're just a burden to everyone, so it would be better if you weren't here anymore," and "You should just do everyone a favor and off yourself." It tricks you into thinking that your children would actually be OK or even BETTER OFF without the "burden of you" in their lives. And you actually believe that B.S.! Severe depression was telling me this A LOT…I had not only "The Devil" but also Lupus and depression whispering in my ear…

It is still pretty painful for me to go back to "those dark places," but when I realized I could help people by sharing my story, I told myself that I would be brave and do this. I would be brave not just for myself but for others that need help. I'm going to use my experience and voice to educate and advocate because **I remember...** I remember what it feels like all too well. It is burned in my memory and senses forever. I weathered this storm barely. But I'm a warrior, and I will rise again...as a much stronger and wiser version of myself.

Even though I've overcome and I'm "here" now, I still mourn for many things...I mourn for opportunities missed mostly. I missed kids' games and activities, meals I couldn't provide, and just spending time in general just enjoying them and watching them grow. There were times when my children needed me, and I couldn't be there for them. I also mourn for my old "self." That fun-loving, silly, happy, and positive girl of days past. She's still in there. I feel her there all the time, waiting patiently in the shadows, peeking out occasionally to "test the waters" while still nursing and healing her deep, nearly annihilating wounds. She's still trying to make sense of this new reality and path we are on. She's not really sure where she fits in anymore, but she sure is trying. She's always been a really good "tryer" anyway! She wants to be brave, but sometimes it's hard. I still feel like I've been turned on my head, and my life has been literally flipped upside down. Most days, I can deal with that, though. I think I've done a pretty good job of reconciling and making peace with "the dark" time. After all, I'm only four years out of it. I would take the Devil's Hell any day because the one I was living in my own head was much, much too personal....

Source:

Me

<div align="center">~~~~~~~</div>

<u>THINGS I LEARNED ALONG THE WAY...</u>

you don't learn
how strong you are
until you are pushed
beyond what you
thought you could handle
and you emerge on
the other side
with more bravery,
grace and determination
than you realized
you even had.

Rachel Marie Martin
The Brave Art of Motherhood
FindingJoy.net

🌸 It's not your fault that you were abused. Your abuser may say things like, "*Look what you made me do,*" "*Why did you make me do that?*" or "*This is all your fault,*" but regardless of their accusations, it's **NEVER** your fault that you are being abused by someone else. Let me repeat that...***IT IS NEVER YOUR FAULT THAT YOU ARE BEING ABUSED !!!*** This is so important to remember because victims will usually self-blame for elements of the abuse, and self-blame turns into toxic shame really fast! In most cases, the abuser is just 'projecting' their issues onto you anyway. (for example, they accuse you of cheating when they are really the ones cheating.)

🌸 It's never OK for your partner to "tell you how you should feel about things." You are a completely separate person who's had separate experiences that shaped your core beliefs, morals, thoughts, and mindset, and you have a right to express them without prejudice or being made to feel that your beliefs, etc., are wrong. You have a *right* to feel and think how you want, no matter how much someone else tries to convince you otherwise. Don't let anyone be dismissive or disrespectful; try to impose their will onto you or try to change your thoughts, feelings, or beliefs. When someone attempts to do this, it's usually because they are attempting to position themselves above you in order to control you. They may also want you to drop down "*to their level*" if you have higher moral and ethical standards than they do.

❀ Life *ebbs* and *flows*; it's full of ups and downs, but no matter how bad and low things can get.....*it's just temporary!* Sometimes, these awful *ebbs* in life last a lot longer than what we can sometimes tolerate or even mentally or physically bear, but remember...*THERE IS ALWAYS HOPE...*

❀ Watch a person's behavior in relation to their words. When dealing with these types of people, if you pay attention to both words and behavior, you will soon find a big disconnect between the two. These people are not true to their words, they make promises they have no intention of keeping, and they may be saying, "You're the only one for me" while having multiple affairs, as was the case in my marriage.

❀ Many victims of domestic abuse, especially when little or no violence is present, often don't even *realize* they're being verbally, emotionally, psychologically, or financially abused. This happened to me.

❀ It's very difficult to have any kind of perspective when you are in the middle of "it," going through" it," so to speak. I knew my ex-husband could be very mean, even sadistic at times, and his mouth could spew poison that was meant to tear at your self-esteem, self-worth, spirit, and soul, but I never REALIZED or actually even knew that these kinds of things were considered "domestic abuse' or "domestic violence." I thought laws all had to do with "physical/sexual/neglect" abuse. I learned all of this "the hard way" and don't want you to make the same mistakes!

❀ Not only are verbal, emotional, psychological, financial, gender, elder, religious, and reproductive abuse recognized as "against the law," but so are oppression and isolation. You can even sue someone in Civil Court for these abuses as "torts"! I did not know that either! "Law" was an area I never ventured into, and I never had any experience with courts or anything, so I was just unfamiliar and unaware of many things in this area. Not anymore, though...I educated myself!

❀ No matter how hard you try to be the best you can for your partner, it's a lost cause if they have a personality disorder, especially one of the more severe ones, where apathy and narcissism prevail, you will never please or satisfy them because they are always looking for more, more, more. They can never be "still," and their empty emotional gas tanks always need refilling. They don't have any deep emotions for you, well, because they *can't.* They can't help it- it is in their nature...

❀ Worrying is a waste of time for the most part. I've spent so much time worrying about things that never happened. That's a lot of wasted time! I think people, in general, worry too much. We spend either too much time in our *past* (which can cause depression) or too much time thinking about the *future* (where the majority of worry and anxiety come from). We are not "fortunetellers"-we cannot predict the future! We spend so much time in the "past" or "future" that we are forgetting to be in the "present!"

❀ Don't compare your situation to others. Other people and families may act happy, seem to have it all together in public or on social media, have a beautiful home, and seem to have plenty of money and beautiful things, *but the cold, hard reality is that we are all struggling in our own ways and winning in our own ways. Stop being disappointed and instead be thankful for what you do have.*

❀ Mindfulness is the key to many things in life!

❀ Listen to your gut instinct. It's much smarter than "you" are!

❀ No matter what...you CANNOT change someone. Minor adjustments can be made, but those core personality traits are there to stay.

We have a CHOICE as to whether we want to be positive thinkers or negative thinkers….Thinking positively literally changes the neural pathways in our brain to keep us thinking positively!

Don't be afraid to ask for help! Oh, this one was a hard one for me and probably for a lot of you, too! We are proud people, aren't we? We don't want to ask for help for anything, right? Some people may even see it as a sign of weakness. I used to be a pretty private person who neither needed nor was used to asking for help from anyone for anything, so it was extremely difficult for me to ask for help when I really needed it. To my surprise, people were more than happy to help and do what they could! Remember, people, in general, love to help out friends, family, and even strangers in times of need. Helping others gives a person the "warm and fuzzies" by giving them a sense of importance and purpose and allowing them to show compassion for their fellow humans! You can always pay it back or forward when you are able!

Not everyone in your circle is your "true friend." Some are jealous, manipulative, and do not have your best interests in mind. They are a one-man show, who only care about what they get out of something or pretend to "help" you, but you later find out they have their own agenda. These people have a difficult time helping or doing something for others without expecting anything in return or just out of the goodness of their hearts. There is always a catch or a price to be paid, usually under their unrealistic "conditions." Remember….when someone does something nice for you or helps you without expecting anything in return, it is called 'kindness", but when they expect something in return or to help their own *cause,* it's just called "business as usual."

~~~~~~~
~~~~~~~

LIFE LESSONS LEARNED FROM PLAYING SOFTBALL

If you have never played sports or have never been a member of a group or team that was working toward a common goal, you may not realize that there are very important life lessons that can be learned during your time as a "member" of a team, group, club or military, etc.

🥎 I started playing team sports when I was really young, and I think one of the first lessons I learned was that you need to get along with your teammates! Lol. The truth is that you're going to have to play with, work with, and even live with family members and people who you don't "jive" with, but you have to learn to put those "differences" aside for the sake of the team. Part of being a member of a group or team comes with that responsibility because that is a crucial aspect when striving for a common goal. It is amazing how just one person can be problematic enough to bring the rest of the group or team down. We call these problem people "cancers" because they are toxic to the rest of the team and the process. They must be dealt with or removed altogether! You learn tolerance, patience, trustworthiness, how to look at things from someone else's perspective (empathy), compassion, and how not to be selfish. And if I'm not mistaken, those are also core components of GOOD CHARACTER...

🥎 If you work hard and keep your nose to the grind (especially when your competition isn't), it's easier to "trust in the process," have confidence and believe in yourself during those tough situations and help you to be successful in those "BIG MOMENTS." I liken it to showing up for a final exam knowing you attended every single class, listened to your professor the entire class, took excellent notes, and studied a nausium... you're going to feel very prepared, and that is confidence. That state of mind alone will ensure you have a positive outcome!

🥎 When my college team would practice, we didn't practice to "just be good" or "to be competitive"; we practiced like we were practicing to win a National Championship...and guess what??? It worked-we won the National Championship! 🙆🙆🙆 (I know, I know, it's not usually that simple) To be truly successful, you really need to have the mindset, conviction, and dedication not just to improve but to have a specific goal in mind and then you set smaller, more attainable goals that align you with your ultimate goal. By doing all the things necessary, you are also creating your own luck by lowering the likelihood and 🥎 Don't try to fight power with power. You're inevitably going to face opponents who are much bigger, stronger, and more powerful than you are. Remember, everyone, or the opponent, in this case, has a weakness. Find it and use a good strategy to outsmart them and endurance to outlast them! David vs Goliath!

🥎 In times of weakness or hardship, learn to lean on your teammates, fellow club members, family members, or friends, AND USE THEIR "COLLECTIVE STRENGTH" AS YOUR OWN WHEN YOURS IS LOW-that is what they are there for! In life, your teammates are your family, friends, and co-workers, whether you've even realized it or not. YES-YOU HAVE A TEAM!!! Your team doesn't have to consist of many people; it can just be one person. One person who can lend their strength and hope to you when yours is running low. It's extremely difficult to ask for help, but once I finally reached out when I was really sick and getting a divorce, I found that not only were people sympathetic to my situation, but they were ready to help in any way they could! We humans (or 'Yumans,' as people from my hometown are called) have a tendency to think that whatever we are going through, others will neither understand nor have experience with it. Actually, the opposite is true...We are all fighting battles, every single one of us, and once you open yourself up and start sharing your story, others will do the same, and you will find that others have much more in common with you than you ever thought! This is when real bonding happens...

🥎 You have a responsibility to others...because they are depending on you. If you are feeling out of sorts, having problems, etc., and it's not only affecting you but those around you, *you have a responsibility* to try to correct the problem. Whether that means seeking counseling, learning behavior modification, or emotional regulation strategies, we owe it to our loved ones and those around us to be the best version of ourselves. Most of all, we owe that to ourselves…

🥎 Have pride in what you do, no matter how small the task, because it matters overall and to "the big picture." Many times, we can get disenchanted with where we are in life or careers because we feel we aren't making a big enough difference or our contributions don't mean much if anything. One reason we tend to have these discouraging thoughts is because we are just looking at that one part: a job. Or aspect all by itself. Instead, try re-framing how you look at your situation, job, etc., as being a part of a larger picture, where all parts are important for the entire process to happen. Without your contributions, no matter how small, the bigger picture can't happen or wouldn't be the same. You are part of something bigger; you just may not realize it!

🥎 Preparation is KEY…you better show up prepared! Not only should you have your "i's" dotted and your "t's" crossed but you had better practice doing it at nauseam, and at that point, you should probably still keep practicing!

🥎 THERE. IS. ALWAYS. SOMETHING. TO. WORK. ON…

🥎 IF IT'S NOT BROKEN, DON'T "FIX" IT. If your way of doing something is serving you well and is successful, don't try to change it just because someone else comes along and tries to tell you otherwise. People like to do that stuff….come along and try to change you, something about you or what it is you're doing. Many times, it is just to benefit themselves in some way or to justify their position or what they do. There is always room for improvement or to make a few modifications, but good lord, don't change yourself or what you are doing (if you believe in it, of course) just because another "thinks" you should!

🥎 *IF YOU DON'T HAVE A PLAY-HOLD THE DAMN BALL!* This also applies to life!

~~~~~~~
~~~~~~~

TIPS FOR HEALTHY PERSONAL BOUNDARIES

"Hey, get outta my lane!"

Personal boundaries are an important way for us to keep ourselves physically and emotionally safe from others. They are the rules and limits we can set for ourselves within relationships. They allow a person to say "no" to experiences or others that make us uncomfortable while still maintaining healthy relationships. Establishing healthy boundaries for yourself can lead to more positive and productive social and interpersonal experiences that encourage self-respect and personal growth and discourage being taken advantage of and mistreated. Below are some tips that can help you achieve these goals!

KNOW YOUR LIMITS- Before becoming involved in a situation, know what's acceptable to you and what isn't. It's best to be as specific as possible, or you might be pulled into the trap of giving just a little bit more over and over until you've given too much.

KNOW YOUR VALUES- Every person's limits are different, and they're often determined by their personal values. For example, if you value family above all else, this might lead to stricter limits on how late you will stay at work, away from family. Know what's most important to you, and protect it.

LISTEN TO YOUR EMOTIONS- If you notice feelings of discomfort or resentment, don't bury them. Try to understand what your feelings are telling you. Resentment, for example, can often be traced to feelings of being taken advantage of.

HAVE SELF-RESPECT- If you always give in to others, ask if you are showing as much respect to yourself as you show to others. Boundaries that are too open might be due to misguided attempts to be liked by elevating other people's needs above one's own.

HAVE RESPECT FOR OTHERS- Be sure that your actions are not self-serving at the expense of others. Interactions should not be about winning or taking as much as possible. Instead, consider what's fair to everyone, given the setting and relationship. You might "win," but at the cost of a relationship's long-term health.

BE ASSERTIVE- When you know it's time to set a boundary, don't be shy. Say "NO" respectfully but without ambiguity. If you can make a compromise while respecting your own boundaries, try it. This is a good way to soften the "NO" while showing respect to everyone involved.

CONSIDER THE LONG VIEW- Some days, you will give more than you take and other days, you will take more than you give. Be willing to take a longer view of relationships when appropriate. But if you're always the one who's giving or taking, there might be a problem.

Sources:

(2017). Tips For Healthy Personal Boundaries. Therapist Aid. https://www.therapistaid.com/worksheets/healthy-boundaries-tips

(2019). Setting Boundaries. Therapist Aid. https://www.therapistaid.com/worksheets/setting-boundaries

<div align="center">~~~~~~~</div>

WHY MINDFULNESS IS SO IMPORTANT FOR EVERYTHING!

"If you get the inside right, the outside will fall into place. Primary reality is within; secondary reality without."~ Eckhart Tolle

"The Human Superpower"

I think "mindfulness" just might be the Holy Grail, the real Holy Grail...of everything! Here, let me explain...When I began my research into the psyche, emotions, and the mind-body connection through psychology, neuroscience, and related fields, I quickly realized how important mindfulness and the ability to "have" or "practice" it actually is! Mindfulness can literally mean the difference between sanity and insanity, overcoming and not overcoming, body and mind attunement or misattunement, and being in sync with the people around you. It has the capacity to make you feel "human" again when you feel numb and detached from your own body as a result of trauma. It regulates emotions, decreases stress, anxiety, and depression, and improves cognitive flexibility and working memory. Mindfulness helps us to focus our attention and be "present" in the moment. Those moments you are playing with your kids, the moments you are having an important conversation with a loved one, or those moments you're supposed to be paying attention in class or at work. Not being mindful and self-aware robs us of being able to fully enjoy life, feel fully alive, and learn from and take note of these important occasions. It can also leave a person unable to properly integrate new experiences. Lack of mindfulness keeps us locked in the past, causing depression, dysfunctional thinking patterns, or thinking about the future, which tends to fill us with anxiety because of its uncertainty.

So, what is "mindfulness" exactly? It can be described as the practice of being fully aware and present in any given moment or time frame. It's the idea that you are aware of what is going on around you and in your immediate surroundings and how it is affecting your inner sensations and experiences. It is the consciousness of being present and aware of your own thoughts and emotions.

For those with PTSD and others who've endured and suffered trauma and abuse, the mind is constantly hyper-focused on "looking for and reacting to danger," whether it's real or perceived. Being in this state of constant hyperarousal keeps people from being "aware" of the smaller, more peripheral information and stimulus, which can be just as important. Mindfulness can help correct this problem! Being in a "mindful state" activates your "medial prefrontal cortex," which is the gateway to activating your limbic system (emotional brain). This is crucial because it facilitates healing and the re-calibrating and calming of the limbic system, which is a major factor in people with PTSD and others who have suffered trauma and abuse.

Mindfulness has other benefits as well. They include reducing autoimmune arthritis (inflammation) and the risk of heart disease, irritable bowel syndrome, and chronic pain. It also aids in weight loss and HIV symptom severity, lessens the effects of cold and flu, and improves sleep.

Those are some pretty compelling reasons to practice mindfulness! Below are some simple ways to practice and implement it into your everyday lives. Best of luck to you, and happy healing!

For people who have been traumatized and their brain and central nervous systems changed because of it, "self-awareness" is at the very core of the recovery process. Self-awareness is achieved by "mindfulness". It calms the sympathetic nervous system, so it's less likely to go into "fight or flight mode," which is an ongoing problem for many of these folks, including myself. Dr. Bessel Van Der Kolk, in his bestselling book, "The Body Keeps The Score; Brain, Mind, and Body in the Healing of Trauma," discusses how mindfulness also gives these people a "lense" to collect those fragmented and scattered reactive energies of the mind and allows it (those potent energies) to transform into focused efforts to coherently categorize their inner experiences for well-adjusted living and problem-solving.

Here are some simple ways to practice mindfulness in your daily life that don't involve having to go into full-blown "meditative mode," which can be very difficult for victims of abuse or trauma because, well, our minds bounce all over the place and are very difficult to quiet and clear!

1. **Take a walk 🚶🚶🚶 and walk like you have no destination in mind.** ➡

We are constantly on the "Go,"... which means we are always preoccupied with what we need to do, and we have those long checklists in our minds that must be checked off in a timely manner. Deadlines and time constraints define us. Life gets crazy. We never feel like we can just "be" for a while; just soak in that present moment and reap all it has to offer. Taking a walk with no destination in mind is a great way to do just that! Walk at any pace that feels most comfortable to you, and try to focus on the sounds around you (birds chirping, kids laughing, cars driving by) and the different smells you encounter. You don't have to worry about which direction you need to go or what time you need to be anywhere. I love walking and do it often. I have found that not only does it facilitate mindfulness and clear my mind, but it's a great way to release anxiety and that extra "nervous energy" that plagues people like us. The act of walking itself is great for the heart, lungs, muscles, and joints. Walking as exercise also releases serotonin (the feel-good hormone), which increases mood and self-esteem!

1. **Give gratitude at mealtime. 🍓🥦🥩**

When we are "hangry" or starving, we tend to shovel our food down before we can really even taste it, especially if we are busy multi-tasking, as many of us are when we eat. We do not usually think about the process of how the food got to our plate or how the nutrients derived from that food fuel, heal and protect our bodies in various ways. A great way to practice mindfulness, slow yourself down, and get re-centered is during mealtime. "Conscious Chewing" is a great way to accomplish that! As you chew, think about the process of how the food was grown or raised, how it was delivered to the store, the method of preparation, and how it looks on your plate. Think about the taste of the food in your mouth as you are chewing it, and finally, give gratitude for all the important nutrients that will fuel your body.

2. Unwind Before Bedtime. 😴

Approximately 30 minutes before you go to bed, turn off all electronics, including the TV. By doing this, you are allowing your mind and body to relax a bit. Allow your body to just relax and sprawl on the bed in a comfortable position. Take a few long, slow, deep breaths, which will allow your body to further melt into the bed. As you begin to relax, focus on feeling the tension and stress leaving each muscle and actually visualize this happening. Try not to think about what happened that day or anything else that may distress or re-direct your attention from this peaceful state. Try to stay in this "zone' as long as you can. Soon, you will feel the tension melt away, and you'll hopefully be off to a good night's rest!

3. Be "Mindfully Mobile" 🚗

Being in your car is the perfect time to practice mindfulness! This will also keep you more focused on the task at hand, namely getting safely to your desired destination. The next time you are in your vehicle and you are stopped at a red light, instead of reaching for your phone, try focusing on the red light, take a few long, slow, deep breaths, and exhale completely each time. This will slow down your frustration and a corresponding rise in blood pressure and hormones released due to your negative reaction of getting caught in that damn red light!

🌷 *Practicing mindfulness, well...takes practice! Doing a little bit each day will really go a long way in your ability to tap into it at will and have command over it. When you are able to reach this level, mindfulness can be used as a tool to heal and grow. It will be your SUPERPOWER!!!!* 🌷

Sources:

Davis, D. & Hayes, J. (2012). What are the Benefits of Mindfulness? American Psychological Association. https://www.apa.org/monitor/2012/07-08/ce-corner

Pal, P. (2024). 5 Simple Mindfulness Practices for Daily Life. Mindful. https://www.mindful.org/take-a-mindful-moment-5-simple-practices-for-daily-life/

~~~~~~~
~~~~~~~

<u>I SEE… (CONCLUSION)</u>

This process has been nothing short of wildly transformative, to say the very least, and has left me with the ability to *see* and understand the better-known phenomena of a world that we cannot see but that profoundly affects us on a daily basis.

I *see* how it can be used to hurt or heal, cause pain or happiness, good health, illness, and even death. I *see* how it can be used for control and power, good and evil. I *see* how evil likes to masquerade as good. I *see* how it can be used to manifest incredible, awe-inspiring feats and inspire. I also *see* how it can be used to completely annihilate without conscience.

I see how it gives those who have suffered, special gifts. Gifts of song, beautiful singing voices, gifts of creativity, art and imagination. A way for them to escape, self-soothe, and heal from within because those who have been traumatized have lost much of that innate ability to do so. Once again, the universe knows what it's doing. It will give balance and compensation where they are needed. I have also *seen* it unleash both positive and negative karma at a moment's notice.

And finally, I *see* how the healing energies created by my own positive intentions, directed thoughts, beliefs, and behaviors that align with healing, actually healed me. I didn't just *see* myself heal; I *felt* myself heal, and that was the most amazing part.

I am very proud of my journey and what it has not just taught me but the truth it has revealed to others as well. It's been a long and arduous one. One hell of a ride, I'd say! I am just thankful every day that I am still here to enjoy it. Today, I am happy, healthy and thriving. I am thankful every single morning when I wake up. It is now obviously hard to trust people at this point, but if any of you are wondering if I have found someone special through this journey to trust and fall in love with, well, I sure did. Someone from my past that I used to love, but we lost touch for a while-someone I ended up coming full-circle with...*ME*.

****Moral of my story here is, DON'T STOP BELIEVING. DON'T EVER STOP BELIEVING!!!**

WORDS TO LIVE BY;

WATCH YOUR THOUGHTS; THEY BECOME WORDS

WATCH YOUR WORDS; *THEY BECOME ACTIONS*

WATCH YOUR ACTIONS; *THEY BECOME HABITS*

WATCH YOUR HABITS; *THEY BECOME YOUR CHARACTER*

WATCH YOUR CHARACTER; *IT BECOMES YOUR DESTINY*

By, Lau Tzu

~~~~~~~
~~~~~~~

"THE PROCESS"

(photos from along the way…)

*2018

*2023

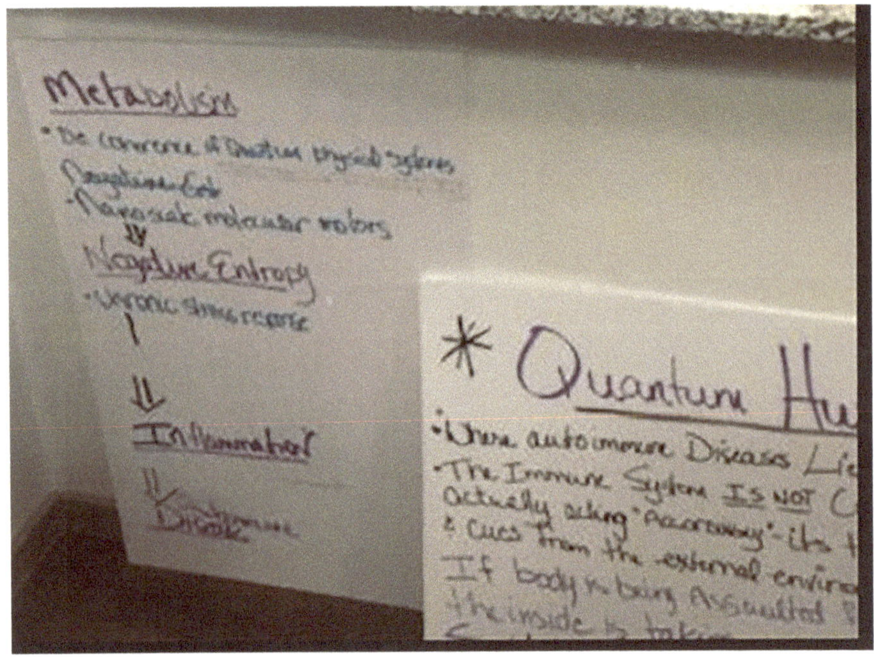

Quantum Field
Spirituality

Quantum Healing

Metabolism

Quantum Hu